Ancient Indian Eugenics, Eroticism and Sex Psychology

ॐ नमो भगवते महासुदर्शन वासुदेवाय धन्वन्तराय अमृतकलश हस्ताय
सकल भयविनाशाय सर्वरोग निवारणाय त्रिलोकपतये त्रिलोकनिधये
ॐ श्री महाविष्णुस्वरूप श्री धन्वन्तरि स्वरूप ॐ श्री श्री औषधचक्रनारायणाय नमः ।

oṁ namo bhagavate mahāsudarśana vāsudevāya dhanvantarāya amṛtakalaśa hastāya sakala bhayavināśāya sarvaroga nivāraṇāya trīlokapataye trilokanidhaye oṁ śrī mahāviṣṇusvarūpa śrī dhanvantari svarūpa oṁ śrī śrī auṣadhacakranārāyaṇāya namaḥ ।

Ancient Indian Eugenics, Eroticism and Sex Psychology

Influence of Āyurveda in the Theory of Kāmaśāstra

Rahul Vishwas Altekar

DK PRINTWORLD®
Publishers of Indian Traditions

Cataloging in Publication Data — DK
[Courtesy: D.K. Agencies (P) Ltd. <docinfo@dkagencies.com>]

Altekar, Rahul Vishwas, 1971- author.
Ancient Indian eugenics, eroticism and sex psychology : influence of āyurveda in the theory of Kāmaśāstra / Rahul Vishwas Altekar.
pages cm
Includes bibliographical references and index.
ISBN 9788124612293 (HB)

1. Sex (Psychology) – India. 2. Eugenics – India. 3. Erotica – India. 4. Medicine, Ayurvedic. 5. Sex in literature. 6. Erotic literature, Sanskrit – History and criticism. I. Title.

LCC HQ21.A48 2025 | DDC 306.7 23

ISBN: 978-81-246-1229-3

First published in India in 2025

Printed and published by:
D.K. Printworld (P) Ltd.
Regd. Office: "Vedaśrī", F-395, Sudarshan Park
ESI Hospital Metro Station, New Delhi - 110015
Phones: (011) 4172 2626, 98713 94815
e-mail: indology@dkprintworld.com
Web: www.dkprintworld.com

धर्मार्थकामेभ्योनमः । (*dharmārthakāmebhyonamaḥ*) – *KS* 1.1.1

Obeisance to Supreme Kāma Puruṣārtha (an elegant framework to fulfil all humanly desires)! which is an outgrowth of Dharma (framework for lawful and moral behaviour) and Artha (framework for economic stability and financial discipline).

तत्सात्म्याद्देशसात्म्याच्च तैस्तैर्भावैः प्रयोजितैः ।
स्त्रीणां स्नेहश्च रागश्च बहुमानश्च जायते ॥

tatsātmyāddeśasātmyācca taistairbhāvaiḥ prayojitaiḥ ।
strīṇāṁ snehaśca rāgaśca bahumānaśca jāyate ।।
– *Kāmasūtra* 2.6.52

A love art performed matching to the customs and climate of a particular region, and the mood, taste and desire of the women that time generates compiling friendship (love), unique sexual orgasm with supreme satistfaction, generating permanent respect in the hearts of women.

Foreword

Dr Rahul Vishwas Altekar has taken up the study to "felicitate the fusion between the ancient and the modern sciences emphasizing the outlook to learn from the past to shape the future". Let me begin with the basics.

Is there really a need to learn "Kāmaśāstra"? Sex is absolutely an individual natural urge and what is there to "learn"?. Sex is a proven thing known to everyone without any formal training. "Is there any teacher who teaches the animals and birds to entertain their own wives?", asks *Kāmasūtra* 2.1.21. It is a very primary and basic question. The answer by Vātsyāyana is not casual but has a potential treasure in it. He has attached some societal values to the natural urge. One of the values is "sex only in youth" (2.1.3). Another is "one has to follow abstinence till the completion of study" (2.1.6) and at last he concludes with, "whoever masters this *śāstra*, becomes the controller of his sense organs, controls one's position of the *dharma*, *artha* in the society (2.7.58).

What about sex in Āyurveda! Is there really a need to juxtapose Āyurveda and Kāmaśāstra? Why not let them become stand alone entities? Why do we need such interdisciplinary study when:

- Āyurveda has *vājīkaraṇa* as a specialized branch of Aṣṭāṅga Āyurveda, along with the other seven, viz. *kāya*, *bala*, *graha*, *ūrdhvaṅga*, *śalya*, *agad* and *rasāyana*?
- Āyurveda has discussed having children, safe birth. Not only that, it has discussed the "preparation" of male and female to become competent to "expect" pregnancy. It has instructed about the diet and medicines, and therapeutics. It has also

instructed about the quality and quantity of intercourses in order to conceive a healthy baby.

- Āyurveda has described about the generation of semen and the ovulation process, and has guided about individual's sexual health.
- At the same time, Āyurveda has refrained from discussing at length about the *kāmeṣaṇā* and the commentator says:

> कामैषणा तु प्राणैषणाधनैषणयोरन्तर्भावनीया,
> शरीरसम्पत्तिधनसम्पत्तिसाध्यत्वात् कामस्य।
> यदि वा कामैषणायां स्वत एव पुरुषः प्रवृत्तो भवति
> नोपदेशमपेक्षत इति तदेषणोपदेशो न कृतः ॥३॥

> *kāmaiṣaṇā tu prāṇaiṣaṇādhanaiṣaṇayorantarbhāvanīyā,*
> *śarīrasampattidhanasampattisādhyatvāt kāmasya* ।
> *yadi vā kāmaiṣaṇāyāṁ svata eva puruṣaḥ pravṛtto bhavati*
> *nopadeśamapekṣata iti tadeṣaṇopadeśo na kṛtaḥ* ॥ 3 ॥

Now, the answer is:

> What Āyurveda has described so far about the sex procedure, sex organ anatomy, physiology, etc. is but a subset of a huge set.

Āyurveda considers *brahmacarya* as one of the legs of tripod. The technical term used for it is *trayopastambha*. The other two being the *āhāra* and the *nidrā*. It is said:

> त्रय उपस्तम्भा इति – आहारः, स्वप्नो, ब्रह्मचर्यमिति; एभिस्त्रिभिर्युक्तियुक्तैरुपस्तब्धमुपस्तम्भैः शरीरं बलवर्णोपचयोपचितमनुवर्तते यावदायुःसंस्कारात् संस्कारमहितमनुपसेवमानस्य [१] , य इहैवोपदेक्ष्यते ॥३५॥

> *traya upastambhā iti - āhāraḥ, svapno, brahmacaryamiti; ebhistribhiryuktiyuktairupa-stabdhamupastambhaiḥ śarīraṁ balavarṇopacayopacitamanuvartate yāvadāyuḥsaṁskārāt saṁskāramahitamanupasevamānasya* [1], *ya ihaivopadekṣyate* ॥ 35 ॥

> ... there are three pillars of the life: food, sleep and *brahmacarya*.

> These three, when systematically utilized and nurtured, help the body gain strength and complexion throughout the life, and hamper if not properly utilized and nurtured.

Further, the commentator says:

> ब्रह्मचर्यस्यायुक्तिरनभ्यासादतिमात्रेन्द्रियसंयमनादिरूपा, सा हि मनःक्षोभादि-हेतुर्भवति ।
>
> *brahmacaryasyāyuktiranabhyāsādatimātrendriysaṁyam-anādirūpā, sā hi manaḥkṣobhādiheturbhavati* ।
>
> *Brahmacarya*, if not properly trained, leads to over control of senses and leads to issues like exploitation of mind.

Now the concept of *brahmacarya* is not only the "abstinence". The contemporary philosophies have described Bhagavān Śrīkṛṣṇa as *naiṣṭhika brahmacārī*. Hence, we Āyurvedīya people classify the term *brahmacarya* into two parts: one is *naiṣṭhika brahmacarya* and another is *vaivāhika brahmacarya* (these are colloquial terms and not by any classical text). And, of course, the discussion about *vaivāhika brahmacarya,* i.e. sex as an enjoyment tool in the life of married couples, needs to be done in detail where the discussion about sex life related to progeny is done.

Second, though there is *vājīkaraṇa* as the eighth *aṅga* of Āyurveda, we do not find any dedicated text about this particular *aṅga*. We have the *Caraka Saṁhitā* as the face of *kāya cikitsā* and the *Suśruta Saṁhitā* as the face of *śalya cikitsā* but we lack any face text of *vājīkaraṇa* and it is discussed among the other sacred texts just as another chapter.

Let there be no face text, but we do not either have any *prakaraṇa grantha* on *vājīkaraṇa,* like we have the *Tarkasaṁgraha* on Nyāya philosophy or the *Arthasaṁgraha* on Mīmāṁsā philosophy, or we have the *Vedāntasāra* on Vedānta philosophy (surprisingly we have applied Āyurveda like Vṛkṣāyurveda and Paśu Āyurveda).

In short, the *vājīkaraṇa aṅga* needs to be systematically explored with the help of contemporary expertise.

Does Āyurveda accept such exploration or is Āyurveda adamant enough not to bother anything outside the classical texts?

Āyurvedic texts are in typical *saṁhitā* form and *sūtra* composition. By definition, the *sūtra* expects and enjoys "to be in brief". This accepted briefness brings along many issues. The most important issue is: one cannot discuss everything in detail, which is neither possible in this information technology era. Thus, Āyurvedic texts describe some representative samples and ask to derive on the same lines (*diṣṇya cāpi svayamuhet buddhimān*). Again, the representative sample is not any random one but it has to be *prayopayogī*. Thus, any entity having considerable dominance over some specific "time–space–society" framework is labelled and discussed as *prayopayogī*. Naturally, the entities outside the locus of *prayopayogī* become *anukta* or *leśokta* (not discussed or partly discussed). Since this is an accepted limit of the texts they have given guidelines on including such *anukta* and *leśokta* in the Āyurvedic framework. Thus, we find *amlapitta* disease included in later texts of Āyurveda though not "per se" discussed in the classical texts and we find contemporary researchers taking cognizance of "cheese" and *vaḍā-pāva* and "microwave machine" which are *anukta* in Āyurveda texts because of unavailability within a particular "time–space–society" referendum.

Now, primarily the Āyurvedic discussion about "sex" is about the *santānārtha maithuna* that is the sex for progeny. The term *santānārtha maithuna* is from the *Mahābhārata.*

तृप्त्यर्थं भोजनं येषां सन्तानार्थञ्च मैथुनम् ।
वाक् सत्यवचनार्थाय दुर्गाण्यतितरन्ति ते ॥

tṛptyarthaṁ bhojanaṁ yeṣāṁ santānārthañca maithunam ।
vāk satyavacanārthāya durgāṇyatitaranti te ।।

– Śānti-Parva 12.110.23

And

यज्ञार्थं पशवः सृष्टाः संतानार्थं च मैथुनम् ।
स समाः षोडशाष्टौ च चतस्रोऽष्टौ तथाऽपराः ।
रतिमप्राप्नुवन्स्त्रीषु बभूव वनगोचरः ॥

yajñārthaṁ paśavaḥ sr̥ṣṭāḥ santānārthaṁ ca maithunam ।
sa samāḥ ṣoḍaśāṣṭau ca catasro 'ṣṭau tathā 'parāḥ ।
ratimaprāpnuvanstrīṣu babhūva vanagocaraḥ ॥
– Ādi-Parva 1.107.21

But human beings do have sex for pleasure too. So, sex is of two types: one is *santānārtha maithuna* (sex for progeny) and the other is *ratyārtha maithuna* (sex for pleasure) (this is not a classical categorization, it is my own). As Āyurveda texts emphasize on *santānārtha maithuna*, the topic *ratyārtha maithuna* is both *anukta* at certain points and *leśokta* at certain points.

Another perspective of Āyurveda texts is that they do not describe anything outside their domain mandate and particularly when any other has elaborated the same authentically. We find Āyurvedic texts humbly saying *parādhikareṣu na vistārokti* (no elaboration on other's mandate) and we find such an example in the *Caraka Saṁhitā* refraining at some point saying *tatra dhanvantariyānāma adhikāraḥ* (that is the mandate of the surgeons). Thus, Āyuveda texts might have refrained from elaboration of *ratyārtha maithuna*.

All these points authenticate an acute timely need for a complimentary work on Āyurveda and Kāmaśāstra.

I am immensely pleased to see the work of Dr Rahul Altekar fulfilling that need. First, I congratulate him for taking up such an interdisciplinary subject for his doctoral study. Of course, you have to have a strong academician to guide you. I humbly take this opportunity to congratulate his guide Dr Gauri Mahulikar, a scholar par excellence.

I am again pleased to see that the author has not limited himself to classroom studies. He has visited some Āyurvedic clinicians and academics, and some other academics. He also visited some temples. It has surely made a considerable impact on his vision and his insight on the subject. His information technology background and his work profile have helped him in the research process. And it is evident in the thesis. His work is really what Māgha says as the *anujhitārtha sambandha prabandha*. He is a good example of a person having "work–passion–life" balance.

I do have some points of disagreement, but those really do not need public attention and can be resolved.

Now the question arises: what is next? What is the forward linkage of this work?

The society is changing, grossly changing and the speed of change is exponential. "Information" is getting spread at an astonishing pace and the "digestion" of information is becoming poor, poorer and poorest. As about the topic "sex", there is a subtle taboo for discussion on public forums. At the same time, it becomes an important topic of grape vine at every group of societal cross-section. The social media and the virtual platforms are multiplying both the taboo and the grape vine. A clinician has to face absolutely anything related to the topic "sex". To share the personal experience, some ten years ago, I was not keen about enquiring about sex life of a patient unless it was quintessential. But now enquiry of sex life of every patient has become a necessary part as it manifests some way or the other in the diseases. Surprisingly, we cannot avoid asking about sex life and sexual preferences to unmarried patients also (with and under due ethical norms and code of conduct). Plastic surgeons are casually demanded organ enhancements and orthopaedic surgeons are demanded "structural changes" to suit sex life. Informally, sexologists are advocating availability of "sex space" and "contraceptive vending machines" within the offices. And what the psychiatrists are not facing?

All this needs some value-based multidisciplinary intervention. And since we Indians have a rich culture over thousands of years, history tells us that we have found value-based answers to such contemporary societal problems. We owe this to our cultural heritage.

I can see this book providing some food for thought to Āyurvedic undergraduate and postgraduate students, and the Āyurvedic clinicians. I can see this book as a value addition to the efforts that the sexologist are doing to improve the sexual health of the society. I can see this book proving some hypotheses to interdisciplinary researchers including medical research, sociological research and researches among Sanskrit faculty.

I also foresee this book as a tool in making future policy on sex education at various levels. Some recommendations like "scientmatic tourism" are worth giving a thought.

The author has started his journey. Let this work be a "comma" and not a "full stop" to his journey.

Recalling author's Preamble, he is trying "to learn from the past to shape the future"!

I wish him a bright future!

Dr Shriprasad Bavadekar
Former Professor of Sanskrit
and scholar in Kāmaśāstra, Belgaum
BAMS, PhD (Ayurveda)
BA, MA, MPhil (Sanskrit)
Diploma in Yoga and Ayurveda

Prologue

It gives me immense pleasure to write a Prologue to this book entitled *Ancient Indian Eugenics, Eroticism and Sex Psychology* (*Theory of Kāmaśāstra*): *An Āyurvedic Perspective* written by Dr Rahul Vishwas Altekar. The subject matter of the book is unique in the Indian knowledge world. Although India is known for its ancient knowledge, we find a lot of hesitation to discuss about sex openly even today. No doubt, sex is a powerful instinct in human beings like in all beings. It is considered as one of the basic needs of man like food, sleep, water and so on. There are different opinions and different attitudes regarding sex throughout the world. Even in India, it is a debatable topic since a long time. Some consider it as one of the human goals and other treat it is an enemy of the man. According to some, copulation is a heinous act, at the same time, for others it is a procreational sacrifice. Sex was censured as lust by some and glorified as love by others. Some perform *kāma-pūjā* and some perform *kāmadahana*. In this paradoxical situation, the author has taken a bold step to deal with this delicate matter openly. I appreciate his open-mindedness which is one of the important characteristics of ancient scholars.

Āyurveda, which is another essential branch of ancient Indian knowledge, is gaining more popularity in the medical field. It has a long history in our country. It deals with human health, hygiene and longevity of the life. Although the process of Āyurveda is slow, it roots out the diseases completely. Hence it carry more attraction among the people in this era. The study of Āyurveda and research therein are going on rapidly. The texts composed on

Āyurveda instruct *dinacaryā* and *ṛtucaryā* for a common man to lead a happy life. Thus, Āyurveda deal with both, a healthy body and a sound mind.

Kāmaśāstra concerns with mind and body; Āyurveda concerns with body and mind. Body and mind are inseparable and in the same way Kāmaśāstra and Āyurveda are also inseparable. Both sciences are helpful for the betterment of human life. The objectives of both Śāstras are to guide human beings for healthy and satisfied life in all respects. The author has made a comparative study of both sciences and showed how they are beneficial to the human life. The concepts of *aṣṭāṅga-yoga* and *aṣṭāṅga kāmaśāstra*, discussed in the third chapter, reveal not only ancient wisdom but also shed the light on human behaviour.

The interdisciplinary study of Dr Altekar indicates the importance of the subject. The modern world is endowed with a materialistic approach. People are running behind sensual pleasures. They are not satisfied with what is available. They need more and more pleasures, making them weak physically and psychologically. They need a control over mind. Such control is possible by reading such books. In this regard, the author has done an appreciable work. I congratulate him and expect more such research works from him in the days to come.

Dharwad
26 April 2022

Dr V.K. Hampiholi
Rtd Principal, A.V. Baliga College of Arts and Sciences, Kumta (Karnataka), and Emeritus Fellow (UGC)

V.K. Hampiholi is a renowned scholar and an author on Kāmaśāstra topic: https://www.amazon.in/Books-V-K_Hampiholi/s?rh=n%3A976389031%2Cp 27%3AV.+K.+Hampiholi

Preamble

DURING my studies and profession throughout, I was keenly interested in espying the fact that the living of our ancestors was scientific and still devoid of all the artificial means. Those archaic styles have been so immensely intriguing me that I strongly developed a natural inclination and urge to explore the depth of ancient Indian wisdom.

Most of the literature which throws light on the stalwart bonding between the behavioural patterns of ancient Indians and the principles of pure sciences such as physics, chemistry, mathematics as well as applied sciences like metallurgy, mechanics and architecture are being observed transcript in Sanskrit. Therefore, after acquiring my graduate degree in engineering and postgraduation in business management, I decided to pursue MA (Sanskrit) with grammar as further specialization. Later, in my quest for knowledge I was looking for the research subject that would invoke challenging attempts to reveal the eco-friendly lifestyles followed in ancient India.

As an engineer and as an admirer of Sanskrit literature, I always felt sorry about the reality that no (or very few) scientific efforts were put on a large scale to decipher ancient Indian technology. Hence, I felt a need to carry out a much-needed research, a research that would facilitate the fusion between ancient and modern sciences emphasizing the outlook to learn from the past to shape the future.

With this motto, I completed my research and thesis in the most relevant area, viz. "Ancient Indian Architecture and Civil

Engineering, i.e. Vāstuśāstra". Later, the research was published as a textbook and placed as a key reference material in many national and international universities. The research could successfully demystify the auspicious (and hence non-scientific) aura of Vāstuśāstra and proved it to be a much scientific and social-friendly engineering.

On the success of this endeavour, I felt to focus on the other misinterpreted ancient Indian social science, the Kāmaśāstra. This science is misinterpreted today as less than pornography or the text that deals with postures of copulation. The essence of social science and eugenics is completely found ignored. Probably this was developed due to the aggression of the foreign culture and false morality on the original and matured culture of this soil.

With my study of Āyurvedic texts and a formal diploma in the subject, I strongly developed a hypothesis on the close relationship of Āyurveda and Kāmaśāstra. This was much intriguing to me and was in line with my objectives and with the interest of pursuing my third PhD.

My research had been fulfilling and enriching to me in terms of both, the knowledge and the skills. I had the wonderful opportunity to discuss Kāmaśāstra aspects with field scholars and to know the practical aspects of Āyurveda from leading practising professional doctors.

My research was further embellished through several site visits, which I made to the places of historic importance. I have seen the multiform temples, houses and other structures located at Khajurāho, the sun Temple at Koṇārk and Sri Chenna Keshava Swamy Temple at Bellur (built by the Vatsal dynasty of Karnataka). The key purpose of these site visits was to discover the clues from erotic architecture of these temples that may support or contradict the theoretical views gathered from literature. This analysis was very important to understand the Kāmaśāstra concepts, especially those regarding the descriptions of various *āsanas* appear in there.

My humble efforts to compile the collected information and its analysis are presented in the form of this book. I hope to make it a monumental work, which will show a pathway for the better understanding and appreciation of our culture, especially with reference to ancient Indian social sciences and medical science.

Contents

Acknowledgements

I AM deeply indebted to my guide Dr Gauri Mahulikar and would like to express my profound respect and sincere gratitude for her valuable guidance, moral support and encouragement, which was a constant source of inspiration for me.

My search for literature granted me the pleasure of being introduced to other eminent personalities in this field like Dr V.K. Hampiholi, Dr Eli Coleman, late Vaidya P.Y. Khadiwale, Dr Subhash Ranade, Dr Sameer Jamadagni and Dr Nitin Kamat. I would like to express my heartfelt gratitude to all these distinguished personalities for their expert guidance and fruitful discussions that I had with them during my course of work.

I owe special thanks to Vaidya Shreeprasad Bavadekar for his kind help in providing his articles on Āyurveda texts.

I would like to thank Dr Marc Halpern and Yogini Shambhavi Devi for providing me with international perspective on Āyurveda.

Thanks are also due to Dr Bharat Gupt for his generous help extended to me in interpreting Kāmaśāstra theme vis-à-vis social bearing. It has further helped me understanding the mysterious aspects of Khajurāho sculptures and its social, scientific and contemporary relevance.

Also, I wish to thank the library staff of the University of Mumbai and all the staff, faculty of the Department of Sanskrit for the extensive support I received from them.

I will be failing in my duty if I do not thank my family members, especially my mother and my wife for putting those extra hours and giving new angles to my thought processes.

Further, my thanks are due to all those who, at some time or the other, have helped me directly or indirectly during my course of work.

Abbreviations

AR	*Anaṅga Raṅga*
ARS	*Arthaśāstra*
AV	*Atharvaveda*
AYD	Āyurveda
BRS	*Bṛhat Saṁhitā*
CS	*Caraka Saṁhitā*
KS	*Kāmasūtra*
NS	*Nāgarasarvasva*
NYS	Nyāya School
RR	*Rati Rahasya*
ṚV	*Ṛgveda*
SS	*Suśruta Saṁhitā*
VAYD	Vāgbhaṭa's *Aṣṭāṅga Hṛdayam*
YS	*Yājñavalkya Smṛti*
YV	*Yajurveda*

List of Tables

List of Figures

1

Introduction

1.1 Context

EVERY culture and civilization of the world has its own history, especially related to various sciences prevailed in that civilization. The scope and applications of these sciences may range from pure sciences like physics, chemistry or mathematics and also spread in the integrated form of pure science applications like cosmology and philosophy, geology and geography, astrology and astronomy, psychology and sexology, algebra and geometry, ergonomics and ecology, mechanical and civil engineering, as well as biology and medical sciences. We could clearly mark the existence and prevalence of these sciences in Indian, Chinese and Greek cultures. India may be one of the few unique countries, where she has her own traditional science of sexology and social behaviour, which can be referred as Kāmaśāstra. Also, it is the general acceptance among the scholars that Āyurveda is the oldest known medical science prevailed in the world. We could find many such unique features of Indian sciences.

Among all Hindu sciences, we find interdisciplinary learning approach and principle-based evolution. Although we see quite a few schools of thoughts for any one Hindu science in the form of many treatises, we could also observe the common theme among them. The present research is an attempt to discover the common understanding between Kāmaśāstra and Āyurveda. The key motive is to analyse how Kāmaśāstra has adopted the key Āyurveda principles in its own theory. Although Kāmaśāstra must have evolved in its own way with rich tradition from the divine sources, like other Hindu sciences, it has its complete coherence with other Hindu sciences like Vāstuśāstra, Jyotiṣaśāstra, Rasaśāstra and Āyurveda.

Here, attempts are made to explain the Kāmaśāstra theory based on Āyurveda. The approach taken is very subject oriented and no chronological elements are considered to conclude on the cross influences. The key motto is to show the compliance of Kāmaśāstra on Āyurveda principles.

1.2 Brief Overview of Āyurveda and Current Trends

Āyurveda can be regarded as the oldest treatises on medicine in the world. It is India's traditional, natural system of medicine that has been practised for more than 5,000 years (Bagde 2013: 1). Āyurveda can be literally translated as "science of life" or "practices of longevity" (*svasthasya svāsthya rakṣaṇaṁ, āturasya vikāra praśamanaṁ* – *CS* 30.26).

The word *āyurveda* is made of two words *āyu* and *veda*. The word *āyu* does not mean just life, instead it means *śarīrendiya satvātmā saṁyogo* – the union of *śarīra* (body), *indriya* (sense organs), *satva* (mind) and *ātmā* (soul) (*CS* 1.42).

Thus, Āyurveda has two aims, one is to protect and promote health; the other is to cure from diseases. It uses the inherent principles of nature to help maintain health in a person by keeping the individual's body, mind and spirit in perfect equilibrium with nature. It emphasizes prevention of disease, rejuvenation of body systems and extension of lifespan. The profound premise and promise of Āyurveda is that through certain practices, not only can a human prevent diseases but can also better understand self and the world, and live a long healthy life in balance and harmony, achieving fullest potential and express true inner nature daily.

Thus, Āyurveda provides an integrated approach (mind and body) for preventing and treating illness through lifestyle interventions and natural therapies. In fact, it is one of the most renowned traditional systems of medicine that has survived and flourished from ages till date. It has enormous knowledge of nature-based medicine, the relationship of human body constitution and function to nature and the elements of the universe. Āyurveda believes that all these variables act in coordination and affect the living beings.

Āyurveda system is getting much more global attention now. Cancer therapy is the latest interest in Āyurveda studies these days. Cancer is related to the adversity of modernization and advanced pattern of irregular and stressed life, dominated by Western medicines (Ganguly 2014). The excruciating experience of dying cancer patients can be ameliorated by making use of Āyurveda principles. It can be helpful in the management of cancer in many ways such as prophylactic, palliative, curative and supportive. Āyurveda medicines help to improve the quality of life of the patients through various pharmacokinetic mechanisms. Āyurvedic drugs act as supplements with chemotherapy and radiation therapy in ameliorating cancer. Interestingly, *snehana*, i.e. intake of various medicated oil preparations in a classical way a week or ten days prior to the start of chemotherapy or radiotherapy, has been found to reduce the toxic effects of such therapies.

In this regard, it is interesting to note (Thomas et al. 2019) in today's context that Āyurveda's medical heritage is spread across two streams of experiential knowledge, viz. the classical (codified) and folk (oral). Both these streams reveal an incredible range and depth of knowledge of medicinal plants. In the classical stream of Āyurveda, across the period from 1500 BCE to 1900 CE, there is information of more than 12,000 distinct Sanskrit plant names with overlaps across texts. This information is captured in more than 200 texts, viz. six *saṁhitās*, fifty-seven *nighaṇṭus* and 140 *vyākhyās*.

There are many avenues of Āyurveda still to be explored by the researchers, practitioners and experts in the field to contribute towards global human health and overall social development in the future.

1.3 History and Legacy of Āyurveda

The popular and available treatises on Āyurveda are the *Caraka Saṁhitā*, Suśruta's *śalya cikitsā*, Vāgbhaṭa's *Aṣṭāṅga Hṛdayam* and a few on *rasa-cikitsā.*

Vāgbhata's *Aṣṭāṅga Hṛdayam* provides with comprehensive overview of eight branches of Āyurveda touching all aspects of diagnosis (*nidāna*), symptoms (*lakṣaṇa*) and therapy (*cikitsā*) for a patient and a healthy person. It details the history of Āyurveda, its fundamental principles, human anatomy, hygiene, materia medica, therapeutics, diseases, diagnostic approach, surgery and surgical diseases, *pañca-karma*, paediatrics, etc. It can be considered as the synopsis of the entire Āyurveda literature. However, the *Caraka Saṁhitā* is the oldest monument on the topic. We will revisit these significant texts later in Chapter 2 in the literature review.

While describing the history of this science, the *Caraka Saṁhitā* (*CS*) says:

> ब्रह्मणा हि यथा प्रोक्तमायुर्वेदं प्रजापतिः ।
> *brahmaṇā hi yathā proktamāyurvedaṁ prajāpatiḥ* । – 1.4
>
> Dakṣa Prajāpati first obtained the science of life (Āyurveda) in its entirety, as promulgated by Brahmā.

From him Aśvin twins obtained it. From Aśvin twins Indra acquired it (*CS* 1.5, 7-9). Bharadvāja, the mighty ascetic, in search of the science of longevity approached Indra and understood Āyurveda. Later, it was spread over the world and we see today various treatises on Āyurveda. We observe Vasiṣṭha, Kaśyapa, Ātreya, Nārada, Agastya, Bharadvāja, Gārgya, etc. enlisted as the authorities on Āyurveda.

It indicates from above that Āyurveda has an age-old history and many scholars believe that it flourished at least from the second century BCE (Jaiswal et al. 2017). Āyurveda has its foundations laid by the ancient schools of Hindu philosophical teachings named Vaiśeṣika and the school of logic named Nyāya.

It is also related to the manifestation framework, well known as Sāṁkhya, and it was established in the same period when Nyāya school and Vaiśeṣika school flourished.

The Vaiśeṣika school preached about inferences and perceptions that should be obtained about a patient's pathological condition for treatment. Whereas, the Nyāya school propagated its teachings on the basis that one should have an extensive knowledge of the patient's condition, and the disease condition before proceeding for treatment. The Vaiśeṣika school classifies the attributes of any object into six types: substance, particularity, activity, generality, inherence and quality called as *dravya*, *viśeṣa*, *karma*, *sāmānya*, *samavāya* and *guṇa* respectively. Later, both these schools merged and brought glory to the ancient Hindu philosophy and helped in disseminating the knowledge about Āyurveda.

As discussed already, the origin of Āyurveda is divine, i.e from Brahmā who is called as the creator of the universe. It is believed that the creator of the universe passed on this holistic knowledge of healing onto the sages for the well-being of mankind. From the sages the knowledge of traditional medicines was passed on to the disciples and then to the common man by various writings and oral narrations. The information about the healing properties of the herbs was composed in the poetic form which was used by sages to describe the use of medicinal plants.

Āyurveda system is believed to be based on four Vedas (ibid.: 51). The *R̥gveda* is the most well known of all the four Vedas and describes sixty-seven plants in 1,028 hymns. The *Atharvaveda* and *Yajurveda* describe 293 and eighty-one medicinally useful plants. The practice of Āyurveda is based upon the knowledge gained from these Vedas. The writings in the *R̥gveda* and *Atharvaveda* are attributed to Ātreya who is believed to have been conferred with this knowledge from Lord Indra, who initially received it from Lord Brahmā.

Agniveśa compiled the knowledge from the Vedas, and it was edited by Caraka and some other scholars and is presently available as the *Caraka Saṁhitā*. It describes all aspects of Āyurvedic medicines, whereas the *Suśruta Saṁhitā* describes the science of surgery.There are several other allied minor compilations like the *Nighaṇṭu*, *Mādhava Nidāna* and *Bhāva Prakāśa* composed to enrich the legacy of Āyurveda.

1.4 Theory of Āyurveda: Basic Building Blocks

Āyurveda believes that the entire universe is composed of five elements: *vāyu* (air), *jala* (water), *ākāśa* (space or ether), *pr̥thvī* (earth) and *teja* (fire). These five elements (referred to as *pañca-mahābhūta* in Āyurveda) are believed to form the three basic humours of human body in varying combinations. The three humours – *vāta-doṣa*, *pitta-doṣa* and *kapha-doṣa* – are collectively called as *tridoṣa* and they control the basic physiological functions of the body along with five sub-*doṣa* for each of the principal *doṣas*. Āyurveda believes that the human body consists of *sapta-dhātus* (seven tissues): *rasa* (tissue fluids), *meda* (fat and connective tissue), *rakta* (blood), *asthi* (bones), *majjā* (marrow), *māṁsa* (muscle) and *śukra* (semen); and three *malas* (waste products) of the body, viz. *puriṣa* (faeces), *mūtra* (urine) and *sveda* (sweat). *Vāta-doṣa* maintains the cellular transport, electrolyte balance, elimination of waste products and its effect is increased by dryness. *Pitta-doṣa* regulates the body temperature, optic nerve coordination, and hunger and thirst management. Heat conditions of the body aggravate *pitta*. *Kapha-doṣa* is increased due to sweet and fatty food and it provides lubrication to the joints for proper functioning. The catabolism of the body is believed to be governed by *vāta*, metabolism by *pitta* and anabolism by *kapha* (Heinrich et al. 2004: 203).

For a healthy state of health, a balance between the three *doṣas* and other factors should be maintained.

Any imbalance between the three causes a state of illness or disease (Ravishankar and Shukla 2007). In Āyurveda, it is believed, that a perfect balance between the natural elements of the human body should be maintained for a healthy state of living by following the principles of divine wisdom. The seven tissues work in coordination with each for proper physiological functioning of the human body. The *rakta-dhātu* resembles the blood and regulates the circulation of blood cells and provision of blood components to the body. The *māṁsa-dhātu* provides supports in the form of skeletal muscles for the adipose fat. The *asthi-dhātu* comprises the bones of the body and the *majjā-dhātu* is made up of the bone marrow and fluids required for the oleation of the bones and their functioning. The *śukra-dhātu* is responsible for functions of the reproductive organs.

Apart from these, the other important factors considered in the doctrine of Āyurveda are the *tri-mala* and *traya doṣa agni*. *Mala*s are the three types of waste products formed in the body due to metabolic and digestive functions. They comprise of urine, faeces and sweat. Āyurveda explains that if the balance between *tridoṣa* is not maintained, the waste products of the body are not effectively eliminated and these lead to further complications like diarrhoea, constipation, asthma and rheumatoid arthritis. If the urine is not removed from the body, it can lead to urinary tract infections, cystitis and gastric pain. If the sweat is not cleared from the body, it can lead to skin irritation and improper fluid balance. As per the principles of Āyurveda, the biological fire of the body for all the metabolic function is called as *agni*. There are thirteen categories of *agni* in a human body and the most important is the one responsible for digestive fire, called as *jaṭharāgni*.

It has a close relation with *pitta* and ultimately *vāta* of the body. If the digestive fire of the body is increased in the body by increased acidity conditions, the elevation in *pitta* levels and its relative symptoms are observed. Digestive fire is important in controlling the normal microflora, proper digestive functions and provision of energy to the entire body. Any disturbance in its balance creates discomfort to the gastrointestinal tract and results in pathological complications like ulcers, diarrhoea and constipation.

Considering the bodily constitution and pathological history, the characteristics, lifestyle and environmental conditions in an individual's routine lifestyle, Āyurveda provides with many treatment strategies for promoting well-being to individuals.

One famous therapy is *pañca-karma*. This therapy applies various processes for the rejuvenation of the body, cleansing and enhancing longevity. It is composed of five actions that are used for the removal of toxins from the body tissues. They are the *virecana* (purgation through the use of powders, pastes or decoction), *vamana* (forced therapeutic emesis by the use of some medicines), *basti* (use of enemas prepared from medicated oils), *rakta-mokṣaṇa* (detoxification of blood) and *nāsya* (administration of medicines like decoctions, oils and fumes through nasal route).

Primarily, it consists of three steps: preparatory process of the body for the therapy, the main process of therapy and the last step consisting of regimens to be followed to restore digestive and other absorptive procedures of the body, back to the normal state. Clarified butter and medicated oils are used in the oleation process. Sweating is brought about by exposure to steam for areas of treatment. Forced emesis is brought about by administration of decoction of liquorice, honey with a few hours of prior administration of curd and rice. These substances are believed to cause elevation in the emesis effect. The laxative therapy is carried out by administration of herbs and liquids like senna, cow milk, psyllium seed and castor oil. The enemas used here can be prepared from medicated oils or decoction of herbs like sesame or anise.

In practice, Āyurveda has eight disciplines called as *Aṣṭāṅga Āyurveda*. They are *kāya-cikitsā* (internal medicine treatment), *bhūta-vidyā* (treatment of psychological disorders), *kaumāra-bhṛtya* (paediatric treatment), *rasāyana* (study of geriatrics), *vājīkaraṇa* (treatment through aphrodisiacs and eugenics), *śalya* (surgical treatment), *śālākya* (otorhinolaryngological and ophthalmological treatment), and *agada tantra* (toxicological studies).

With a rich knowledge of plants, minerals and animal-based products, and the above-mentioned principles of doctrine, Āyurveda has achieved its widespread acceptance globally.

1.5 Literature Review of Āyurvedic Texts

Investigator has used structured methods of literature review to identify the core concepts of Āyurveda. It will be interesting to understand that the core concepts of Āyurveda theory in the light of its basic building blocks. The same are presented below in different sections. The discussions on literature review are primarily around those aspects of Āyurveda where Kāmaśāstra possibly has direct or indirect dependencies.

1.5.1 CONCEPT OF HOMEOSTASIS: BALANCE AND IMBALANCE (SAMĀVASTHĀ VICĀRA)

Imbalance in the state of bodily tissues is known as "disease" and equilibrium is called "health" (Patwardhan 2008). The aim of Āyurveda is to re-establish the state of equilibrium among different tissues. *Dhātu-sāmya* is the term given for homeostasis in Āyurveda.

In Suśruta's view (ibid.), the life on this universe is maintained because of three opposing factors known as the sun, moon and air. The sun exerts a drying effect on earth whereas the moon is coolant and strengthening in nature. The air brings about all types of movements. In exactly similar manner, the body is sustained by three opposing factors called *vāta*, *pitta* and *kapha*.

Āyurveda places great emphasis on prevention of diseases and encourages the maintenance of health through close attention to balance in one's life: right thinking, diet, lifestyle and the use of herbs. Knowledge of Āyurveda enables one to understand how to create this balance of body, mind and consciousness according to one's own individual constitution and how to make lifestyle changes to bring about and maintain this balance.[1]

Just as everyone has a unique fingerprint, each person has a pattern of energy – an individual combination of physical, mental and emotional characteristics – which comprises her/his own constitution. This constitution is determined at conception by several factors and remains the same throughout one's life.[2]

Many factors, both internal and external, act upon us to disturb this balance and are reflected as a change in one's constitution from the balanced state.

Examples of these emotional and physical stresses include one's emotional state, diet and food choices, seasons and weather, physical trauma, work and family relationships.

Once these factors are understood, one can take appropriate actions to nullify or minimize their effects or eliminate the causes of imbalance and re-establish one's original constitution. Balance is the natural order; imbalance is disorder. Health is order; disease is disorder. Within the body there is a constant interaction between order and disorder. When one understands the nature and structure of disorder, one can re-establish order.

In Āyurveda, body, mind and consciousness work together in maintaining balance. They are simply viewed as different facets of one's being. To learn how to balance the body, mind and consciousness requires an understanding of how *vāta, pitta* and *kapha* work together. According to Āyurvedic philosophy, the entire cosmos is an interplay of the energies of the five great elements – space, air, fire, water and earth. *Vāta, pitta* and *kapha* are combinations and permutations of these five elements that manifest as patterns present in all creation. In the physical body, *vāta* is

[1] Vasant Lad, "Ayurveda: A Brief Introduction and Guide", p. 1, available online: https://www.ayurveda.com/resources/articles/reading-list-and-references-about-ayurveda.

[2] Ibid., p. 3.

the subtle energy of movement, *pitta* the energy of digestion and metabolism, and *kapha* the energy that forms the body's structure.

Āyurveda clearly advocates (Patwardhan 2008) that there can be no mental health without physical health and vice versa. The symptoms and diseases that could be categorized as mental thoughts or feelings are just as important as symptoms and diseases of the physical body. Both are due to imbalances within a person and both are treated by restoring the natural balance mentally and physically.

Lifestyle interventions are considered as the major preventive and therapeutic approach.

1.5.2 CONCEPTUAL ELEMENTS IN THERAPY (SĀTMYA VICĀRA)

Āyurveda deals with holistic principles of treatment and believes in complete health. The definition of health in Āyurveda is not limited up to physical well-being only but it includes the mental, spiritual and social well-being also (Paliwal 2014: 16). Moreover, it is not only concentrated on the treatment of diseases but has laid proper emphasis on the care of diseased person also. It advocates to examine the constitution, morbidity, constitution of the *dhātu*, compactness, measurement, suitability, psyche, power of intake and digestion of food, power of exercise and age of the patient before application of medicine (ibid.: 17). It is because the strong, moderate or mild medicines are advised according to the superior, medium and inferior strength of the patient as well as disease respectively.

Sātmya is one of the important considerable issues during application of medicine or diet. Efficacy of medicine depends upon it, as the diet or medicine which is not *sātmya* to the person does not act properly and sometimes it may cause reactions also (ibid.: 18). A physician must advise the diet or medicine considering all the *sātmya* for the rational use.

Sātmya may be sometime wholesome entity while sometime unwholesome also (ibid.: 18). If unwholesome entity is accustomed due to habitual use, it should be gradually withdrawn and wholesome at its place should be used. All types of *sātmya* are considerable for the maintenance of health (ibid.: 19).

If anybody ignores the *sātmya* of the person, he/she will not get success in treatment and homeostasis cannot be maintained.

1.5.3 CONCEPT OF ANATOMY AND PHYSIOLOGY (ŚĀRĪRA VICĀRA)

Śārīra vicāra is the Āyurvedic term that represents both anatomy and physiology. *Vicāra* means the special or detailed knowledge (Patwardhan 2008). As per the *Caraka Saṁhitā*, the detailed knowledge of normal human body is helpful to understand the factors influencing health and, therefore, such knowledge is widely appreciated by experts (*CS* 6. 3).

1.5.3.1 *Concept of a Cell*

The *Caraka Saṁhitā* has explained that the body parts can be divided and redivided into innumerable individual components called *paramāṇu*' (Patwardhan 2008: 55). These are innumerable because of their huge number, highly minute structure and limited perceptive ability of sense organs (*CS* 7.17). This statement indicates that there existed a concept of minute and numerous individual living units in the body. Today, we call such microscopic units by the name "cell". "*Aṇu srota*" is another such very similar term, probably indicative of a cell (ibid.: 56). Some scholars even hold the view that the living body is nothing but the resultant of aggregation of such innumerable *srota* (*CS* 5.4). A tissue is a group of structurally and functionally similar cells. These are structurally like their corresponding tissues. Also, each *srota* is functionally (metabolically) related to its corresponding tissue (Patwardhan 2008: 61).

1.5.3.2 *Basic Tissues*

Plasma and lymph, blood cells, muscular and general connective tissues, body lipids including adipose tissue, tissues resisting easy degradation like bones, bone marrow and nervous tissue, and tissues responsible for reproductive functions are the basic tissues from which the body is formed. Tissues producing breast milk, female reproductive tissues, tendons, blood vessels, muscle fat, six layers of skin and sinews are the subsidiary tissues (*CS* 15.17).

Classification of tissues described in Āyurveda is based on some rational observations (Patwardhan 2008: 61). For example, *rasa-dhātu* includes both plasma and lymph (intravascular fluid). *Rakta-dhātu* mainly stands for RBCs. *Māṁsa-dhātu* stands for muscular tissue in general but also includes general connective tissue and parenchymal and stromal tissues of different viscera. *Majjā-dhātu* stands for everything that fills bony cavities. So, apart from bone marrow, it also stands for brain substance because this fills up a cavity formed by the union of several cranial bones. *Śukra-dhātu* mainly stands for all hormones of hypothalamus–pituitary–gonadal axis (Patwardhan 2008: 55).

'Medo Dhātu' includes adipose tissue and circulating lipids of blood because it is of two types: 'Baddha' (bound) and 'Abaddha' (free). 'Asthi Dhātu' includes all those structures of the body, which resist easy degradation. So, teeth and nails also are included under this 'Dhātu'.

Supplying the nourishment, delivery of life-principle, providing covering or coating, providing lubrication, giving mechanical support, filling - in the bony cavities and reproduction - are the most important functions of these seven *dhātus* respectively (Patwardhan 2008: 68).

1.5.3.3 *Role of Vāta*

All functions of nervous system in human body are represented by *vāta* in Āyurveda (Patwardhan 2008). In general, the functions ascribed to *vāta* are: Control and coordinationof different parts of the body, initiation of all movements, regulation of psychological processes, initiation of all activities of sense organs, transmission of different sensations, production of speech, secret motor functions in the gut, expulsion of wastes from the body and control of respiration (*CS* 12.8).

Vāta is divided into five subtypes (Patwardhan 2008: 57) – *prāṇa*, *udāna*, *vyāna*, *samāna* and *apāna*.

Prāṇa Vāta: This is situated in head and is responsible for the control over intellectual functions, cardiovascular functions, sense organs, psychological activities, respiration, and reflex activities like sneezing, belching and deglutition.

Udāna Vāta: Its active site is the chest region. It is basically responsible for production of speech. The effort and strength required for speech are also the functions of this element. It also helps in recall of vocabulary required for a well-articulated speech.

Vyāna Vāta: The active site of *vyāna vāta* is the heart. It makes the circulation of blood possible by controlling the heart. It makes the intravascular fluid including plasma and lymph to get forcefully ejected out of the heart and makes it circulate throughout the body (*CS* 15.36). The sympathetic and parasympathetic control of heart is indicated by this element (Patwardhan 2008: 62). Some authors have ascribed the functions of somatic nervous system also to *vyāna vāta* as movements like flexion, extension, opening and closure of eyelids have been said to be under its control (*CS* 28.9).

Samāna Vāta: Active site of *samāna* is adjacent to the gastrointestinal tract. It performs the functions like reception of food, its digestion through the activation of *agni*, its division into useful and waste parts, and its onward propulsion. All these functions are either those of parasympathetic nerves supplying the gut or those of enteric nervous system.

Apāna Vāta: This is active in the pelvic region. It governs physiological processes like micturition, defecation, ejaculation, menstruation and parturition. Autonomic nervous system has got a definite role in most of these activities.

1.5.3.4 *Reflexes*

The *Caraka Saṁhitā* has opined that one should not suppress the natural urges related to micturition, defecation, ejaculation, flatus, vomiting, sneezing, eructation, yawning, hunger, thirst, tears, sleep and dyspnoea developed after exertion (*CS* 7.3-4). It should be noted (Patwardhan 2008) that one or the other reflex is involved in all these activities. So, the term *vega* stands almost equivalent to reflex.

1.5.3.5 *Physiology of Male Reproductive System*

The roots of *śukravāha srotas* are the testicles and penis (*CS* 5.10). Testicles synthesize the hormone testosterone and, also, they are the sites of spermatogenesis. Penis is the male copulatory organ through which the seminal fluid is deposited in the female reproductive tract. The factor, which is responsible for the formation of embryo, is known as *śukra* (*CS* 2.4).

All hormones of hypothalamus–pituitary–gonadal axis can thus be included under the term *śukra*. In some references, *śukra* stands (Patwardhan 2008: 57) for only semen.

1.5.3.6 *Ejaculation*

When the person gets excited because of the sexual urge, determination and romantic mental attitude, *śukra* comes out through the urethra (with which the bladder is connected) as if the melted *ghee* (Patwardhan 2008). This occurs because of the heat produced by the physical exertion during copulation. The simile given to describe this process is the flow of water from a place of lower altitude to a place of higher altitude (*CS* 15.34-35). Generalized sympathetic stimulation is an essential feature of sexual activity. Erection requires parasympathetic stimulation, whereas ejaculation is dependent on sympathetic one. Also, ejaculation is brought about by *apāna vāta*, which represents the sympathetic activity in this case.

1.5.3.7 *Physiology of Female Reproductive System*

Menstrual blood (*raja*) also is a derivative of *rasa* only (Patwardhan 2008: 56). Menstruation occurs in females once in every month and lasts for about three days. This process of menstrual cycle begins at the age of twelve years and stops at about fifty years of age (*SS* 14. 6). During the act of copulation, production of *śukra* occurs in females also; and it should not be thought that it is of no use in the process of production of embryo, i.e. it is also of definite use (Patwardhan 2008: 58). *Ārtava* is responsible for the production of embryo (*SS* 15.5). It denotes ovum in this context. After getting nourished over the period of a month, it enters the uterus and then vagina through the specialized structures called *dhamanī* meant for the transportation of the same. *Vāta* is responsible for this movement (*SS* 3.10). This is the explanation regarding the process of ovum entering the uterus through the Fallopian tube. If not fertilized, it is shed off through menstrual fluid.

1.5.4 CONCEPT OF HEALTHY LIFESTYLE (SVASTHA-VṚTTA)

Maintenance of a healthy life by one's own ethical code of conduct is called *svastha-vṛtta*, which literally means the regime of abiding by one's own nature (Dewan 2014). One who stands in the balanced status of one's own self is called *svastha* – the state of equilibrium of *dhātu* (ibid.: 212). It raises the limit and standard of life to enable man fulfil his personal and social obligations perfectly. In other words, it improves both qualitative and quantitative aspects of man not only in individual perspective but also in relation to social environment.

Āyurveda suggests practical approach to improve immunity by getting proper nutrition, minimal exposure to pollutants, reducing stress in one's life. The *Caraka Saṁhitā* suggests (ibid.: 214) the ways to live in accordance with the nature termed as *sukhāyu* and *hitāyu*, and recommends the preventive and social medicine (ibid.: 213). It explains the advantages of prevention in indulgence of three basic ideas: *ati-yoga*, *hīna-yoga*, *a-yoga* of the *kāla*, *prajñā* and *indriya*. Human body is greatly influenced by external environment. Many of the exogenous rhythms and endogenous rhythms have specific phase relationship with each other; which means that they interact and synchronize with each other. Any change in the external environment causes change in one's body. Hence, it is advised to follow such a regimen which helps in adapting the external environment smoothly (ibid.: 216).

Characteristics of a healthy person are:

- Person having proportionate musculature and compactness of the body with strong sensory organs will overcome onslaught of diseases.
- Can withstand hunger and thirst.
- Can withstand heat of the sun and cold.
- Can withstand physical exercises.
- Can digest and assimilate the food properly.

Thus, a happy and healthy life should be leading to the fulfilment of four main objectives of human life (Dewan 2014) – service to society (*dharma*), service to family (*artha*), service to self (*kāma*) and self-emancipation (*mokṣa*).

The topic includes the avoidance of excessive utilization, non-utilization and wrong utilization of sense organs and mind. It suggests the following elements:

1. Daily regimen (*dinacaryā*);
2. seasonal regimen (*ṛtucaryā*);
3. occasional occupational duties;
4. precautionary observances in sexual activity;
5. general rules of conduct for the well-being of society (ethical regimen);
6. precautionary measures against untimely old age; and
7. conduct and practices to achieve self-realization.

The other perspective is to cluster all these recommendations into three broad categories as mentioned below (ibid.):

a. *Personal Hygiene*: This consists of the appropriate daily routine, seasonal regimen and ethical conduct. *Svastha* means physically, psychologically and spiritually harmonious condition. Hence, various methods, which increase physical, mental and spiritual strength, are included in this branch.

b. *Rejuvenation* (*Rasāyana*) and *Invigoration* (*Vājīkaraṇa*): There are special foods and herbs to prevent ageing, strengthen immunity, improve mental faculties and increase vitality. *Vājīkaraṇa* drugs are specifically used as aphrodisiac and fertility improving agents.

c. *Yoga*: *Yoga* is considered as part of a rejuvenation practice of Ayurveda. The regular practice of *yoga* keeps body and mind fit, which provides a feeling of well-being, prevents ageing and inhibits disease.

Āyurveda says misconduct is the cause of diseases (Dewan 2014: 217). There are three important causes of the diseases, which encompass broadly of all diseases. They are:

- Incompatible core relation of the senses with their objects.
- Volitional transgression that is wrong use of the will which ultimately occurs due to disregard of advice for the physical and mental health respectively.
- Effect of time.

Effect of time is unavoidable, and prior two causes make the situation worse. This means if we avoid the misconducts, the probability of occurrence of diseases will be less (ibid.: 218). Also, to train each individual for treating diseases is not possible but to understand preventive measures to avoid diseases is much easy.

The key to health does not lie in the application of drugs, but in the prime factors on which our life and vitality are based. The three most important ones are food, sleep and sexual energy. While considering these pillars one should include daily routines like oil massage, etc. in addition to diet. If one can comply all the three pillars in proper way, it can be very beneficial for one's life (Dewan 2014).

1.5.5 CONCEPT OF DIGESTION AND METABOLISM (AGNI VICĀRA)

Āyurveda has described an important factor of digestion and metabolism in our body as *agni* (Agrawal et al. 2010). Āyurveda uses the term *agni* in the sense of digestion of food and metabolic products.

Ingested food is to be digested, absorbed and assimilated, which is essential for the maintenance of life and is performed by *agni*. It converts food into energy, which is responsible for all the vital functions of our body. Therefore, the *Caraka Saṁhitā* mentions that *dehāgni* is the cause of life, complexion, strength, health, nourishment, lustre, *oja*, *teja* (energy) and *prāṇa* (life energy) (*CS* 15.3).

About the importance of Agni, the *Caraka Saṁhitā* has mentioned that after stoppage of the function of *agni*, the individual dies and when the *agni* of an individual is in the state of harmony, then that person would be absolutely healthy and would lead a long, happy, healthy life. But, if the *agni* of a person is vitiated, the whole metabolism in his body would be disturbed, resulting in ill health and disease. Hence, *agni* is said to be the base of life (*CS* 15.4).

Agni is innumerable because of its presence in each cell of the body. However, Āyurveda texts provide classification of the same.

The *Caraka Saṁhitā* has mentioned that the seven *dhātus* that support the body contain their own *agni*, and by their own they digest and transform the materials supplied to them to make the substances alike to them for assimilation and nourishment (*CS* 28.15).

1.5.6 CONCEPT OF VITAL POINTS AND TRAUMATIC EFFECTS (MARMA VICĀRA)

Marma (vital points) is one of the important aspects described in various ancient texts of Āyurveda. Knowledge of *marma* has been used since long time in surgery (Rathod et al. 2016). The *Suśruta Saṁhitā* defined *marma* as the vital points of the body which shows various fatal signs and symptoms on traumatic injury (ibid.: 19). Depending upon traumatic effects and prognosis, various types of such points are mentioned in Āyurveda, like sudden death, death within short period, deformity due to trauma, person lives until removal of foreign body, continuous pain due to trauma.

These are superficial and deeply-seated points on body that involves artery, vein, bone, muscle, ligament and joint, where vital energy resides or flows through (ibid.: 20). *Marma* therapy involves utilization of these points for the purpose of gentle massage with oil. *Marma* points can be used to balance the basic components at physical level and even at mental level.

The *Suśruta Saṁhitā* mentions 107 vital points which on injury generate various symptoms. It has classified them based on location, prognosis, etc. For example, the hand region contains five vital points. These points are supposed to be related with the function of various organs (ibid.).

Human body when exposed to trauma shows various signs and symptoms depending on severity and types of trauma. The *Suśruta Saṁhitā* mentions that such deep or superficial points on body surface, when get traumatized, produce various signs and symptoms not only based on the type of injury but based on its constituents also. Our physic comprises vessels, muscles, bones, joints, nerves, ligaments, etc. everywhere in proportion. According to the *Suśruta Saṁhitā* (ibid.: 21), the point where all the above structures meet and is the site of *prāṇa* (vitality) is nothing but *marma*. Vāgbhaṭa's *Aṣṭāṅga Hṛdayam* consideres *marma* as the points where special and unusual pulsation feels. Depending on this composition, traumatic effects develop.

Marmas are classified again on the basis of regions of body (Rathod et al. 2016: 22). Upper extremities contain twenty-two *marmas*. In each hand region, there is the presence of five vital points of different prognostic value when one is in trauma.

As these are vital points, knowledge is of great importance

during surgical procedures. In fact, it is half knowledge of surgery (ibid.: 19). Āyurveda provides with the ideas for avoidance of these trauma. *Hṛdbasti* is one of the best examples applied in cardiac disorder. These procedures proved to be effective due to their action on component like muscle, nerve, vessels, at the site of *marma* by improving tone, circulation, etc.

1.5.7 CONCEPT OF MATERIA MEDICA AND PHARMACOLOGY (DRAVYA-GUṆA VICĀRA)

The word *dravya-guṇa* means the science dealing with properties and actions of drugs (Kumar et al. 2011). This is counterpart of modern pharmacology. It would be necessary, at first, to understand the fundamentals of Āyurveda in general before one can grasp the concepts of its pharmacology.

Pañcabhūtas are regarded as physio-chemical basis of the material objects (Kumar et al. 2011: 147). When life evolved, out of these five, three came forward to control and regulate the biological functions. These three (*vāta, pitta, kapha*) are known as *tridhātu* (*tridoṣa* in pathological state) having specific functions of *vikṣepa* (movement), *ādāna* (assimilation) and *visarga* (growth) respectively.

Primarily based on this fundamental background, the following concepts were developed to explain the drug action (ibid.: 148).

1. *Dravya* (substance – drug and diet)
2. *Guṇa* (property)
3. *Rasa* (taste)
4. *Vipāka* (final transformation)
5. *Vīrya* (potency)
6. *Prabhāva* (specific potency)
7. *Karma* (action)

The *Caraka Saṁhitā* has classified drugs from various angles, e.g. according to source, effect on constituents, composition, properties, actions, etc. Marvellous piece (ibid.: 150) in the *Caraka Saṁhitā* is the description of fifty groups of drugs according to their main action.

In this connection, two broad propositions are established by Āyurveda:

1. There is no substance which cannot be used as drug.
2. All drugs are composed of five *bhūtas.*

1.5.7.1 *Psychic Qualities*

These are six in number (ibid.) such as desire, aversion, pleasure, pain, will and determinative intellect.

1.5.7.2 *Physical or Material Qualities*

These are five in numbers such as sound, touch, vision, taste and smell. They are specific objects of five sensory organs (ibid.: 151).

Interrelation of basic principles of drug action must be kept in mind with two basic fundaments (ibid.):

- Concept of macrocosm and microcosm-continuum.
- Properties are similar in substances and the body and as such, normally, increase and decrease in the body are caused by substances.

Following principles affect the drug action (ibid.: 149):

- In general, drug possessing *madhrua rasa* will have *madhura vipāka* and *śīta vīrya*. Similarly, *āmla rasa* will have *āmla vipāka, uṣṇa vīrya* and *kaṭu rasa* will have *kaṭu vipāka* and *uṣṇa vīrya.* Drug possessing *lavaṇa rasa* will have *madhura vipāka* and *uṣṇa vīrya.* But drugs containing *tikta* and *kaṣāya rasa* possess *katu vipāka* and *śīta vīrya.*
- Naturally when *rasa,* etc. are of in equal strength, *rasa* is subdued by *vipāka*, both by *vīrya* and all by *prabhāva.*
- In case the *rasa*, etc. are of unequal strength, the potent overcomes the weaker one, which is governed by the rule of

nature as the stronger overpowers the weaker in case of incompatible combination.

- Even in case of inequality of strength, *rasa*, etc. perform their own action due to their inherent property.

1.5.8 CONCEPT OF DIET (ĀHĀRA VICĀRA)

As per Āyurveda, diet is believed to be one of the major pillars of life (Borakhade et al. 2018). Faulty diet results in disturbed functions of the body. That is the reason why while describing causative factors of diseases, dietary articles have been given prime importance. The *Caraka Saṁhitā* has stated that diet sustains life if taken with discipline in a proper manner. Diet has a prime role in maintaining health and also in treating various disorders. Āyurveda considers diet as the great medicine (ibid.:47). It emphasizes that the diet is the nourisher of the body elements, vital essence, vitality, complexion and other things, but its action is dependent on the proper function of *jaṭharāgni* (ibid.: 48).

Complexion, clarity, good voice, longevity, astuteness, happiness, satisfaction, nourishment, strength and intellect are all conditioned by food. Diet supports the body constantly just like the house (is supported) by the pillars. Complete nutritional diet or the wholesome food is responsible for the growth of the living beings while unwholesome food for the growth of diseases. Proper growth and maintenance of the body depends on the balanced diet (ibid.: 49).

Diet and the dietetic rules are basic factors among the causes of disease. Hence, it is an important part of the treatment by avoiding the causative factors of a disease.

As per Āyurveda, the factor those take part in the digestion are (ibid.):

- Digestive enzymes
- Nervous mechanism of digestion
- Hydrolyzing agent

- Softening agent
- Time factor
- Rules for proper digestion

The diet and regimen which are beneficial to the body, also give happiness to the mind (ibid.: 52). Āyurveda gives a lot of importance to the diet regarding its processing, quality, quantity because it plays an important role in healthy, diseased and convalescent states. It is more important than the medicine itself.

The body can be nourished and maintained in good health status, by adopting suitable diet and full benefits of life can also be reaped by adherence to proper mental hygiene.

The *Caraka Saṁhitā* states that the ideal diet is that which rebuilds the worn-out systems, nourishes *dhātu* and maintains equilibrium of the body constituents. Irrational diet acts, otherwise, producing disease (ibid.: 47).

One should eat food, which is hot, unctuous, in due measure, after the digestion of previous food and non-antagonistic in potency. It should be eaten in a hygienic place, provided with all accessories, neither too hurriedly, nor too leisurely, without talking or laughing with full concentration and having proper regard to oneself (ibid.: 52).

1.5.9 Concepts in Therapeutical Approach (Cikitsā Vicāra)

Cikitsā is defined as the process in which the vitiated *doṣas* are brought to normal state and their equilibrium state will be maintained (Bagali et al. 2016).

It is classified on different basis, as *dvividha*, *trividha*, *caturvidha*, etc. Among these, *trividha* is given much importance. The method of treatment in Āyurveda has been classified into three categories by the *Caraka Saṁhitā* (ibid.: 56):

- Divine therapy
- Rational therapy
- Psychotherapy

1.5.9.1 *Divine Therapy*

It is a faith therapy used in management of mental diseases. Faith is a part and parcel of human psychology and this treatment is a play of faith where in patient should have full belief in the medicine and the method of treatment (ibid.: 58). This therapy is designed to exhaust evil acts of the past to combat diseases. As a matter of fact, it is concerned with all the unknown circumstances, which are beyond the purview of reasoning. Hence this treatment is often referred to as spiritual therapy. The methods adopted (ibid.: 59) by the *Caraka Saṁhitā* here are like hymns, amulets, talisman, wearing of gems, auspicious ceremony, offering to God, gift, oblations, observance of scriptural rules, atonement, fasting, chanting of auspicious hymns, observance to God, going to pilgrimage.

1.5.9.2 *Rational Therapy*

This type of therapy refers to union, connection, reasoning device, strategy, artifice, expedients and application (ibid.: 60). In medical context, it makes the sense of application of reason to diagnose and treat the diseases. It relies on the valid knowledge and defines it as utilization of rational faculties by the physician, both for understanding the causes and the nature of the diseases, and for deciding upon proper course of treatment.

Therapy is based on the rational thinking and represents careful and purposeful employment of a drug or a method of treatment. It is by far the most scientific of the methods inasmuch as it removes the causes and undertakes to diffuse the pathogenesis.

1.5.9.3 *Psychotherapy*

The rational therapy is primarily used for the treatment of somatic diseases in Āyurveda (Bagali et al. 2016: 61). A specific line of treatment is essential for the management of mental diseases to normalize *doṣa* like bodily disorders. It should be, different from divine therapy, which to some extent, also includes treatment of psychiatric disorders.

This therapy deploys (ibid.: 62) a special method of treatment, which is a non-pharmacological approach equivalent to modern psychotherapy; especially for mental diseases and has been found very effective. It literally means overcoming of mind or victory over mind or control of mind (ibid.: 60).

The perfect balance of mind, body and soul is considered as complete health in Āyurveda.

The reason for any unhealthy condition is the toxins created by the accumulated *doṣas*. These negative feelings are emotional toxins accumulate in the mind. If they are not driven out of the body in a stipulated period, they give rise to or may lead into various chronic mental disorders like anxiety, neurosis, depression, insomnia (Behere et al. 2013). If this is further ignored, it turns into permanent disorders like *unmāda*, the unreasonable and irrational state of mind like hysteria and epilepsy.

Every person has got his own individuality and capability to respond to normal variations. This forms his constitution, which distinguishes him from other individuals. Hence, every therapy must be applied keeping in view the constitution of the person concerned and his suitability (ibid.: 312).

There are specific mental treatments described in Āyurveda to cure physical problems as well as mental disorders. The mental attitude, mental status of a person has a great role in the curing process of every disease. The *Caraka Saṁhitā* describes (ibid.: 314) the disorders Spermaturia in which the patient passes semen resembling urine or urine mixed with semen. Semen is considered as the most important *dhātu* among all. This syndrome is a clinical condition in which the patient is preoccupied with excessive loss of semen by nocturnal emissions and this leads to severe anxiety, hypochondriasis, lack of concentration, bodily weakness and is often associated with sexual impotency. Āyurveda provides with apt techniques of psychotherapy here. The effectiveness of traditional mental-health-promoting practices was identified as health regimens, correct behaviour and *yoga*. Psychotherapy is the mental restraint, or "mind control" as referred by the *Caraka Saṁhitā*, which cab be achieved achieved through "spiritual knowledge, philosophy, fortitude, remembrance and concentration".

1.5.10 CONCEPTS IN SURGICAL APPROACH (ŚALYA-TANTRA VICĀRA)

Suśruta was the first person, who learnt and practised various surgical procedures in approximately 300 BCE (Joshi et al. 2016). He compiled a surgical compendium including other branches of medicine which is known as the *Suśruta Saṁhitā*. It describes eight types of surgical procedures. We are discussing them same below (ibid.: 226-27).

1.5.10.1 *Incision and Exploration*

It is a procedure to be made to expose underlying structures and to let out the content by using scalpel, single-edged knife. For example, to manage a case of abscess, an adequate incision and proper exploration is an essential step. To learn this technique, incision should be practised on a leather bag, urinary bladder or leathern pot containing full of water and slime.

1.5.10.2 *Scraping and Scooping*

This is carried out to remove undesired tissues like hyper-granulations, epithelized tissue and sequestrum. To gain clinical experience, this should be practised on piece of hairy skin. It is a very small surgical procedure, but highest attention is needed to avoid injury to nearby structures. For example, during surgical scrapping of an ulcer, there is a chance of damage to its base, arteries, veins, etc.

1.5.10.3 *Puncturing*

It is a procedure to pierce the epithelial surface, superficial veins, etc. For this purpose, very fine hand is necessary. This procedure should be practised using veins of animals or on the lotus stalks which are smooth, spongy in nature. This procedure is applicable to remove the fluids from any cavity. Example – abdominal paracentesis.

1.5.10.4 *Probing*

This should be practised using holes in pieces of wood eaten by moths, bamboos and mouth of dried gourd. These materials are containing multiple holes and passages through which a probe can be passed without any resistance or least of resistance. By this procedure, a scholar can develop clinical skills to assess the pathway of sinuses and cavities in humans.

1.5.10.5 *Extraction and Pick-up*

This is the act of removal of a foreign body by pulling. This technique can be practised on fruits containing seeds like jackfruit, pulp of *bilva* or on the teeth of dead animals. This procedure is followed to remove the impacted foreign body, stone, fecalith, etc. in surgical practice.

1.5.10.6 *Drainage and Removal of Vitiated Doṣa*

This method is used to remove the abnormal collection of fluids in body cavities and to let out the vitiated *rakta-doṣa* (vitiation of blood). The procedure should be practised on a piece of *śālmali* wood coated with beeswax.

1.5.10.7 *Suturing*

This technique is defined for approximation of cut margins of wound, which are produced by a surgical or a non-surgical process. Approximation of margins anatomically has paramount of importance in surgical practice. This technique should be practised on the borders of fine, closely-knitted cloths and on the borders of soft leather.

1.5.10.8 *Bandaging Technique*

Total fourteen bandaging techniques are mentioned in the *Suśruta Saṁhitā* considering the nature of disease and season. A suitable method helps for early healing of crushed, lacerated wound and to stabilize the fracture, dislocation, etc. so that a wounded person can sleep well, able to walk and sit comfortably. The scholar, who desires to learn this, should practise on different parts of the dummies made up of cloth.

1.5.10.9 *Kṣāra and Agni Karma*

These are the most important para-surgical tools mentioned in Āyurveda.

One, who desires to become skilful to use the alkaline therapy and thermal cautery, should practise on similar objects like a suitable soft muscle piece.

1.5.10.10 *Miscellaneous Procedures*

The *Suśruta Saṁhitā* includes enema therapy, wound cleaning, irrigation, etc. under this category. The scholar should practise this on the side hole of an earthen pot containing full of water or on the mouth of a gourd.

1.5.11 CONCEPTS IN MEDICATION (BHEṢAJA VICĀRA)

Āyurveda suggests (Patil et al. 2017) transforming natural materials into easily administrable pharmaceutical preparations leading to Āyurveda concept of *bhiṣajya kalpanā*. It deploys the five pharmaceutical processes. These are *svarasa*, *kalka*, *śṛta*, *śīta* and *pānta*. Mechanically expressed juice of a plant is called the *svarasa*. *Jalī-yāṁśa* and *pārthivāṁśa* predominant drugs are preferred for the preparation of *svarasa*. It is most potent and heavy among the five. The soft mass of the drug prepared by pounding it in *khalva* machine is called *kalka*. It can be prepared from both wet and dry drugs. Liquid, boiled over *agni*, is *śrutā* or *kvātha*. *Hima kalpanā* is a simple preparation where the drugs in coarse powder form are kept soaked in water for a stipulated time period to facilitate the transfer of water-solubles active principles from drug to the liquid media. In *pānta* preparation, the water-soluble extractives are brought into the liquid media and the liquid is used as medicament. This processing results in the transformation of inherent attributes of substances. Transformation (Joshi et al. 2016: 227) of the attributes is affected by dilution, application of heat, cleansing, churning, storing, maturing, flavouring, impregnation, preservation, and the container.

1.5.11.1 *Concept of Personalized Medicine*

Āyurveda encompasses the belief that one's genotype can be influenced by environment, maternal diet, lifestyle and the age of parents at the time of conception (Sumantran et al. 2012). Conversely, Āyurveda believes that an individual's phenotype can vary because one's *prakr̥ti* constantly interacts with diet and environmental factors. Hence, the drug tolerance and drug response depend on specific interactions between the patient (host) and drug. Notably, in addition to one's *prakr̥ti*, there are twelve other host factors and twelve drug-related parameters to be considered (ibid.: 3). Āyurveda accounts for all permutations and combinations of these host and drug factors, and accordingly select appropriate drugs for the patient. The final choice of drugs is highly personalized because additional parameters such as the patient's overall health, diet, digestive status, immunity and response to environmental factors are also considered (ibid.: 5).

1.5.12 CONCEPTS IN EUGENICS, VIRILITY AND APHRODISIAC THERAPY (VĀJĪKARAṆA VICĀRA)

The word *vājīkaraṇa* is composed of two words. *Vājī* means horse, the symbol of sexual potency and performance, and *karaṇa* means power (Bagde 2013). By proper use of the *vājīkaraṇa* formulations, one becomes endowed with good physique, potency, strength and complexion, and sexually strong as like an eight years old horse.

It has been mentioned (ibid.) in the *Caraka Saṁhitā* that if a person receives these medicines then his erection time will be so long that he can perform in sexual activity for a long time and frequently he can satisfy hundred female partners in a day.

This therapy improves the function of the reproductive organs and vitalizes reproductive tissues increasing semen count and strengthening sperm motility in men and making eggs more viable for conception in women. This process enhances not only the quality and longevity of one's individual life but also the health and vitality of his or her offspring (ibid.: 6).

The *Caraka Saṁhitā* mentions benefits of this therapy as:

- It increases the timespan of erection and helps in curing erectile dysfunction and prevents premature ejaculation.
- It facilitates in reproducing vigorous offsprings.
- It stimulates man for sexual acts and helps to cohabit with females without getting tired.
- It makes females satisfied in sex.
- It transforms a lean, thin and impotent man into a powerful and vigorou person.
- Just as a tree has many branches, similarly man gets many descendants by use of this therapy and provides success, power, riches and fulfilment to an individual.
- It increases the willpower, intellect and memory in addition to promoting a healthy body (ibid.: 7).

This therapy primarily deals with sexuality. However, it talks about anatomy, physiology, pathology, diet and medicines involved in sex. There are two main objectives, viz. maintenance and augmentation of sexual potency of a healthy man and creation of a healthy progeny, and the other is the management of disturbed sexual potency and treatment of seminal related disorders in a person (Bagde 2013).

This therapy claims to minimize the occurrence of congenital disorders; besides, it may also boost the genetic constitution of the offspring.

The therapy rejuvenates male reproductive system and helps to increase sperm count and sperm motility. It increases body energy level and retards the ageing process. Men who undergo this therapy look attractive and never get tired. The *vājīkaraṇa* medicines do not aim only at having offsprings but healthy and strong offsprings, who are physically as well as mentally fit and prove to be good citizens.

This therapy advises the couple about the right time, place and method of copulation which can determine the certain characters of the baby. Therefore,*vājīkaraṇa* is a must for all those partners going to start the sexual life and who wish to continue the sexual life in a better way (ibid.: 6).

1.5.13 COMMON MEDICINAL PLANTS IN ĀYURVEDA

Āyurveda seeks to diagnose patients' conditions first before treating them with internal preparations, diet and habit restrictions. Plant-based preparations play a major role in the Āyurvedic healing process (Syal 2017). In broad terms, there is no substance in the world that cannot be used as a potential medicine.

However, Āyurveda texts warn against the use of substances that are notadequately understood (ibid.). Thus, any plant, animal or mineral substance can be incorporated into the Āyurvedic pharmacopoeia, but only if it is understood fully, in terms of its nomenclature, identity, properties and applications.

The texts also warn against the abuse of well-known medicines, emphasizing the point that even poisons can have medicinal properties when used appropriately, whereas the best of medicines can be harmful if improperly used (ibid.: 496).

Of nearly 10,000 plants used for medicinal purposes in the Indian subcontinent, only 1,200 to 1,500 have been incorporated into the official Āyurvedic pharmacopoeia in more than 3,000 years. All plants must be studied thoroughly before becoming part of the Āyurvedic pharmacopoeia (ibid.: 499).

1.5.13.1 *The Role of Food as Medicine*

Food plays a major role in Āyurveda practice by supporting the body's healing processes. Metabolic diseases and diseases of the gastrointestinal tract are directly influenced by food. Food can also indirectly affect diseases of the skin, muscles and joints, as well as neurological, gynaecological and psychological disease. Infrequent consumption is unlikely to cause a problem, but frequent consumption of inappropriate foods will cause disease or worsen existing disease. Advice on food depends not only on the disease but also on the disease condition and the *doṣa* involved. Because of this, food advice may change throughout the course of a disease, depending on the stage reached. Interactions between foods and medicines are a major issue. The advice given about food must take account of the medicines prescribed, otherwise, potential interactions may worsen patient's condition.

1.5.13.2 *The Action of Indian Spices*

The second strongest influence on patients' *doṣa*, after food, is spices (Syal 2017). Many spices are strong by nature. Spices are obtained from the roots, flowers, fruits, seeds or bark of plants or herbs.

Spices are native to warm, tropical climates. The action of spices within the body differs according to the ways that they are used. The phytochemicals within spices are secondary metabolites, which serve to protect the plants from damage by insects, animals, fungi, pathogens and parasites.

Before consumption, most spices are dried to degrade these chemicals. In addition to adding taste, some spices (cumin, ginger, coriander) also have preventative effects, aiding digestion through the production of digestive enzymes.

When mixed with digestive juices, these substances aid absorption. Such spices have individual effects, their actions depending on the constitution of the persons concerned and their diseases.

1.5.14 CONCEPTS IN EIGHT WINGS OF ĀYURVEDA (AṢṬĀṄGA ĀYURVEDA)

Āyurveda is also frequently referred as Aṣṭāṅga Āyurveda which is divided into eight branches, which are carefully chiselled out to meet specific needs in the process of maintaining health and preventing diseases (Garde 1983).

These include the following parts:

1. *Kāya-Cikitsā*: Internal and external treatments of the body.
2. *Bāla Cikitsā*: Diseases related to infants.
3. *Graha Cikitsā*: Healing of psychological problems.
4. *Ūrdhvāṅga Cikitsā*: Treatments related to the ear, nose and throat region.
5. *Śalya Cikitsā*: Surgeries and operations.
6. *Viṣa Cikitsā*: Toxicology.
7. *Rasāyana Cikitsā*: Methods to rejuvenate the *dhātu.*
8. *Vṛṣya Cikitsā*: Science of aphrodisiacs, virility and improving the health of the progeny.

The topics of *vājīkaraṇa, rasāyana, śalya* and *kāya* are already discussed earlier. The rest are having less imperative from the Kāmaśāstra perspective. The related discussions of the rest of the Āyurveda branches are carried out in the relevant chapters.

The author has reviewed the Āyurveda literature further and identified the concepts of auspicious elements of Āyurveda (*śubhāśubha*) and modular approach of Āyurveda (*trisūtra*). Āyurveda follows three main modules of treatment called *hetu, liṅga, cikitsā* – etiology, symptoms and treatment. He has used these concepts in the further chapters to examine the influence of Āyurveda on Kāmaśāstra.

1.6 Overview of Kāmaśāstra and Its Key Texts

Kāmaśāstra is considered as one of the sacred sciences of the Hindu tradition. It talks about the social behavioural aspects of human with special reference to sexology.

Brahmā considered being the first who composed a text of one lakh chapters dealing with the guidelines of lifestyles of the people[3] (Shastri 1992). Later, Nandī segregated thousand chapters from it and compiled the text called *Kāmaśāstra*. Śvetaketu further edited it into a smaller version of 500 chapters. Later, Bābhravya compiled it into seven books containing fifty chapters. The later tradition continued with Dattaka, Cārāyaṇa, Suvarṇanābha, Ghoṭakamukha, Goṇarda, Goṇikaputra, Kūcumāra, who composed their own treatises focusing on the one or more issues presented by Bābhravya.

Vātsyāyana composed a treatise called *Kāmasūtra*, which is a general text based on all above. It contains total seven books arranged in sixty-four chapters with 1,250 verses. We find very lucid and detailed description of all the issues pertaining to the matured and cultured lifestyles focusing on male–female relationships. Typically, it includes discussions on the history of Kāmaśāstra, objectives of life, connubial relationships, nature of females, duties and expectations of wives, extramarital relationships, prostitution and guidelines, sexual power increase, use of instruments and medicines, and guidelines for successful and fruitful life.

Similarly, the *Nāgarasarvasva* is the monumental work by a Buddhist Monk Padmaśrī composed in tenth century CE. It incorporated several new conceptions of the body and related para-technologies as well as elements of material and aesthetic culture which had become prominent in the cosmopolitan, courtly milieu. Rather than seeing this development as an attenuation of the earlier science as constituted by Vātsyāyana's *Kāmasūtra*, it is possible to see that Kāmaśāstra developed closer relations with fields of knowledge that had long developed alongside it.

The most recent authentic work on Kāmaśāstra is the *Rati Rahasya* by Kokkoka, composed around tenth to twelfth century detailing the metrical descriptions of sexual and mind management

3 प्रजापतिर्हि: प्रजाः सृष्ट्वा तासां स्थितिनिबन्धनं त्रिवर्गस्य साधनमध्यायानां शतसहस्रेणाग्रे प्रोवाच।

techniques. Interestingly, Kokkoka writes about the applicability of Kāmaśāstra even for the gods:

> Manmatha, son of Lord Viṣṇu, is responsible to produce sexual excitement not only in the humans but also within gods themselves. He is personified as travelling in the chariot of the cool southern winds, with the cool moon as his flag, sugar cane as his bow and five flowers as his arrows. The roaring of the sea is his drumbeat and the music of the Gokila as another accompaniment; the humming of the bees as the ambassadors of ecstasy and the bevy of beautiful girls as his army.

Shastri (1992: 136) interpreted the word *kalā* referred in Kāmaśāstra as the skills that is used to attract males or females. It also creates aesthetic value (*rasa*) in the mind of performer. Thus, Kāmaśāstra deals with the management of psychological imbalances that irrupt due to various sexual feelings. Love includes both physical and mental feelings. It is true that emotional feeling is a characteristic of only human beings. Most of the creatures other than man are attracted to each other physically only, that is also a sex-oriented relationship. That may be the reason why in human society sex-oriented love is not taken in a good sense. But this is the fact and reality of life, and it is so even for the existence of the world. Humans cannot continue to exist without physical love. For making it viable, purely human physical love must be combined with emotions. In this case, the best form of love is a good combination of physical and emotional relationships. Kāmaśāstra is considered as one of the major social sciences in the Hindu tradition. It talks about the social behavioural aspects of human being with special reference to sexology. It corresponds with the third human goal, viz. *kāma*. The key theme behind Kāmaśāstra is to guide and provide with prescriptions for the happy and sustained married life. This interpretation helps us in understanding the meaning of Kāmaśāstra in Āyurveda perspective.

2

Areas of Āyurveda Influence

2.1 Introduction

It is indeed very interesting to study the interdisciplinary learning and relationships across these two sciences, Āyurveda and Kāmaśāstra. Shastri (1992: 10) explains the positioning of Kāmaśāstra literature in overall Hindu value system. His approach of interpretation is depicted in *fig.* 2.1. A human being should achieve four objectives in his life in different phases. These objectives are achieved by four different tools. Kāmaśāstra aims at helping human achieve *kāma* through satisfaction (management) of mind.

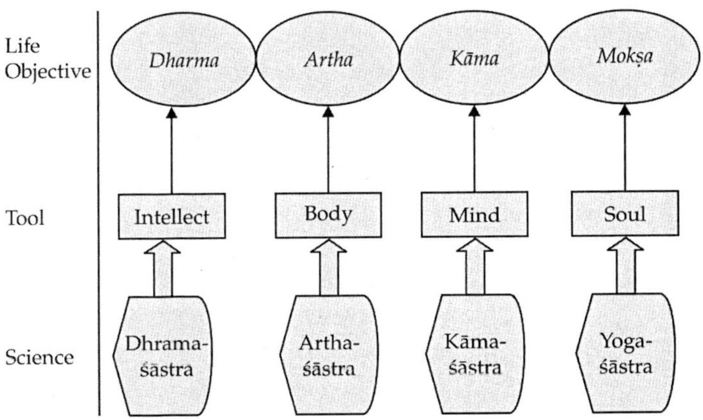

fig. 2.1: Positioning of Kāmaśāstra in Indian (Hindu) Value System

On the other side, we find Āyurveda advocates the balance of mind and body to manage diseases. In fact, Vāgbhaṭa's *Aṣṭāṅga Hṛdayam* categorically mentions (Uttarasthāna, chap. 40, v. 41) the adoption of Kāmaśāstra principles along with Āyurveda prescriptions for better achieving *kāma.*

Another eminent conceptual parity is observed between the *dinacaryā* and *ṛtucaryā* prescribed by Āyurveda (Vāgbhaṭa's *Aṣṭāṅga Hṛdayam*, Sūtrasthāna, chaps 2-3) and the *dinacaryā* and *rātricaryā* described by the *Kāmasūtra* (chap. 4). Both mentions similar thoughts and processes. In fact, it would not be an exaggeration if we say that Kāmaśāstra describes the process and Āyurveda provides the reasoning behind prescription mentioned in Kāmaśāstra.

Vāgbhaṭa's *Aṣṭāṅga Hṛdayam* **(I.12.34-35)** describes that *doṣa prakopa* causes the diseases and it happens due to three major reasons, viz. unknown *āhāra/vihāra, duṣṭa ṛtu* and *duṣṭa kriyā. Duṣṭa kriyā* comprises of *kāyika, vācika* and *mānasika karma* which typically consists of non-equilibrium status of copulation process as mentioned in Kāmaśāstra. The *asātmya* behavioural pattern leading to physical and mental diseases due to *hīna-yoga* (less consumption), *ati-yoga* (extra consumption), *mithyā-yoga* (undesirable consumption) directly leads to *apāna vayū* deterioration which determines the movements of sperm and menstrual. Thus, we find the strong base of Āyurveda theory in the Kāmaśāstra prescription of *nāyaka–nāyikā* match matrix.

Moreover, the *tridoṣa, dravya vidyānam, śārīra, vājīkaraṇa, ṛtucaryā, dinacaryā, bheṣaja* and *śalya-tantra* provides the basic building blocks for the recommendations prescribed in Kāmaśāstra.

Kāmaśāstra also deals in detail with the diet, medication and cosmetic treatments (*KS* 1.7). The present research has shown various aspects of similarities between these virgin areas to prove the cross-learning dependencies between these two sciences.

I have shown further the confluence between these two sciences in the areas of human anatomy of Āyurveda and physical description of males and females appearing in Kāmaśāstra, Āyurveda outlook on *āsana* which are prescribed by Kāmaśāstra, importance of human character and philosophical approach assumed in both sciences.

2.2 Review of Literature on Kāmaśāstra

In the previous chapter, we have already reviewed the key Kāmaśāstra text on the subject. Ancient Indian sages had appropriately understood the significance of the social behavioural science in the life cycle of human beings. Right from the *R̥gveda* hymns, we find relevant references of Kāmaśāstra topics. In fact, Āyurveda is regarded as the origination of Kāmaśāstra. This tradition of open and evolutionary discussions right from the *R̥gveda* must have helped to develop full-fledged texts of Kāmaśāstra, especially the *Kāmasūtra*. "The first urge of a creature is hunger or thirst and the next is sex", is what one gets to read in *Chāndogyopaniṣad* III.17.1.3. (Incidentally, according to Kane, the period of Upaniṣads is thought to be roughly around 1000 BCE.) Hence, *kāma* was placed as one of the four objectives of life along with *dharma*, *artha* and *mokṣa*. These objectives are to be attained by man (human) to have perfection in his life. *Mokṣa* (freedom from the cycle of birth and rebirth) is of the other world and is attained after death, if one were fit for it. The three worldly objects of life were treated as "sciences" and hence one finds the scholarly works on these topics written and perfected by many sages and scholars.

This basic thought process and theme of Kāmaśāstra is very ancient and can be traced back to Brahmā himself. Since we do not get any authentic texts by those ancient sages, I have taken a rational approach of relying on the *Kāmasūtra* itself for Kāmaśāstra.

Tables 2.1 and 2.2 provide brief visualization of the evolution and ownerships of Kāmaśāstra texts. We will discuss this in later chapters as the reference appears.

Table 2.1: Brief History of Kāmaśāstra Literature

Creator/Author (Key)	*Text*	*Approximate Timeline*
Brahmā	*Kāmaśāstra* (Original)	Unknown and before *Kāmasūtra*
Nandin	*Kāmasūtra* (Edition)	Unknown and before *Kāmasūtra*
Śvetaketu	*Kāmasūtra* (Concise)	Unknown and before *Kāmasūtra*
Bābhravya	*Kāmasūtra* (Collated)	Unknown and before *Kāmasūtra*
Vātsyāyana	*Kāmasūtra* (Available)	Forth or third century BCE

Table 2.2: Later Tradition in Kāmaśāstra Texts

Creator/Author	*Text*	*Approx. Timeline* (CE)
Dāmodaragupta	*Kuṭṭanī-Matam*	779–813
Kokkoka	*Rati Rahasya*	950
Padmaśrī	*Nāgara-Sarvasvam*	1351
Ananta	*Kāma-Samūha*	1457
Kalyāṇa Malla	*Anaṅga-Raṅga*	1488-1517
Jayadeva	*Rati Mañjarī*	1500
Harihara	*Śṛṅgārarasa-prabandhadīpikā*	1500

The Rati Rahasya provides a detailed listing and chronology about the Kāmaśāstra authors and their texts (Appendix 2). I have purposely avoided those discussions in the interest of keeping focus on the technical details of the subject. Hampiholi (1988: v-xii) has provided a similar synopsis on Kāmaśāstra literature.

All these Kāmaśāstra texts are dealing with the common topics like types of *nāyaka*, *nāyikā*, their characteristics, aphrodisiac recipes, copulation and position details, auspicious elements and sexual instruments. A good collection of less known eleven Kāmaśāstra texts is available in the *Kāmakuñjalatā* (Chouhan 2008). Along with the popular topics, it also talks about the liquor consumption and sex, exciting techniques for partners and overall copulation process details.

The *Kāmasūtra* is the only text which has compiled the entire knowledge of Kāmaśāstra as a social science. Apart from the common topics, it deals with multiple aspects like *rasa* and *bhāva*, venues, food consumption rules, rituals, specific treatment to adultery and prostitution, and an overall therapeutic approach towards the subject. Hence, I have used the *Kāmasūtra* as the prime source of literature. The same principle and approach has been taken while relying primarily on Vāgbhaṭa's *Aṣṭāṅga Hṛdayam* among Āyurveda texts.

2.3 Kāmaśāstra in Classical Sanskrit Literature

Kāmaśāstra is the earliest available text on erotic, composed by Mallanāga Vatsyāyana in fourth or third century BCE. However, we find the influence of the Kāmaśāstra on poets right from the first century CE. Although, classical Sanskrit texts are not directly relevant to the current research, I have taken the liberty in reviewing and identifying any specific references within these texts related to Kāmaśāstra.

Krishnamachariar (1974: 888) mentions that Aśvaghoṣa, the earliest known writer, describes love in the light of the *Kāmasūtra* only. His three major texts, which are composed to teach Buddhism, are full of *śṛṅgāra* element. Similarly, we find laureates like Bhāsa, Śūdraka, Kālidāsa, Kumāradāsa, Bhāravi, Māgha, Bhartṛhari, Bāṇa, Harṣa, Daṇḍin, Amarūka, Dāmodaragupta, Bhavabhūti, Rājaśekhara, Bilhaṇa, Śrīharṣa, Jayadeva and even later authors have consumed the Kāmaśāstra content aptly in their literature compositions. However, as mentioned by De (1959), all these authors have picked up the concepts from Kāmaśāstra for its relevance, embellishment of their own text and as a vogue or fashion during their time. I have completely aligned with this argument and briefly used those references in the current study. Since the prime objective of my research is to decipher the technical and medicinal aspects of Kāmaśāstra, this approach served its purpose.

2.4 Hypothesis Design

We will now see the influence of Āyurveda on the various aspects of Kāmaśāstra. Various hypotheses can be investigated to examine the Āyurveda's influence on Kāmaśāstra. Here is a list of hypotheses:

- Kāmaśāstra has used similar sequence of chapetrization theme as that of Āyurveda texts.
- Kāmaśāstra has adopted similar style of narration as observed typically and in general in Āyurveda texts.
- Kāmaśāstra has deployed Āyurveda terms and direct examples from Āyurveda texts thus leading to Āyurveda's influence.
- *Concept of Homeostasis* (*Balance and Imbalance*) – The Āyurveda theory believes in a perfect balance between the nature elements and the *tridoṣa* to maintain a healthy state of living by following the principles of divine wisdom. Kāmaśāstra adopts the same concept of balance for the healthy state of mind and sustainable connubial relationships.
- *Concept of Anatomy* – Kāmaśāstra has adopted Āyurveda anatomy as its base for the classifications of male and females.
- *Conceptual Elements in Therapy* (*Sātmya Vicāra*) – Āyurveda advocates to examine the constitution, morbidity, proportion of the elements, compactness and measurement as the key considerations before any therapy. Kāmaśāstra has adopted the same concept in its theory of pleasure maximization.
- Kāmaśāstra has prescribed daily routine and night routine which is in line with Āyurveda recommendations.
- Kāmaśāstra has adopted methods of *āsana* based on the Āyurveda theory of prescribed behaviour and motions.
- Kāmaśāstra has prescribed the usage of similar medicinal plants and materials as Āyurveda mentions for sexual power development.
- Kāmaśāstra has adopted Āyurveda's is coherent ideas

of maintaining body hygiene, caring body organs and consumption of food and its quality.

- The regional significance on human behaviour and pleasure preference described in Kāmaśāstra is based on the regional considerations in the Āyurveda theory.
- There is a symbolic parity between Āyurveda model of patient, doctor, messenger and medicine, and Kāmaśāstra model of male, female, messenger and pleasure techniques.
- Auspicious elements and description in Kāmaśāstra are in line with Āyurveda recommendations.

The author has adopted a structured research methodology here. This included the following methods for data collection and analysis:

- Literature survey keeping the research objectives in mind.
- Development of detailed research framework.
- Critical literature review keeping the research questions in mind.
- Site visits.
- Interviews with field scholars.
- Theorizing the finding.

The surveying of various popular and available literatures on the subject is the first step here. This included various treatises, research papers, research articles and relevant texts.

Second, visits to various sites are significant from the investigation standpoint. The list includes Khajurāho, Sun Temple at Koṇārk and Śrī Cennakeśava Svāmī Temple at Bellur (built by the Vatsal dynasty in Karnataka). The key purpose of site visit was to discover the clues from erotic architecture of these temples that may support or contradict the theoretical views gathered from literature. This analysis was important to understand the Kāmaśāstra concepts especially regarding the descriptions of various postures (*āsanas*) appearing in Kāmaśāstra and its depiction in architecture. These endeavours opened new dimensions of investigation within the research scope that led to enrich the overall research conclusions.

Further, interviews and discussions were conducted with renowned subject scholars. This helped in validation of the theory that was used to build the project outcome. These outcomes are presented below.

2.5 Areas of Āyurveda Influence

Four broad areas are considered here, which include structural, conceptual, prescriptive and symbolic influence of Āyurveda on Kāmaśāstra.

2.5.1 STRUCTURAL INFLUENCE ON THE FOUNDATION OF KĀMAŚĀSTRA TEXTS

While Kāmaśāstra begins with the texts of providing strong reasoning of its composition, it further states very clearly the scope and coverage of its discussions compiled as per Āyurveda. The *Kāmasūtra* (Shastri 1992: 368-69)[1] clearly refers to Āyurveda and mentions about the scoping of any scientific literature. Āyurveda does describe the properties of the meat of dog, however it is not intended for prescribed consumption; similarly, Kāmaśāstra also discusses the topics like oral sex, however not in prescription. We could mark the apt baselining work Kāmaśāstra has done referring to Āyurveda. It is interesting to note that Kāmaśāstra has selected Āyurveda referencing and not *Yājñavalkya Smṛti.*

This connection can be traced to the common originator of Āyurveda[2] and Kāmaśāstra (Shastri 1992: 11)[3] as same, i.e. Brahmā.

---

[1] रसविर्यविपाका हि श्वमांसस्यापि वैद्यके (*rasaviryavipākā hi śvamāṁsasyāpi vaidyak*)।

[2] ब्रह्मणा हि यथा प्रोक्तमायुर्वेदं प्रजापतिः (*brahmaṇā hi yathā proktamāyurvedaṁ prajāpatiḥ*)। – *CS* 1.4

[3] प्रजापतिर्हि प्रजाः सृष्ट्वा तासां स्थितिनिबन्धनं त्रिवर्गस्य साधनमध्यायानां शतसहस्रेणाग्रे प्रोवाच। →

Table 2.3: Sequence of Topics in Āyurveda and Kāmaśāstra

Chaps	*Āyurveda Texts*	*Key Discussions in Āyurveda*	*Kāmaśāstra Texts*	*Key Discussions in Kāmaśāstra*
1	Sūtrasthāna	General introduction	Sādhāraṇa	General introduction
2	Śārīrasthāna	Anatomy	Sāmprāyogika	Anatomy
3	Nidānasthāna	Diagnosis	Kanyā related	Diagnosis and therapy
4	Vimānasthāna	Measurement and Standardization	Bhāryā related	Diagnosis and therapy
5	Cikitsāsthāna	Therapy	Paradārā related	Diagnosis and therapy
6	Kalpāsthāna	Pharmacology	Vaiśika related	Diagnosis and therapy
7	Uttarasthāna	Special treatments	Miscellaneous	Special treatments

The structure of composition of Āyurveda and Kāmaśāstra texts reflects unique parity between them. Table 2.3 shows emphasizes on the same.

We could see the conceptual alignment in placing the sequence for chapterization between these two sciences. Āyurveda generally arranges its content of *svasthasya svāsthya rakṣanam* in the initial sections followed by *āturasya vikāra praśamanam* discussions. We find the similar flow in Kāmaśāstra. The *Kāmasūtra* describes all the natural- and moral-based pleasure-generating techniques in first four *adhikaraṇas* (sections) followed by special pleasure techniques in last three sections. The *Kāmasūtra* discusses the general male and female classification, routines, aspects of selection of bride, creating synergic relationships with newly wedded, maintaining the marital happiness with wife in the first four sections leading to the sustenance of healthy connubial relationships. In the last three sections, it discusses the specifics of adultery, prostitutions, sexuual instruments and special techniques of sexual acts. These narrations are related to the treatment for psychological disorders and can be interpreted as diseases.

We can conclude that the Kāmaśāstra has picked up the

← *(prajāpatihiḥ prajāḥ sṛṣṭvā tāsāṁ sthitinibandhanaṁ trivargasya sādhanamadhyāyānāṁ śatasahasreṇāgre provāca)* ।

sequence of narration from Āyurveda. This can also be further taken to the optimistic view to state a hypothesis that – One can understand Kāmaśāstra better if he or she understands Āyurveda first in a reasonable way. Investigator proved the argument in the further discussions.

Interesting simile with Āyurveda is observed in the diction of Kāmaśāstra texts. Many a time while reading Kāmaśāstra, we may feel we are reading Āyurveda verses. For example, the word – *viparyayeṇa* (Shastri 1992: 184)[4] is widely used in Āyurveda (Garde 1983).[5] It appears[6] in multiple times in the Nidānasthāna of Vāgbhaṭa's *Aṣṭāṅga Hṛdayam* in the similar sense.

The interesting part is the usage of this word vis-à-vis the topic of discussions. Kāmaśāstra uses this word to efficiently describe the multiple possible combinations based on the male and female types. The discussions further go in the direction of the best and the worst combination from healthy connubial relationships. This topic is nothing but the diagnostics approach of Kāmaśāstra discussed in Table 2.4 further. As mentioned earlier, Āyurveda uses this word multiple times under its diagnostics (Nidānasthāna). It shows the coherence of Kāmaśāstra thought process with Āyurveda very apparently.

We find the Āyurveda word *prakṛti* used in Kāmaśāstra (Shastri 1992: 356)[7] in the similar sense. According to Āyurveda, the basic constitution is determined at the time of conception. This constitution is called *prakṛti*. Its literary meaning is "nature", "creativity" or "the first creation". One of the very important propositions of Āyurveda is that one's basic constitution is fixed throughout his lifetime. The combination of *vāta*, *pitta* and *kapha*

4 विपर्ययेण विषमाणि षट् (*viparyayeṇa viṣamāṇi ṣaṭ*) । – *KS* 2.1.3 ।

5 हेतुव्याधिविपर्यस्तविपर्यस्तार्थकारिणाम (*hetuvyādhiviparyastaviparyastā-rthakāriṇāma*) । – VAYD 3.1.6

6 Ibid. 3.6.13; 3.13.47; 3.16.30 (Grade 1983: 180, 203, 214 respectively).

7 द्विविधा तृतियाप्रकृतिः (*dvividhā tṛtiyāprakṛtiḥ*) । – *KS* 2.9.1

that was present in the individual at the time of conception is maintained throughout his lifetime. Different persons can have different combinations hence differ in their basic constitution (*prakṛti*). Thus, Āyurveda acknowledges the subtle differences between individuals and considers everyone is unique and that two persons can react very differently when exposed to the same environment or stimuli. In a symbolic way, the constitution is like the fingerprint and DNA.

The therapeutic principles of Āyurveda focus on *prakṛti* and these principles emphasize on the individual and his uniqueness. It determines the characteristic response of everyone to medications, environmental conditions and dietary factors. Further, it helps (Jaiswal and Williams 2017) for the individualized therapies and managing the potential side effects and lack of desired therapeutic efficacy.

Kāmaśāstra has adopted an entire theme of above-mentioned Āyurveda therapy and very meaningfully used the word *prakṛti* for describing the Kāmaśāstra therapy to third genders. These persons (third genders) are of two types – one more inclined towards masculine and other towards the feminine. The *Kāmasūtra* describes the details of the behavioural patterns and pleasure treatments with minute details for both the types. The narration acknowledges the subtle differences between the two and clearly proposes individual treatment to each type.

Interestingly, the *Nāgarasarvasva*[8] uses the Āyurveda word *cikitsā* in the sense of behaviour of a husband towards his wife. The very usage of this word is a significant evidence of Āyurveda's influence on the entire Kāmaśāstra approach wherein it deploys the behavioural treatment equivalent to the therapeutic approach of Āyurveda. Kāmaśāstra scopes the psychological and physiological aspects of treatments along with medication based on Āyurveda.

---

8 चिकित्सयति यो नित्यं पदं प्राप्नोति कामिकम् (*cikitsayati yo nityaṁ padaṁ prāpnoti kāmikam*)। – *NS* 1.5 (Jha, 1929: 12)

The *Kāmasūtra* uses the Āyurveda term धातुक्षय (Shastri 1992: 199)[9] indicating the ejaculation and not used any other common word like *skhalana*. This is again a strong evidence of Āyurveda's influence on Kāmaśāstra authors. In fact, the earlier verse uses typical classical Sanskrit romantic words for describing the copulation and pleasure-generation mechanics. We could mark the unique style here of Kāmaśāstra narration, wherein Āyurveda-oriented medical terms are blended within romantic classical Sanskrit styled description.

While concluding the fifth section, the *Kāmasūtra* typically follows the Āyurveda's style of narration on causes, symptoms and remedies on adultery disease. It mentions (ibid.: 597, 5.6. 45-47) initially all the possible reasons why and how married women could be deceived, followed by a clear indication on its remedies. It finally concludes the prescriptive way of taboos. The narration is structured in such a way that the reader must get a feel of reading an Āyurveda text on psychotherapy.

The *Kāmasūtra* categorically describes the conditional remedies in the style of Āyurveda. It talks (ibid.: 379, 2.10.18) about the earlier referred remedies in the current discussions using the phrases like "as suggested earlier". This style of narration is very pertinent with Āyurveda and its topics of discussions. Vāgbhaṭa's *Aṣṭāṅga Hṛdayam* 2.1.97/100/123 (Garde 1983) at many places uses this style especially in the *Cikitsā Sthāna* like पूर्वक्तं रेतसावृते (*pūrvaktaṁ retasāvṛte*) (VAYD 4.22.60; Garde 1983: 333).

This is highly popular, efficient and scientific style of science texts. The authors use this effectively to connect various concepts and avoid repetition of words and texts. We can conclude here that Kāmaśāstra should not be regarded as classical Sanskrit literature but aptly as scientific literature of medical essence.

Interestingly, we see the poetic diction in Āyurveda, although

---

[9] धातुक्षयनिमित्ता च विरामेच्छोपजायते (*dhātukṣayanimittā ca virāmecchopajāyate*) ।
– *KS* 2.1.22

not surprising, as such is always a common ethos of ancient Indian Sanskrit texts on sciences. We know that even mathematics is narrated in poetic ways in the *Līlāvatī*. Āyurveda becomes much romantic when it narrates the prescribed consumption (Garde 1983: 257; VYAD 4.7 54-67) of liquor. It further becomes a romantic classical Sanskrit literature, perhaps Kālidāsa styled, when it narrates (ibid.: 6.40.39-40; ibid.: 489) aphrodisiac methods. It is much of an overwhelming experience when we see Āyurveda texts tastes like Kāmaśāstra texts and recommends woman as medicine. We are discussing these aspects under Symbolic Influence section of this chapter.

The entire seventh section of Kāmaśāstra is very close to Āyurveda from topic, narration and utility perspective. In fact, the *Kāmasūtra* opens with the topic in section 7, as if, saying (Shastri 1992: 704)[10] "here ends the Kāmaśāstra and starts Āyurveda".

This Kāmaśāstra section has two chapters and deal with multiple topics. The similarities with Āyurveda can be observed as tabulated in Table 2.4.

The topic flows in this section like typical Āyurveda way, wherein first, the causes are discussed, followed by remedies. We see prodigal usage of Āyurveda medico terms like अक्षतैलम् (*akṣatailam*), सिद्धतैलम् (*siddhatailam*), चूर्णम् (*cūrṇam*) and अनुलिप्य (*anulipya*). (*KS* 7.1. 5-6, 8-9; Shastri 1992: 705). The entire diction is of medical textbook.

Table 2.4: Parity in the Style between Kāmaśāstra and Āyurveda

Topic	*Narration Style in Kāmaśāstra*	*Āyurveda Resemblance*
Miscellaneous therapy and description of herbal medicines	*Cikitsā* and a little bit like *Nidāna*	More as the *kalpa* section of Āyurveda

10 व्याख्यातं च कामसूत्रम् (*vyākhyātaṁ ca kāmasūtram*) । – *KS* 7.1.1

Similarly, we find Āyurveda terms like शीतवीर्याणि (*śītavīryāṇi*)and कर्मणि (*karmaṇi*) used in the same sense (ibid. 7.2.6; ibid.: 724).

Moreover, we could mark the Āyurveda narrative style for the penis surgery process (ibid. 2.7, 16-18; ibid.: 727), perhaps due to its close connection with the Āyurveda topic. It details the process, practice, prescription and even disinfecting ideas. From the above-mentioned text, if we expose this to any reader, who never read Kāmaśāstra, certainly will qualify this as a medical science matter.

We find the Āyurveda style of symptoms description (ibid. 5.1. 4-5; ibid.: 512) while Kāmaśāstra narrates adultery. The text gives a feel as if an Āyurveda practitioner has written the complete sets of symptoms step by step for the disease of adultery. In fact, the *Kāmasūtra* uses the Āyurveda term लिङ्गानि (*liṅgāni*) for the symptoms (ibid. 5.1.5; ibid.).

Āyurveda, while talking about the auspicious elements (Garde 1983: 163; VAYD 2.6.71-72), finally summarizes the scientific outlook and emphasizes on the logical and practical aspects. We find the similar approach in narration Kāmaśāstra has taken at multiple places. For example, while concluding the adultery section (*KS* 5.6.47-48; Shastri 1992: 407), its final recommendation on the controlled behaviour and precautions resembles with the Āyurveda example cited above.

Kāmaśāstra has picked up the Āyurveda style of providing the alternate (synonyms) words for the technical terms to facilitate easy interpretation and clarity of concepts. We find Vāgbhaṭa's *Aṣṭāṅga Hṛdayam* (Garde 1983: 334) mentioning:

> चिकित्सितं हितं पथ्यं प्रायश्चितं भिषग्जितम् ।
> भेषजं शमनं शस्तं पर्यायैः स्मृतमौषधम् ॥
>
> *cikitsitaṁ hitaṁ pathyaṁ prāyaścitaṁ bhiṣagjitam* ।
> *bheṣajaṁ śamanaṁ śastaṁ paryayaiḥ smṛtamauṣadham* ॥
>
> – VAYD 4.22.74

and the the *Kāmasūtra* (Shastri 1992: 407) mentioning:

रसो रतिः प्रीतिर्भावो रागो वेगः समाप्तिरिति रतिपर्यायाः ।
संप्रयोगो रतं रहः शयनं मोहनं सुरतपर्यायाः ॥

raso ratiḥ prītirbhāvo rāgo vegaḥ samāptiriti ratiparyāyāḥ ।
saṁprayogo rataṁ rahaḥ śayanaṁ mohanaṁ surataparyāyāḥ ॥
– *KS* 2.1.32

Āyurveda mentions the alternate words for the physical medicines, whereas Kāmaśāstra mentions the alternate words for the psychological medicines.

It will not be an exaggeration to say that Kāmaśāstra authors followed and adopted minutely the structural elements of Āyurveda texts and their ethos of composition.

2.5.2 CONCEPTUAL INFLUENCE ON KĀMAŚĀSTRA THEORY

2.5.2.1 *Core Objectives, Applications and Relevance*

As explained in *fig.* 2.1, Āyurveda and Kāmaśāstra have tight alignment in its core objectives and applications. Āyurveda describes its relevance as an essential knowledge base for longevity; wherein longevity in turn aims at achieving life objectives (Garde 1983).[11]

Kāmaśāstra, in similar tone, mentions its relevance as to provide foundation for achieving the life objectives. In fact, the *Kāmasūtra* in its first verse propitiates three life objectives.

Āyurveda knowledge ensures the proper treatment of diseases and ensures the health of the person. Lack of Kāmaśāstra knowledge leads a person to be petrified, nervous and dependent (needy/contingent) which makes him or her emotionally tasteless or revolting. The sexual pleasure in this situation resembles more like a mechanical physical process we observe in animals. Longevity for such person is a not less than a life imprisonment.

I have proved that while Āyurveda ensures longevity of life,

---

11 आयुः कामयमानेन धर्मार्थसुखसाधनम् (*āyuḥ kāmayamānena dharmārthasukha-sādhanam*) । – VAYD 1.1.2

Kāmaśāstra ensures the fulfilment within it. Āyurveda provides means and prescriptions of keeping a healthy body and mind, whereas Kāmaśāstra describes the fruitful utilization of the same in generating social health and individual pleasure. The boundaries of behavioural freedom and maximum degree of pleasure consumption recommended in Kāmaśāstra have clear sanctity with Āyurveda principles. Thus, the Āyurveda influence on Kāmaśāstra is clearly visible in the entire Kāmaśāstra theory across different notions and models described in Kāmaśāstra.

2.5.2.2 *Concept of Balance*

We have discussed that the Āyurveda theory believes in a perfect balance between the nature elements and the *tridoṣa* to maintain a healthy state of living by following the principles of divine wisdom. Kāmaśāstra adopts the same concept of balance for the healthy state of mind and sustainable connubial relationships.

While suggesting the criteria for marriage Kāmaśāstra suggests (Shastri 1992: 407) to maintain balance between education, wealth and family culture of both, the bride and groom. These three dimensions are like the *tridoṣa* concept of Āyurveda. We see a detailed treatment of this topic in the *Kāmasūtra*. The approach of balance is much visible when *Kāmasūtra* 3.1.2 categorically mentions (ibid.: 391) the selection criteria for a bride as someone whose physical dimensions should neither be small nor too big and never have absence of any organ. In fact, *Kāmasūtra* 3.1.3 further refers (ibid.: 392) the possible "illness" of social disgrace and ignominy due to such imbalance between the bride and groom. We could clearly see here the Āyurveda style of narration of diseases erupts from imbalance in *tridoṣa*. The idea of Āyurveda to avoid diseases by ensuring the right balance between the *tridoṣa* is well observed here.

Interestingly, the *Vātsyāyana Kāmasūtra* depicts (ibid.: 66)[12]

[12] शरीरस्थितिहेतुत्वादाहारसधर्माणो हि कामाः (*śarīrasthitihetutvādāhārasa-dharmāṇo hi kāmāḥ*) ।
– *KS* 1.2.37

the entire concept of pleasure as the consumption of food. In this regard, it is interesting to note Vāgbhaṭa's *Aṣṭāṅga Hṛdayam* (Garde 1983: 179)[13] giving significance of the apt food consumption. The over, under and no consumption of food will lead to diseases and ultimately the death of human. Moreover, it recommends consuming food only when a person feels hungry; otherwise, it will lead to diseases. Kāmaśāstra talks the same concept of balance in pleasure consumption; pleasure is necessary but need to be consumed in right degree to create a balance between desire and health. Only a medical practitioner can think of depicting such an idea of food equivalent for pleasure and recommends its apt consumption.

We find the word – *samaratāni* (*KS* 2.1.2; Shastri 1992: 183) – used in the *Vātsyāyana Kāmasūtra* and its significance for the copulation. The idea is very much like the *samadhātu* concept of Āyurveda.

2.5.2.3 *Concept of Modular Approach* (*Trisūtra*)

The modular approach of Āyurveda has apparent influence on the Kāmaśāstra theory. While describing any topic, Kāmaśāstra follows the three main modules of Āyurveda – etiology, symptoms and treatment. A mentally disturbed society leads to multiple social diseases like all forms of sexual coercion and sexual violence (including rape, sexual abuse and harassment), body mutilations, contracting or transmitting sexually transmitted infections (STIs), consequences of physical or mental disabilities and increased impact of medical and surgical conditions. Such a situation overall leads to the loss of culture and possible chaos. Interestingly, we see Kāmaśāstra adopts modular approach of Āyurveda to arrest these social diseases (Shastri 1992: 11). Table 2.5 presents the Kāmaśāstra approach.

---

13 आमोद्भवा च भक्तस्य संरोधाद्वातपित्तजा (*āmodbhavā ca bhaktasya saṁrothā-dvātapittajā*) । – VAYD 3.5.54

Table 2.5: Modular Approach in Kāmaśāstra

Etiology	*Symptoms*	*Treatment/Therapy*
Lack of below feelings in human: • Respect for sex, reproduction and genital organ • Accountability of humanhood • Respect, love, attraction for partner(s)	Leads to: • Conflicts and dissatisfactions between couples • Brake ups of relationships • Criminal behaviours like rapes, tortures and kidnapping • Adultery and secret relationships • Prostitution and its consumption • Unnatural urge or sexual arousal	Kāmaśāstra follows a structured approach of treatment that typically includes: • Scientific selection process of partners • Suggested routine and food consumption • Guidelines on partner appeasement and behaviours • Recommended process of pre- and post-copulation

Kāmaśāstra categorically follows the modular approach step by step as mentioned in Table 2.5. No short-cuts and skipping of any steps are allowed in the Kāmaśāstra therapy for its reasonable outcome. We see a clear recommendation (Shastri 1992: 418)[14] to complete the diagnostic study of woman mind before any next step of going ahead with her. It further describes the positive aspects of following the steps and provides warnings of possible conflicts (can lead to psychological diseases) in case of opposite approach. The entire narration suits to a clinical and scientific text.

2.5.2.4 *Conceptual Elements in Therapy and Medication*

Kāmaśāstra is significantly influenced by the *sātmya vicāra* of Āyurveda. Its aims at bringing harmony within the human body and mind to balance the natural urge. In this regard it does not hesitate to recommend (ibid.: 357; *KS* 2.9.4) specific sexual methods or activities like oral sex. For the third gender persons, Kāmaśāstra

---

14 सहसा वाप्युपक्रान्ता कन्याचित्तमविन्दता।
भयं वित्रासमुद्वेगं सद्यो द्वेषं च गच्छति।।

sahasā vāpyupakrāntā kanyācittamavindatā ।
bhayaṁ vitrāsamudvegaṁ sadyo dveṣaṁ ca gacchati ।। – *KS* 3.2.34

suggests oral sex for the pleasure and even for his (her) economic survival. We are discussing these aspects in detail in the next chapter.

The idea of considering every type of the persons (whatever the physical status) and recommending the process of pleasure generation itself shows the clinical maturity and therapeutic approach of Āyurveda.

While Kāmaśāstra focuses on each person's constitution, we find an interesting generic approach that Kāmaśāstra takes regarding the pleasure generation across genders. Kāmaśāstra says (ibid.: 202)[15] that there is no difference in the experience of pleasure within the human genders; it means men get the same quality of sex satisfaction as women get. Kāmaśāstra categorically proposes that the same species will get the same quality of sexual pleasure and satisfaction. This is a fundamental hypothesis which Kāmaśāstra brings in based on the Āyurveda concept. Āyurveda never differentiates on the gender basis the therapy and the medication especially from the health protection perspective. This is a strong evidence of conceptual parity between these two sciences and how Kāmaśāstra has naturally adopted clinically appropriate view of Āyurveda. We can also note the maturity of understanding between these two sciences.

We see the Āyurveda influence on Kāmaśāstra in adopting the systemic way of describing the symptoms first before its treatment. Kāmaśāstra enlists (Shastri 1992: 512)[16-17] the ten causes (*nidānas*) of adultery disease. In fact, it uses the Āyurveda (ibid., Garde 1983: 370)[18] term *unmāda* in the exact sense. The Āyurveda influence is quite apparent here in the Kāmaśāstra therapeutic approach.

---

15 आकृतेरभेदादिति (*ākṛterabhedāditi*) । – *KS* 2.1.27

16 दशः तु कामस्य स्थानानि (*daśaḥ tu kāmasya sthānāni*) । – *KS* 5.1.4

17 उन्मादो मूर्छा मरणमिति तेषां लिङ्गानि (*unmādo murchā maraṇamiti teṣāṁ liṅgāni*) । – *KS* 5.1.5

18 उन्मादाः षट् (*unmādāḥ ṣaṭ*) । – VAYD 6.6.1

Kāmaśāstra further uses the Āyurveda (ibid.: 371; VAYD 6.6.6-9) concept of physical body examination for the symptomatic analysis to diagnose disease. Kāmaśāstra (Shastri 1992: 512 *KS* 5.1.7) clearly suggests examining the women symptoms before adultery.

Interestingly, we find that Vāgbhaṭa's *Aṣṭāṅga Hṛdayam* mentions (ibid.: 617, *KS* 6.2.9) a trick for prostitutes to quickly close the meeting with her lover. She should lie about a pain (diseases) that might make her uncomfortable suddenly, cannot be diagnosed easily and seen in the form of any symptoms, not much harmful or shameful and still will not have any permanency in it. Such *vyādhi* will help her scuttle from the place. The verse describes the symptoms as if a medical practitioner has composed it.

Kāmaśāstra propounds a special concept of "women on top" posture during intercourse. This is to be used for a specific type of women. Kāmaśāstra suggests (Shastri 1992: 349)[19] to diagnose women nature first to understand her preferences about the specific posture. It further provides symptoms of such women. Then as if like a doctor, a man should treat her with those techniques to pacify her desires (ibid.: 347[20]) . We see the typical *nidāna* and *cikitsā* approach of Āyurveda in these narratives.

Similar recommendations we could see in the third section of Kāmaśāstra, where it categorically mentions (ibid.: 418; *KS* 3.2.31-34) how to treat women before love exercise. It recommends moderate approach to build love, respect and create trust in the mind of women. Kāmaśāstra specifically emphasizes to learn the women psychology before establishing any sexual relations even with wife. It further warns (ibid.: 419; *KS* 3.2.35) about the mishap in relationships due to disdaining by women. The entire approach is more inclined towards the proper *nidāna* and then following the *cikitsā* for the copulation with scientific description.

---

19 यथाशीला भवेन्नारी यथा च रतिलालसा (*yathāśīlā bhavennārī yathā ca ratilālasā*) ।
– *KS* 2.8.40

20 तेषां स्त्रीसात्म्याव्दिकल्पेन प्रयोगः (*teṣāṁ strīsātmyāvdikalpena prayogaḥ*) ।
– *KS* 2.8.31

The Āyurveda *cikitsā* concept is much apparent in chapter 3 of section 3 of Vāgbhaṭa's *Aṣṭāṅga Hṛdayam*. It advocates (ibid.: 444-50; *KS* 3.4.2-18) slow advances as per *rasābhāva* creation model (discussed in the next chapter). It ensures the administration of all techniques in a proper pace as if like the consumption of dosages. Further, it warns about the precautions to be taken while advances (ibid.: 447).[21] It recommends men should not present themselves and advance in manner when women might suffer from annoyance. From this, we can conclude that Kāmaśāstra has resorted to many Āyurveda concepts and we feel that it is written by Vaidya Vātsyāyana. This is a much acceptable proposition when we see Vāgbhaṭa's *Aṣṭāṅga Hṛdayam* uses the medical related aspects even while explaining core Kāmaśāstra topics. For example, Vāgbhaṭa's *Aṣṭāṅga Hṛdayam* says (Shastri 1992: 447; *KS* 3.4.22) man should use headache as good reason to call woman at home and request her head massage for the remedy. Vāgbhaṭa's *Aṣṭāṅga Hṛdayam* very specifically recommends passing her hands through eyes and forehead. Further, it recommends (ibid.: 448; *KS* 3.4.24) admitting to her that her touch itself is a medicine. The essence of this entire approach can be termed as therapeutic romance which is in line with Āyurveda philosophy. Vāgbhaṭa's *Aṣṭāṅga Hṛdayam* (Garde 1983: 489)[22] in clear words says: "woman is a real medicine for man". We can observe the undoubtful influence of Āyurveda and coherence between these two sciences.

Kāmaśāstra discusses marriage types and partner matching logic in detail. It concludes *gāndharva* type marriage is the best type due to right proportion of love, passion and attraction (Shastri 1992: 467; *KS* 3.5.29). The outlook of Kāmaśāstra about marriage is like medicine on social and individual psychological issues. Interestingly, Āyurveda says to use medicine cautiously and

---

21 तत्र यथार्थमनुव्देजयतोभावनिवेदनम् (*tatra yathārthamanuvdejayatobhāva-nivedanam*) । – *KS* 3.4.20

22 सा स्त्री वृषत्वाय परं नरस्य (*sā strī vṛṣatvāya paraṁ narasya*) । – VAYD 6.40.40

wisely. There is no absolute good or bad medicine as such; it is to be selected based upon the fitness of the patient conditions and properties of the medicine (Garde 1983: 348).[23] The *Caraka Saṁhitā*[24] mentions that nothing is useless from medicinal perspective; what is required is the right application.

We see the exact concept Kāmaśāstra propounded while describing the eight types of marriage and its situational fitness. We could see the multiple processes and possibilities Kāmaśāstra describes in this regard with reference to situational dimensions. While emphasizing the core objective as love and corresponding recommendation on the possible best marriage type as *gāndharva*, Kāmaśāstra still recognizes the other marriage types as most applicable in appropriate situations. Further, it inclined to prohibit a few marriage types like *paiśāca* and *rāksaṣa*; but still calibrates between them and comments the latter is better (Shastri 1992: 466; *KS* 3.5.28).

Moreover, we become astonished when we read (ibid.: 467; *KS* 3.5.30) the typical medical approach mentioned to support the *gāndharva* type marriage as superior due to its inherent elements of pleasure creation, easiness due to natural forces, less painful and does not demand any tedious rituals. This description is apt for medicine.

An interesting comparison below might make the point clearer:

We find Vāgbhaṭa's *Aṣṭāṅga Hṛdayam* 5.1.44 (Garde 1983: 337) mentioning arranging the apt and suitable medicine for a delicate person:

कुटजं सुकुमारेषु पित्तरक्तकफोदये ।
ज्वरे विसर्पे हृद्रोगे खुडे कुष्ठे च पूजितम् ॥

---

23 तद्योग्यौषधयुक्तान् (*tadyogyauṣadhayuktān*) । – VAYD 5.5.71

24 अनेनोपदेशेन नानौषधिभूतं जगति किंचिद् द्रव्यमुलभयते तां तां युक्तिमर्थं च तं तमभिप्रेत्य (*anenopadeśena nānauṣadhibhūtaṁ jagati kiñcid dravyamula-bhayate tāṁ tāṁ yuktimarthaṁ ca taṁ tamabhipretya*) । – *CS* 1.26.11

kuṭajaṁ sukumāreṣu pittaraktakaphodaye ।
jvare visarpe hr̥droge khuḍe kuṣṭhe ca pūjitam ॥

The *Kāmasūtra* (3.5.19) mentions the "conditional remedy" for a delicate (incapable) woman who herself cannot catch hold of a man: She should use a middle person (Shastri 1992: 464):

अप्रतिपद्यमानायामन्तश्चारिणीमन्यां कुलप्रमदां पूर्व संसृष्टांप्रीयमाणां चोपगृह्य तया सह विषह्यमवकाशमेनामन्यकार्यापदेशेनानाययेत् ।

apratipadyamānāyāmantaścāriṇīmanyāṁ kulpramadāṁ purva saṁsr̥ṣṭāprīyamāṇāṁ copagr̥hya tayā saha viṣa-hyamava-kāśamenāmanyakāryāpadeśenānāyayet ।

Āyurveda always emphasizes on the adequacy (Garde 1983: 352; VAYD 5.6.11-12) of medicine based on patient's fitness to it; whereas Kāmaśāstra, while adducing the similar concept, emphasizes on the right technique of marriage based on the partner's fitness to it.

Conceptually, we could see very fascinating simile between Āyurveda and Kāmaśāstra footings regarding the *rasa* and *śukra*. The Āyurveda concept of food digestion starts with *rasa* and ends with *śukra* creation; and the Kāmaśāstra concept also starts with *rasa* and ends with *śukra* utilization.

Section 7 of *Kāmasūtra* can be considered as the extension of Āyurveda itself. Several Āyurveda therapeutic concepts like *bhāvanā* (Shastri 1992: 732; *KS* 7.2.41) and *lepana* (ibid.: 733; *KS* 7.2.43) are directly used here in the same sense. We are discussing these aspects in detail in the next section. Further, Vāgbhaṭa's *Aṣṭāṅga Hr̥dayam* uses typical Āyurveda style of describing reversing impacts by using the word *pratyānayanam* (ibid.: 733).[25] The Āyurveda concept of reverse therapy is flawlessly used here. It also shows the command of Kāmaśāstra authors on physiology and pharmacology subjects.

While the concluding section Kāmaśāstra clearly-indicates (ibid.: 734; *KS* 7.2.53) that the theory of Kāmaśāstra should lead to a person towards the religious, confident and social-friendly

25 गुडो जीर्णितश्च प्रत्यानयनम् (*guḍo jīrṇitaśca pratyānayanam*) । – *KS* 7.2.45

behaviour. This means that the Kāmaśāstra techniques should be used scientifically to achieve (Shastri 1992: 735; *KS* 7.2.57) a healthy society (*lokayātrārtham*) and not just aiming at the pleasure (*rati-rāga*) of an individual. In fact, the key idea (ibid.: 736; *KS* 7.2.58) of Kāmaśāstra is to ensure that the people should become *jitendriya* in turn protecting the balanced state (*sātmyāvasthā*) of the society. We can draw below conclusions from these discussions.

The Āyurveda influence on Kāmaśāstra is very apparent from below table 2.6 and 2.7.

Table 2.6: Āyurveda Framework of Therapy and Medication

Therapeutic Theme	*Āyurveda*	
	Prevention	*Curation*
Subject	Healthy person	Patient/unwell
Objective	To retain health	To treat diseases
Treatment approach	Routine guidelines (*svastha-vṛtta*)	*Nidāna, cikitsā, kalpa*
Focus	Ensures balance within *trodoṣa**	
Key principles/techniques	Common base like *pathya* and *tristambha*	

* Along with *sapta-dhātu, mala, agni, indriya*

Table 2.7: Kāmaśāstra Framework of Therapy and Medication

Therapeutic Theme	*Kāmaśāstra*	
	Prevention	*Curation*
Subject	Healthy person	Patient/unwell
Objective	To retain health	To treat diseases
Treatment approach	Routine guidelines (*nāgaraka vṛtta*)	*Nidāna, unmāda, cikitsā*, adultery, prostitution, oral, *kalpa*, instruments
Focus	Ensures balance within three *puruṣārthas*	
Key principles/techniques	Common base like *rasābhāva, āsana* and aphrodidiacs	

* Along with *rasā, bhāva, rāga*.

The Kāmaśāstra adoption of Āyurveda style of *nidāna* and *cikitsā* can be observed when Kāmaśāstra provides remedies and taboos together. Kāmaśāstra categorically mentions (Shastri 1992: 476; *KS* 4.1.20-21) the reason of mistrusts between partners is black magic and strictly recommends avoiding its usage. It says it is better to rebuke husband in privacy or even in front of his friends than using any black magic. It further provides (ibid.: 477; *KS* 4.1.22) directions of *svastha-vṛtta* and recommends that the *sādhvī* should avoid certain types of behaviours like ill talking, standing near door for long, secretly talking with someone in garden. It will avoid the very common reasons of mistrust development.

While describing the duties of a wife, Kāmaśāstra authors had shown the notable knowledge of Āyurveda-compliant medicinal plants. Kāmaśāstra recommends (ibid.: 478; *KS* 4.1.28) a housewife should ensure the proper inventory of all scarce medicines like *pañcamūla*. This is an important medicine (group of drugs) mentioned in Āyurveda.

Pañcamūla means a group of five roots of small herbal plants, viz. *śālaparṇi*, *pṛṣṇiparṇi*, *bṛhati*, *kaṇṭakāri* and *gokṣura* or *eraṇḍa* (Ghildiyal and Joshi 2012). This is known as *laghupañcamūla* under *miśraka varga* (group of drugs). It is used as such or with *mahat pañcamūla*, i.e. *bilva*, *gambhari*, *śyonaka*, *agnimantha* and *paṭala*, constituting *daśamūla*, a well-recognized and popular Āyurveda preparation. *Eraṇḍa* is being considered due to its best *vṛṣya* (spermatogenic and aphrodisiac effect) and *vātahara* property.

Pañcamūla is also used as a key ingredient (in the decoction form) of *mahā yuṣa* (Princy and Yadav 2018: 121). Its therapeutic property and usage found in pacifying *tridoṣa* and curing *atyāgni*, *anidrā*, *stabdhatā* and *atisāra*. According to Ācārya Kaśyapa, *yuṣa* means liquefaction and metabolization. According to Monnier-William dictionary, *yuṣa* means soup, broth, the water in which pulses of various kinds are boiled. The cooked *yuṣa* liquefies the diet. It indicates as a wholesome diet for a healthy or a person under medication, or during and after purification procedures (Singh and Nathani 2018).

Kāmaśāstra not only recommends storing inventory of these medicines but also advises to preserve the seeds of these valuable medicinal plants and cultivate the same during appropriate time (Shastri 1992: 478, *KS* 4.1.29). We get astonished to note the immense knowledge the Kāmaśāstra authors have on Āyurveda concepts and its apt applications. It also provides a strong evidence of therapeutic influence of Āyurveda on the Kāmaśāstra theory, that too very naturally.

While acknowledging the need of multiple marriages, Kāmaśāstra clearly anticipates the risk of loss of harmony in relationships between partners, especially between wives (ibid.: 492, *KS* 4.2.3). This is a serious disease in Kāmaśāstra perspective and can be termed as loss of *rasābhāva*. This will certainly lead to the spoiled mental health of everyone concerned.

We observe a very intelligent therapy Kāmaśāstra suggests in this regard. It suggests a *yuktivyapaśraya* type of *cikitsā*. This is the rational therapeutic view of Āyurveda (ibid.: 493, *KS* 4.2.4-5).

Kāmaśāstra emphasizes the critical role of the first wife (*jyeṣṭhā*) and suggests behaving very responsibly in these circumstances of managing conflicting situations erupted due to polygamy. The first wife should cleverly treat the newly-wedded co-wife like her own sister and help in multiple ways including her make-up, sharing tips on dealing with husband and even educate[26] her on sexology while husband is listening (ibid.: 493).

It does not even hesitate to suggest instigating a conflict between other wives and husband if husband is biased with any one wife. This is absolutely balance creating act between all partners to ensure harmony in polygamy. This is not less than any therapy that Āyurveda recommends for physical diseases. In fact, we could mark the minute and commendable practical knowledge used by Kāmaśāstra authors on the psychotherapies. Like an Āyurveda

---

26 नायकसंश्रवे च रहसि विशेषानधिकान् दर्शयेत् (*nāyakasaṁśrave ca rahasi viśeṣānadhikān darśayet*)। – *KS* 4.2.6

practitioner, Kāmaśāstra expects from the first wife the skills in conducting diagnosis and treatment to manage the mental health of the family.

These narratives are so medically prescriptive that it is surprising and it would take a while for us to realize that we are not reading an Āyurveda text but a Kāmaśāstra text.

Kāmaśāstra has composed a separate section on adultery. The very fact of dealing this topic as a separate section, which itself is a controversial topic from social, religion and even moral point of view, shows the scientific and clinical approach of Kāmaśāstra ensuring that these discussions are strictly pertaining to the psychological and physiological elements. The entire discussions are following the Āyurveda principle of *trisūtra*. Āyurveda conceptualized the three steps therapy approach of diagnosis first based on the symptoms and followed by the right treatment. Kāmaśāstra adhered the same theme in this section. Table 2.8 shows the summary.

While emphasizing the analysis of physical symptoms exhibited by a lady, Kāmaśāstra categorically mentions its significance before proceeding for any action of building relationships with her. Only a professional medical practitioner can recommend such a prescriptive approach. We could see the very high influence of Āyurveda on Kāmaśāstra texts here.

Table 2.8: Adoption of the Āyurveda Trisutra Approach by Kāmaśāstra

Hetu (causes)	If person is subjected to the suicidal feelings without achieving her intimacy*
Liṅga (symptoms)	Kāmaśāstra describes ten symptoms** and uses the exact Āyurveda term – लिङ्गानि (*liṅgāni*)
Cikitsā (treatment)	We find a detailed treatment in the fifth section of the *Kāmasūtra*

* व्याख्यातकारणाः परपरिग्रहोपगमाः (*vyākhyātakāraṇāḥ paraparigrahopagamāḥ*) । – *KS* 5.1.4

** दश तु कामस्य स्थानानि (*daśatu kāmasya sthānāni*) । – *KS* 5.1.4 (Shastri 1992: 512)

Kāmaśāstra further provides with the reasoning behind the suggested therapy by describing the logical interpretation of women's psychology and the her natural behaviour (Shastri 1992: 514). [27] Women doesn't care any "rule book" of morality but very much honest to her feelings and practical possibility of success in love affair.

Kāmaśāstra further provides a list of reasons why women may not proceed in extra-marital relationships (ibid.: 515-18; *KS* 5.1.18-42). It also suggests a few remedies to counter the resistance of women especially related to fear (ibid.: 518-19; *KS* 5.1.43-49). Kāmaśāstra details the qualities of man that leads to the successful task of achieving love in extra-marital relationships (ibid.: 520; *KS* 5.1.50). We get the very interesting account on consumption of quick effect and low side-effect "medicine" type of women who are easily acquired with high probability (अयत्नसाध्या – *ayatnasādhyā*) (Shastri 1992: 521, *KS* 5.1.52).

We could see the deep psychological analysis on promiscuity and monogamy here. the Kāmaśāstra theory does not incline too much on morality-based extreme prescriptions, it however, does not warrant the unlimited monstrous[28] liberty leading to social disasters of being "free society pandemic". It strongly endorses the clinical ethos of conjugal relationships with permitted dilution that ensures the medically and psychologically correct behaviours of the human society. Hence, the narrative of Kāmaśāstra theory is exactly in line with Āyurveda philosophy.

Interestingly, Kāmaśāstra begins this section (ibid.: 511; *KS* 5.1.2) by clearly making a statement like the medical declaration,

---

27 न स्त्रीधर्ममधर्मं चापेक्षते कामयत एव (*na stridharmamadharma cāpekṣate kāmayata eva*) ।
– *KS* 5.1.10

28 "What freedom men and women could have, were they not constantly tricked and trapped and enslaved and tortured by their sexuality! The only drawback in that freedom is that without it one would not be a human. One would be a monster." – Steinbeck 1952

which patient signs before risky operation that the success is probabilistic and no guarantee on the result.

We observe the entire *Bhāvaparīkṣā* chapter of Kāmaśāstra is like the *vikṛtividnāniyam* chapter of *Āyurveda*. The depth of topic and style of Vāgbhaṭa's *Aṣṭāṅga Hṛdayam* is seen apparently in the *Kāmasūtra* while it details out the psychological and behavioural symptoms of *paradārā*. Vāgbhaṭa's *Aṣṭāṅga Hṛdayam* categorically mentions to master the art of understanding the physical symptoms (Garde 1983: 158).[29] This is crucial for the success of medical profession especially for the disease diagnosis and severity management.

We find a similar approach in Kāmaśāstra. It mentions the importance of physical examination and behavioural symptoms to decide systematic course of the remedial action (Shastri 1992: 543).[30] It theorizes a hypothesis that even if *bhāva* is invisible, the physical and behavioural gestures, which it produce, are much conclusive about the very condition of a person. This approach is very much therapeutic and influenced by Āyurveda. It perfectly qualifies the medical diagnostic theory.

Āyurveda mentions the *trivarga anvekṣaṇam* while treating the mental diseases (Bagali et al. 2016: 59). It is the course of conduct relating to *trivarga*, i.e. three objectives of life, viz. *dharma* (virtue), *artha* (wealth) and *kāma* (desire), should be attended. This can be achieved by knowledge or cognition. It means one should go in the service of those who are well versed in nature and treatment of mental diseases, i.e. specialties of the therapy and the therapy

---

29 आयुर्वेदफलं कृत्स्नं यदायुर्ज्ञे प्रतिष्ठितम्।
रिष्ठज्ञानाहृतस्तस्मात्सर्वदैव भवेभ्दिषक्॥ – VAYD 2.5.131
āyurvedaphalaṁ kṛtsraṁ yadāyurjñe pratiṣṭhitam ।
riṣṭhajñānāhṛtastasmātsarvadaiva bhavebhdiṣak ।।

30 अभियुञ्जानो योषितः प्रवृत्तिं परीक्षेत।
तया भावः परीक्षितो भवति॥ – *KS* 5.3.1
abhiyuñjāno yoṣitaḥ pravṛttiṁ parīkṣeta ।
tayā bhāvaḥ parīkṣito bhavati ।।

should be done by them. This way, Āyurveda clearly suggests the services of an expert and specialty person for mental diseases (*tadvidyāsevā*).

We could see the messenger's role mentioned in Kāmaśāstra is very much in line with the above recommendation prescribed by Āyurveda. Kāmaśāstra has adopted this concept of expert usage of messenger and categorically mentions (Shastri 1992: 552; *KS* 5.4.1) as the best option, especially in the case of dealing with an extraordinary woman (*apūrva strī*), unknown women and the one who is not showing any symptoms (*pragalbhā*). All these are difficult cases to handle for a man.

Further, it can be also seen (ibid.: 552-53, *KS* 5.4.3-8) that Kāmaśāstra has used the *hetuviparīta* type of therapy, prescribed in Āyurveda, while describing the suggestive actions of messenger.

Kāmaśāstra follows the unbiased discussions on the grounds of gender, religion, caste, ritual and recommends its prescriptions predominantly on the scientific propositions. Hence, we find clear recommendations like *gāndharva* type marriage, freedom for women to choose her partner, and daily and night routines.

Moreover, Kāmaśāstra considers adultery as an extreme and uncommon option to choose and imposes several restrictions to achieve love from such an extra-marital affair. While considering the exceptional need of such affair, Kāmaśāstra is gender unbiased. It talks that both men and women can be seduced.

Similarly, Kāmaśāstra talks about the topic (section 5, chapter 5) wherein a higher status man wishes to seduce a lower status woman; and immediately in the next chapter (section 5, chapter 6) composes the reverse possibilities wherein queens seduce men from other statuses. This is the testimonial of scientific approach and more importantly Āyurveda's clinical approach of non-discrimination based on gender or status of persons. Therapy should be given to the person who needs it and not about any irrelevant prejudice.

Interestingly, Kāmaśāstra, like Āyurveda, never deviates in

recommending its step by step and sequential process of pleasure creation that largely includes detailed sub-steps of *rasābhāva* creation followed by *āsana*, etc. We see this consistency even in case of engaging all types of women including prostitutes. It clearly shows the scientific emphasis and therapeutic romance leading to a strong Āyurveda process compliance.

Thus, we could see the great level of parity between the themes of therapy suggested by these two sciences.

2.5.2.5 *Concept of Classification and Precision*

In this section, we will discuss the Āyurveda influence on Kāmaśāstra with reference to the two specific areas, viz. classification theory and depth of discussions (precision). The classification theory deals with arranging diagnosis and prescription topics based on the key identified elements; whereas precision is all about the minute considerations within the theory.

Āyurveda recognizes three basic and four combinatory constitutional types based on different combinations of the *doṣa* at conception. Individuals of the three extreme constitutional types express a single dominant *doṣa* and are said to have *vāta prakṛti*, *pitta prakṛti* or *kapha prakṛti* respectively (Venil and Girish 2012). However, most individuals have constitutional types arising from combinations of the three basics in varying proportions. Accordingly, most individuals have one of seven main types, viz. – *vāta*, *pitta*, *kapha*, *vāta-pitta*, *pitta-kapha*, *vāta-kapha* and *vāta-pitta-kapha*, which results in a wide range of phenotypic variation.

Kāmaśāstra has picked up the similar idea of classifying males and females based on three basics constituents followed by multiple combinations. Kāmaśāstra classifies (Shastri 1992: 183; *KS* 2.1.1) males as hare, bull or stallion according to the size of their sexual organ. And women are defined as deer, mare and elephant, based on the size of their genital. Kāmaśāstra further discusses the nine possible combinations of partnerships from this and suitability of the same. The idea of classifying humans into three categories and then reviewing the combinations for the best partnership is very much driven by medical concepts. We are discussing these aspects in detail in the next section.

Moreover, like Āyurveda mentions the infinite possibilities of phenotypic variation, Kāmaśāstra (ibid.: 205)[31] extends the similar concept to connote infinite possibilities of grades of pleasure produced by a variety of male–female combinations.

Āyurveda believes that imbalances or disturbed interactions between the three *doṣas* are the root cause of all disease and optimal function of each *doṣa* and interactions between them are essential for normal health (Venil and Girish 2012: 3). The entire concept of classification of different constitutional types is aimed at laying down the precise therapeutic and clinical foundation.

We see profound influence of this Āyurveda concept on Kāmaśāstra. While classifying the partnership possibilities, Kāmaśāstra creates its foundation of therapy and symptomatic treatments on the psychological diseases erupt out of sexual displeasures and related matters. It classifies (Shastri 1992: 184; *KS* 2.1.3) precisely the displeasure possibilities across different combinations of partnerships and calibrates the recommendations of best matches. The psychological stability of any human governs his physical health. We see a unique influence of Āyurveda on Kāmaśāstra theory in classifying the root causes of diseases precisely.

Like the *doṣa* classification, Āyurveda describes different types of physicians such as *rāja-vaidya* (royal physician), *prāṇābhisāra* (an excellent physician), *bhiṣakacadhamcara* (pseudophysician/who poses himself as a physician), *siddhisādhita* (feigned physician/ who boasts as a successful physician), *vaidyaguṇayukta* (genuine physician) and *mūrkha vaidya* (Bagde et al. 2014: 9). While it is obvious that medical professionals possessing good qualities alone can save a patient's life always, Āyurveda provides all practical possibilities of professional types.

---

31 सुरतसंख्या न शक्यते कर्तुम् (*suratasaṁkhyā na śakyate kartum*) । – *KS* 2.1.33

Kāmaśāstra also classifies men and women on the ground of multiple criteria of age, relationships, morale restrictions, physical marks, body structure, etc. Hence, we find different types of prostitutes, wives, customers, etc. We are discussing these aspects in the next chapter.

Although the aim of Kāmaśāstra is to provide pleasure theory, it considers all real-world possibilities and variations that need to be addressed in the society.

Āyurveda classifies the *vikṛti* (death symptoms) into two broad categories. One is permanent and the other is temporary (Garde 1983: 151, VAYD 2.5.3). Āyurveda clearly proposes here a criterion of permanency or continuity to distinguish between these two broad categories of symptoms. It further warns (ibid.; VAYD 2.5.2) about the difficulty in diagnosing these symptoms when the *vaidya* does not have proper knowledge. Temporary symptoms might be due to *doṣa prakopa* and not conclusive enough to diagnose as life-threatening indicators. But permanent symptoms are conclusive.

Kāmaśāstra has picked up the similar concept for symptom diagnosis of the natural tendency and feelings of women (Shastri 1992: 543; *KS* 5.3.1). It recognizes the two types of possibilities and advocates systematic and sequential steps of remedies (ibid.; *KS* 5.3.3).

Possibility 1: A Woman exposes symptoms and possibly mingles.

Possibility 2: A Woman does not expose any symptoms but possibly mingles.

We have seen that Āyurveda faces a challenging situation to determine the conclusive symptoms which are produced and observed among all those physically, whereas Kāmaśāstra, using Āyurveda baseline, deals with a much challenging situation of judging a woman who might be mingling even though symptoms are not exposed, but willingness and high possibility exist. Hence, Kāmaśāstra recommends a detailed framework of symptoms observation, called *bhāva parīkṣā*. We are discussing these aspects in the next chapter.

2.5.2.6 *Precision Aspects*

Āyurveda recognizes the critical role and responsibility of messenger. Patient deploys messenger for ensuring the proper communication to a doctor and getting the one visited at patient's place. From Āyurveda description, it is apparent that the messenger literally determines the fate of the patient. It suggests the detailed behavioural aspects for messenger including dressing sense, communication, mannerism and decorum, smartness, knowledge of customs, auspicious elements, etc. (Garde 1983: 159-60; VAYD 2.6.1-16).

Kāmaśāstra completely resonates with this theory of messenger and effectively narrates (Shastri 1992: 567; *KS* 5.4.66) the role and reasonability in its own context in a precise way. We are discussing these aspects in the next chapter.

The way messenger in Āyurveda determines the success of medical treatment and life of a patient, Kāmaśāstra believes in the critical and intelligent role of messenger in saving the life of a person by ensuring *paradārā rati bhāva*. Further, it prescribes a well-defined *cikitsā* to be performed by messenger.

We could very clearly relate the behavioural aspects mentioned in Āyurveda as the "forbidden practices" for messenger in Kāmaśāstra. It is not far-stretched to believe that Āyurveda narrates the forbidden behaviour of a messenger which is very much part of Kāmaśāstra and without repeating the same, Kāmaśāstra prescribes the intelligent and sequential therapy to be practised by messenger.

While narrating about the betel leave mixture, its ingredients and consumption, Kāmaśāstra talks about utmost precision like we see in Āyurveda pharmacology. Kāmaśāstra articulates the precise usage and consumption timing of betel mixture in the day and night routine (Shastri 1992: 110). It has clear sense of medicine and taboos for over and under consumption. We are discussing these aspects in detail in the next section.

The *Kāmasūtra* author very naturally and precisely mentions the possibility of first meeting of *nāyaka* and *nāyikā* at the home of a medical professional (ibid.: 530; *KS* 5.2.6). It says that one must take deliberate efforts to make it happen. Looking at the Kāmaśāstra subject, while composing the text, it would be very interesting to note the mention of the home of a medical practitioner when the other places are mentioned like friend's place, celebration occasions, royal houses, religious places and gardens.

We can easily conclude here that the *Kāmasūtra* author had always been mentally connected with the Āyurveda theme while composing its text, otherwise, it would be very irrelevant to mention the home of a medical practitioner when the other places are mentioned.

2.5.3 PRESCRIPTIVE INFLUENCE ON KĀMAŚĀSTRA PRACTICE

Under this section, I have reviewed different postulates of Āyurveda influence on the Kāmaśāstra theory related to the structured guidelines appeared in Kāmaśāstra texts. These prescriptions of Kāmaśāstra span across varied topics like daily routines, behavioural taboos, food consumption, body hygiene, medicines and even regional considerations within the doctrine.

2.5.3.1 *Food Consumption*

Kāmaśāstra recommends strict restrictions on the consumption of salty and acrid-dominant food for the first three days after marriage (Shastri 1992: 408).[32] The examples of these are mentioned as eatables made using sea salts and unwashed jaggery (Madhavacharya 2008: 593). Further, it advises to consume food dominated with sweet, milk and ghee (ibid.).

---

32 संगतयोस्त्रिरात्रमध शय्या ब्रम्हचर्य क्षारलवण (*saṅgatayostrirātnamadha śayyā brahmacarya kṣāralavaṇa*) । – *KS* 3.2.1

The *Suśruta Saṁhitā* describes the unwashed (unrefined) jaggery is slightly alkaline and causes intestinal worms, increases chances of disorder in marrow, blood, fat tissue and muscles (Shastri 1954: 182).[33] It also describes (ibid.: 157) the side effects of salts on genital and copulation performance. The *Caraka Saṁhitā* in clear words describes similar nature of jaggery.[34] It uses the word क्षुद्रो गुडः (*kṣudro guḍaḥ*) (black jaggery) (*CS* 1.27.238) and describes its properties as impure and it will cause more damage than refined one.

The sweet food, milk and ghee are classical catalysts for semen production in Āyurveda.[35]

The first few days after marriage are very important from long-term relationship development. The first impression which bride might catch will be determining factor of respect she extends forever to her husband. The very common first impressions are always about the physical structure and health. While the investigator has captured all physical structure-related discussions in a separate topic, it is worthwhile to understand here the health-related aspects Kāmaśāstra recommends. Kāmaśāstra acknowledges the importance of the honeymoon period and very meticulous about its recommendations during this period. The approach is very prescriptive especially about the food consumption as we have seen. Kāmaśāstra seems to be very careful and highly Āyurveda compliant when recommends the restrictions on the salty and acrid food and promotes usage of sweet, milk and ghee-dominant food during the honeymoon period. This will ensure the reduction of the possibility of intestinal infections, power loss and low semen count in those precious days of honeymoon. While deploying Āyurveda knowledge in very prescriptive way, Kāmaśāstra has

---

33 गुडः सक्षारमधुरो (*guḍaḥ sakṣāramadhuro*)। – *SS* I.42.14

34 प्रभूत कृमिमज्जासृङ् मेदोमांसकरो गुडः (*prabhūta kr̥mimajjāsr̥ṅ medomāṁsakaro guḍaḥ*)। – *CS* 1.27.237

35 नरं विशेषात्क्षीराज्यैर्मधुरौषधसंस्कृतैः (*naraṁ viśeṣātkṣīrājyairmadhurauṣadhasaṁskr̥taiḥ*)। – VAYD 2.1.20

achieved in its narration, the delicate balance between technical medical language and natural inclination of reader towards the simplicity and application orientation. The very usage of the technically sounded word क्षारलवण (*kṣāralavaṇa*) itself denotes the strong Āyurveda knowledge of Kāmaśāstra authors.

Interestingly, Kāmaśāstra suggests the food consumption timings as a protocol (Shastri 1992: 116; *KS* 1.4.7). The food should be consumed two times a day and the dinner should be in the early evening. Āyurveda clearly suggests the bathing before meal consumption and Kāmaśāstra categorically mentions the same as prescription (Garde 1983: 8; VAYD 1.2.17).

Post-copulation, Kāmaśāstra suggests to eat and drink as per one's own *prakṛti*, season and taste (Shastri 1992: 374; *KS* 2.10.7). We get astonished to see such a parity between the prescriptions of these two sciences. A direct mention of Āyurvedic term like *prakṛti* in the same sense proves the command and preferential outlook of Kāmaśāstra authors on Āyurveda subject matter. Moreover, Kāmaśāstra further emphasizes to consume the sweet and fruit dishes post copulation. We have already discussed that the sweet foods are classical catalysts for semen production as per Āyurveda.

We can conclude that the above approach of Kāmaśāstra in its recommendations is completely in line with the Āyurveda theory and its inspiration.

2.5.3.2 *Theory of Conception and Anatomy*

Most of the human physiology concepts mentioned in Āyurveda are like the contemporary medical science. However, some concepts like *ātmā*, *manas* and *prakṛti* are unique (Patwardhan 2008).

The foetus formation process described in Āyurveda is very interesting. The *Caraka Saṁhitā* says:

> What is that of a man which having four constituents and six sources and which coming out of him while cohabiting with a

> woman of a different clan in a lonely place after the period of her menses is converted into an embryo in the women.
>
> – Loon 2013: 512

It further says:

> The wise call it *śukra* (semen), which is implanted for the origin of the embryo. By the excellence of sperm, ovum, the self, uterus and time and by management with wholesome diet the normal foetus gets delivered in fully developed state, in time and with ease.

The *Kāmasūtra* believes this Āyurveda theory of conception (Shastri 1992: 187). The second section of the *Kāmasūtra* (we can say *śārira* section of Kāmaśāstra) describes the human anatomy vis-à-vis copulation fitness between partners. While narrating the basic conception process, the *Caraka Saṁhitā* is referred in the *Kāmasūtra* with above discussions.

Āyurveda clearly warns about the possible risks to the healthy foetus formation. And interestingly, we find the corresponding taboos in Kāmaśāstra. The *Caraka Saṁhitā* says:

> Though fertile, a woman gets conceived after a long time due to defects in genitals, mental worry, derangement of sperm, ovum, diet and behaviour; absence of proper timing and diminution of strength.
>
> – Loon 2013: 513

Further:

> Intellectual error, unbalanced use of senses and consequence of time; these three are the causes of all the disorders. Similarly, the remedy of all disorders consists of the balanced use of intellect, senses and time.

It reads further:

> When the parents have sluggish and diminished reproductive factor, are weak, unstimulated and with damaged genetic portion, they cause the two disorders: male and female sterility. Due to mother's lack of desire (for coitus) or complicated posture (during coitus) and due to genetic deficiency of father, *vakrī* (with curved

organ) is caused. *Īrṣyābhirati* is caused if the parents are subdued by jealousy and have mild passion.

In this regard, it is interesting to note the *Aṣṭāṅga Hr̥dayam*'s prescriptions on the mental health of parents for the sound foetus formation. It emphasizes the purity of mind (*śuddhe hr̥di*) (VAYD 2.1.8; Garde 1983: 121) and mind assimilation of partners (*saṁraktaṁ mithunaṁ*) (VAYD 2.1.19; ibid.: 122) as the key to a healthy foetus.

The Kāmaśāstra theory has used all the Āyurveda propositions in its recommendations. We should observe the few important elements listed by Āyurveda in the above narration – balanced usage of intellect, senses and time, and lack of desires (sluggish behaviour of partners), mild passion, complicated postures during coitus. We find the entire male/female classification system, calibration recommendations, techniques of relaxing wife before copulation, *āsana* theory, *rasa* and *bhāva* theory of Kāmaśāstra are based on this. Kāmaśāstra categorically mentions to avoid awkward postures of copulation to ensure birth of a normal child (Shastri 1992: 353). Moreover, overall copulation process (inclusive of pre and post) details are recommended based on the Āyurveda compliance. These topics are discussed in detail in the next chapter.

We find the direct conceptual referencing of Āyurveda in Kāmaśāstra while describing the female anatomy and nature (Jha 1929: 81-83). The *Nāgarasarvasva* describes the types of females using Āyurveda terms to emphasis the overall clarity. It is the inseparable relationship between Kāmaśāstra and Āyurveda with Āyurveda being its foundation, naturally makes the Kāmaśāstra authors to adduce and apply Āyurveda concepts.

The *Nāgarasarvasva*[36] mentions that a deer woman is of *kapha* type, a mare woman is of *pitta* type, an elephant woman is of *vāta*

---

[36] समधिककफः हरिणी भवेत (*samadhikakaphaḥ hariṇī bhaveta*) । – *NS* 14.15; Jha 1929: 81); पीत्ताधिका वडवा (*pīttādhika vaḍavā*) । – *NS* 14.16; Jha 1929: 82; वातप्रकृतिरकृशै हस्तपादैर्वराङ्गी (*vātaprakr̥tirakr̥śai hastapādairvarāṅgī*) । – *NS* 14.17; Jha 1929: 82

type. The Āyurveda influence is very clearly seen here. Vāgbhaṭa's *Aṣṭāṅga Hṛdayam* (1.1.10-112) mentions the distinct properties of each *doṣa* (Garde 1983). The main properties of *vāta* are dry, cold, light, subtle, clear, rough, astringent taste, responsible for movements and catabolic in nature. *Pitta* possesses properties of hot, unctuous, sharp, liquid, spreading, sour-pungent-bitter taste, responsible for digestion and metabolism. *Kapha* possesses the qualities of cold, heavy, soft, oily, stable, slimy, sweet taste and anabolic in nature. The parity of this description with the *Nāgarasarvasva* description is conclusive on Āyurveda influence.

The *Kāmasūtra* in clear words interprets (Shastri 1992: 191) the Āyurveda influence on partner selection process. While narrating eight different criteria, the *Kāmasūtra* mentions Āyurveda's perspective should be used for age and physical matching criteria of partners. This will lead to a healthy progeny.

Interestingly, the Kāmaśāstra recommendation on the best pair of partners goes completely as per Āyurveda prescription of constituent's theory (see Table 2.9).

Kāmaśāstra proposes restricted pairing for *kapha* to *vāta* and estimates moderate quality for *kapha* to *pitta*. This recommendation is exactly based on Āyurveda philosophy.

Āyurveda mentions that each type of constituent is associated with distinct physiological patterns, energy metabolism and tolerance to external factors. Thus, individuals with the two extreme types of *prakṛti* (*vāta* vs *kapha*) show low vs high body mass index values respectively.

Table 2.9: Adoption of Āyurveda Constituent Theory by Kāmaśāstra

Male Type	*Constituent*	*Female Type*	*Constituent*	*Pair Quality*
Hare	*Kapha*	Deer	*Kapha*	Best
Bull	*Pitta*	Mare	*Pitta*	Best
Horse	*Vāta*	Elephant	*Vāta*	Best

From above discussions we can conclude the sanctity within the process of copulation recommended[37] (Garde 1983: 122)and expected by Āyurveda is detailed by Kāmaśāstra as well. Thus, the hypothesis – it is Āyurveda, which forms the foundation for the Kāmaśāstra theory of anatomy – can be accepted.

Lastly, as described by the *Atharvaveda* and adopted by Āyurveda, one should have a life expectancy of 100 years; Kāmaśāstra's endorsement of this is observed in exact words (Shastri 1992: 294).[38] We can conclude here that Āyurveda tells us how to ensure 100 years of life longevity and Kāmaśāstra tells us what to do in those 100 years.

2.5.3.3 *Copulation Process and Pleasure Enhancement*

Āyurveda strictly recommends to avoid intercourse during the first three days of post menstruation period (Garde 1983: 123; VAYD 2.1.27). It further recommends avoiding eleventh day as well. The idea is to increase the progeny probability along with hygiene. Kāmaśāstra has adopted these recommendations and suggests avoiding the copulation in the first three days post-marriage.

In fact, Āyurveda details the process of copulation including rituals, charity, overall good behaviour and regulation, prior food consumption, how to board on bed, how to ensure the focus and concentration for copulation and getting *tridoṣa* in balanced state during copulation to maximize pleasure and high probability of healthy progeny (ibid.: 123-24; VAYD 2.1.31, 34). Kāmaśāstra must have picked up this theme while detailing the details of different techniques of generating the copulation pleasure. We can conclude here that Āyurveda describes "what to do" and Kāmaśāstra details "how to do" elements.

Kāmaśāstra provides a detailed account on dental hygiene and ideal dental topography. We become absolutely astounded

---

37 क्षीणे शुक्रकरी क्रिया (*kṣīṇe śukrakarī kriyā*) । – VAYD 2.1.14

38 संवत्सरशतेनापि प्रीतिर्न परिहीयते (*saṁvatsaraśatenāpi prītirna parihīyate*) । – *KS* 2.5.43

when see the detailed description like dentistry textbook on dental "virtues" (Shastri 1992: 283; *KS* 2.5.2). Kāmaśāstra defines the ideal dental topography as even sized, naturally shining, lined up without gaps and sharp edged. We see the usage of typical Āyurveda-styled word *daśāṅgunā* as dental qualities. Moreover, it does not stop by mentioning virtues but also describes the defects in dental topography (ibid.: 283; *KS* 2.5.3). This again proves the adoption of Āyurveda approach of narration in terms of completeness in discussions.

We see the Kāmaśāstra prescriptions on teeth bites during copulation. Kāmaśāstra provides detailed recommendations and techniques of bites to accelerate and enhance pleasure (ibid.: 284-86; *KS* 2.5.4-18). Kāmaśāstra mentions various places (points) on body for eight types of bites. These are primarily lips, forehead, ears, neck, arm pits and breasts.

Āyurveda recognizes the concept of *marma*. There are several vital points (Rathod et al. 2016) in the body having importance regarding traumatic effect. These points when exposed to trauma generate the symptoms from pain to fatal effect and should be protected from injury. On the other hand, these points are considered as healing points. There is remarkable research outcome which has proved the strong relationship between Āyurveda and acupressure. The summarized discussions are presented in Table 2.10.

Table 2.10: Highlight of Marma Theory

Āyurveda Concept of Marma	*Related Points as per Acupressure*
Kūrca	Spinal (column), uterus/prostate, bladder, lumbar, thyroid and parathyroid
Kūrcaśira	Ovary and testis, uterus, prostate and stomach
Maṇibandha	Lymph, sciatic nerve, ovary/testis, intestine
Kṣipra	Head and brain, pituitary, pineal and hypothalamus, neck, throat, thyroid and parathyroid
Talahṛdaya	Adrenal, intestine, spleen, kidney, hip, thigh and solar plexus

Further, the touch therapy on *marma* will directly impact the organs in below manner:

- *Kūrca* – Helpful for overall sensory acuity.
- *Kūrcaśira* – Helpful for reproductive function and promotes visual acuity.
- *Maṇibandha* – Energizes the reproductive system and helps maintain functional hand movement.

We find significant impact of this Āyurveda principles on Kāmaśāstra. While advocating the creation of pleasure through biting at different body points, Kāmaśāstra has categorically avoided these fatal portions; and advised caressing the same. Thus, it ensures no mishap is possible during the sensual excitement leading to the life risk.

The hypothesis gets further strengthened when we observe the direct reference in Kāmaśāstra advising to keep *prakṛti* as key focus than any regional taste and preference for biting (Shastri 1992: 291).[39] It clearly proves the clinical influence on the Kāmaśāstra thought process while suggesting the pleasure enhancement techniques. The life is much more important than the copulation pleasure and any custom or formality. It explains the Kāmaśāstra prescriptions strongly based on the Āyurveda theory.

2.5.3.4 *Routine Management*

It is apparent that there is influence of Āyurveda on Kāmaśāstra on the topic of day and night routine management. Āyurveda places tremendous emphasize on the daily routine management. It describes the minute details of the routine to ensure the state of healthier body, mind leading to the less risk of diseases. We observe many references in Āyurveda, and below are a few significant observations (Bargale et al. 2019: 5):

---

39 देशसात्म्यात् प्रकृतिसात्म्यं बलीय (*deśasātmyāt prakṛtisātmyaṁ balīya*)।
– *KS* 2.5.34

मानवो येन विधिना स्वस्थस्तिष्ठति सर्वदा।
तमेव कारयेद्वैद्यो यतः स्वास्थ्यं सदेप्सितम॥

दिनचर्या निशाचर्यामृतुचर्या यथोदिताम।
आचरन्पुरुषः स्वस्थः सदा तिष्ठति नान्यथा॥

mānavo yena vidhinā svasthastiṣṭhati sarvadā ।
tameva kārayedvaidyo yataḥ svāsthyaṁ sadepsitam ॥

dinacaryā niśācaryā mr̥tucaryā yathoditāma ।
ācaranpuruṣaḥ svasthaḥ sadā tiṣṭhati nānyathā ॥

The methods by which men can remain healthy always should be instructed by physician, since health is always desirable. By following day routine, night routine and seasonal routine described for health of mean but not otherwise.

तच्च नित्यं प्रयुञ्जीत स्वास्थ्यं येनानुवर्तते।
अजातानां विकाराणामनुत्पत्तिकरं च यत॥

tacca nityaṁ prayuñjīta svāsthyaṁ yenānuvartate ।
ajātānāṁ vikārāṇāmanutpattikaraṁ ca yata ॥

One should regularly follow diet and regimen, which keep good health and prevent diseases, which are not manifested.

नरो दिनादिचर्याभिर्यो न वर्तेत नित्यशः।
स एव लभते रोग ततः पथ्यं समाचरेत॥

naro dinādicaryābhiryo na varteta nityaśaḥ ।
sa eva labhate roga tataḥ pathyaṁ samācareta ॥

One who does not follow the day routine and night routine regimens properly as stipulated in Āyurveda, is likely to be infected with multiple health problems. Hence, everyone should adhere to these regimens strictly in the interest of his own health.

We find striking resemblance between the day routine advised by Āyurveda and Kāmaśāstra. Let us examine the highlights of day routine suggested by Āyurveda:

Waking up Early: A healthy person should arise one and half hour before sunrise. This is the time when *vāta-doṣa* is predominant and helps in easy evacuation of bowels.

Evacuation of Bowel: To get natures call after getting up from the bed in the morning is a sign of good health.

Body Hygiene: Hands, feet, mouth should be thoroughly washed with soap and water after defecation. This type of cleanliness prevents bacterial contamination.

Dental Hygiene: After defecation proper cleaning of teeth is necessary. Seers have prescribed special herbs for brushing like *vaṭa* (*Ficus bengalensis*), *vijaysara* (*Pterocarpus marsupium*), *jaṭī* (*Myristica fragrans*), *karavīra* (*Nelium indicum*), *arjuna* (*Terminalia arjuna*), *nimba* (*Azadirachta indica*) and *karañja* (*Pongamia pinnata*).

Cleansing of Tongue: It should be cleaned by a flexible and long strip of metal or wood. This stimulates the whole digestive tract and increases the digestive fire.

Cleansing of Mouth: *Gaṇḍūṣa* and *kavala* are both variants of gargling described in Saṁhitās. In *gaṇḍūṣa* one takes such a large quantity of fluid into the mouth that one is unable to move it inside the mouth. Whereas in *kavala* one holds and moves the semisolid paste solution in the mouth. Either practice helps in removing the odour, stimulates the taste buds, strengthens the gums and teeth, and increases the appetite.

Application of Collyrium: Everyday collyrium should be applied in the eyes. Its regular use increases the brightness of the eyes and strengthens their ability to withstand the bright light.

Instillation of Nasal Drops (*Nāsya*): All the medicated medicines whether in the form of liquid, vapours, powder or smoke when applied inside the nose is called *nāsya*. Out of the entire five sense organs, nose is termed as the gateway to the head. Regular use of *nāsya* helps to keep the nose, ears, eyes clean, intact and healthy. Also the voice becomes clear and unobstructed; helps prevent premature graying of hair and baldness, stiffness of neck and jaw.

Smoking of Medicinal Herbs (*Dhūmapāna*): Medicated herbs like *jaṭāmāṁsī* (*Nardostachys jatamansi*), *guggulu* (*Commiphora wightii*), *agāru* (*Aquilaria agallocha*), *lodhra* (*Symplocos racemosa*) and *udumbara* (*Ficus racemosa*) when wrapped in a cigarette form are inhaled through nose or mouth but never the fumes are exhaled from nose unlike normal smoking. This helps alleviating extra *kapha-doṣa* present in the head or nose region. Also it is indicated in many diseases especially *vāta kaphaja* predominant and healthy individual. It prevents premature graying of hair. It is useful in excessive salivation, itching in the mouth, sneezing, sinusitis, pain in the ear and many such diseases pertaining to the head and nose region.

Massage (*Mardana*) *and Oil Massage* (*Abhyaṅga*): Rubbing of the body is called *mardana* and when done while using certain oils is called *abhyaṅga*. Both procedures improve blood circulation in the body, stimulates nervous system, prevents old age and increases longevity.

Exercise (*Vyāyāma*): Everybody should do regular light exercises. With exercise the body grows and becomes proportionate in shape. It also increases muscular strength. It is best when done to the extent of half the exercising capacity of the individual. When sweat appears on the forehead and armpits, and the respiration becomes quick, exercise should be stopped.

We will now review the Kāmaśāstra narrative (Richard et al. 2009: 20) on day routine below. In fact, it is very interesting that Kāmaśāstra uses the Āyurveda terms itself – *dinacaryā* and *rātricaryā*.

The householder having got up in the morning and performed his necessary duties, should wash his teeth, apply a limited quantity of ointments and perfumes to his body, wear some ornaments and put collyrium on his eyelids and below his eyes, colour his lips with *alacktaka* and observe himself in the glass. Having then eaten betel leaves, with other things that give fragrance to the mouth, he should perform his usual business. He should bathe daily, anoint his body with oil every other day, apply a lathering substance to his body every three days, get his head (including face) shaved every four days and the other parts of his body every five or ten days. All these things should be done without fail and the sweat of the armpits should be well taken care of. Meals should be taken in the forenoon, in the afternoon and again at night, according to Caraka. After breakfast, parrots and other birds should be taught to speak and the fighting of cocks, quails and rams should follow. A limited time should be devoted to diversions with *pīṭhamardas*, *viṭas* and *vidūṣakas*, and then should be taken the midday sleep. After this the householder, having put on his clothes and ornaments, should, during the afternoon, converse with his friends. In the evening there should be singing and after that the householder, along with his friend, should await in his room, previously decorated and perfumed, the arrival of the woman that may be attached to him, or he may send a female messenger for her, or go for her himself. After her arrival at his house, he and his friend should welcome her and entertain her with a loving and agreeable conversation. Thus, end the duties of the day.

We could see the significant influence and compliance to Āyurveda in above Kāmaśāstra recommendations. The key areas of influence are, early waking, teeth cleaning, application of collyrium, consumption of betel leaves, significance of bathing everyday, scientific body massage, regular shaving and wearing ornaments.

The *Kāmasūtra* categorically mentions the *anulepana* materials like sandalwood, deer musk, saffron, aloewood along with milk and cream. Further, it supports the usage of the same basic Āyurveda theory (Shastri 1992: 108). Vāgbhaṭa's *Aṣṭāṅga Hṛdayam* 6.24.33 suggests the same for hair care (Garde 1983: 426).

Regarding the betel leaves, *Suśruta Saṁhitā* 1.45.492 clearly mentions its medicinal value to manage *kapha doṣa* (Shastri 1954: 221). *Bṛhat Saṁhitā* 77.35-37 has interestingly put forth linkages of betel leaves consumption with copulation. We see below in the *Bṛhat Saṁhitā*:

> The chewing of *tāmbūla* excites sexual passion, brightens personal appearance, promotes prosperity, causes the mouth to smell sweet, increases strength, removes phlegmatic affections and produces many other benefits. A due admixture of lime reddens the lips. If the nut exceeds its measure it will bring down the colour; if the lime exceeds its measure, the mouth will smell ill and if the leaves exceed their measure the mouth will be of good smell.
>
> If the leaves exceed their measure at night or the nut exceed its measure by day the effect will be good; if the case be otherwise, the *tāmbūla* will not be found sweet. If the *tāmbūla* contains as its ingredients *kakkola*, arecanut, *lavalīphala* and *pārijāta*, it will exhilarate the spirit and excite sexual passion.

Kāmaśāstra has very wisely used the medicinal and aesthetic value of betel leaves and describes its recipe precisely. We can conclude here that the Kāmaśāstra thought process is always based on the Āyurvedic medicinal prescription, which might be less compelling to adopt in its purest form as a health-saving habit, especially when there is no suffering from any disease; hence, Kāmaśāstra embellished those basic recommendations with romantic characteristics to ensure its much captivating adoptions within the society. Advising the regular consumption of the betel leaves for alleviation of cough is less compelling for a general (healthy) person, than prescribing the same based on its romantic characteristic of enhancing the personality appeal with the mouth fragrance and colourful lips.

Regarding wearing ornaments and flowers, the *Caraka Saṁhitā* 1.5.94-95 mentions the benefits of sexual arousal, mind calmness through fragrance and longevity. Kāmaśāstra has adopted the same prescriptions and we could get the reasoning in Āyurveda theory.

Regarding the hair cutting and maintenance, we find the *Caraka*

Saṁhitā[40] recommending proper and decorative teaming. This will lead to enhanced beauty and pleasure in life. We will be discussing these aspects in detail in the next section.

2.5.3.5 *Direct References in Āyurveda*

We find many places both in Āyurveda and Kāmaśāstra, they refer each other for the prescriptive approach. *Nāgarasarvasva* 4.1 clearly refers to Āyurveda for its superiority in collection of various fragrant materials (Jha 1929: 24). It suggests one should effortfully (sincerely) study Āyurveda and understand those recommendations spelled out about fragrance and ensure its assortment for usage. We have many such instances in Kāmaśāstra as discussed already.

Interestingly, we find Vāgbhaṭa's *Aṣṭāṅga Hṛdayam* 6.40.41 categorically mentioning Kāmaśāstra in Vājīkaraṇa chapter and recommends following its prescriptions (Garde 1983: 489). Moreover, the language of Āyurveda becomes very romantic while narrating these aspects and resembles with Kāmaśāstra texts. Same experience we get when Āyurveda describes the liquor consumption prescriptions (Garde 1983: 259; *VAYD* 4.7.87-92). There is absolute synergy in these two sciences, which is predominantly visible in their narration when Āyurveda cuts across the Kāmaśāstra topics and vice versa.

Although Āyurveda can be regarded as the earlier science than Kāmaśāstra, the synergy between these two does not restrict itself to the date of origination but the evolution, which further proves the matured approach of Āyurveda and the significant position of Kāmaśāstra from the medical science perspective. In a way, we can say that if Āyurveda is a graduation level text on basic medical science, then Kāmaśāstra is the specialized post-graduation level

---

40 पौष्टिकं वृष्यमायुष्यं शुचि रूप-विराजनम् ।
केश-श्मश्रु-नखादीनां कल्पनं संप्रसाधनम् ॥
pauṣṭikaṁ vṛṣyamāyuṣyaṁ śuci rūpa-virājanam ।
keśa-śmaśru-nakhādīnāṁ kalpanaṁ saṁprasādhanam ॥ – *CS* 1.5.97

Āyurveda text on therapeutic romance. We are discussing these facets in Chapter 4 in detail.

2.5.3.6 *Coherence in Medicines and Therapy*

We find a special reference of hair maintenance discussed in both the sciences. Interestingly, the objectives of the haircare are almost resembling in both approaches. Kāmaśāstra categorically recommends maintaining the black colour of hair for better appearance and mental health. In this regards, it is relevant to quote *Bṛhat Saṁhitā* 77.1 which is mentioned in the *Kāmasūtra*:

> To a person whose hair are white, flower wreaths, sandal paste, perfumed smoke, clothes and jewels can give no beauty. It is therefore necessary to blacken and embellish the hair.

It talks about the *dhūpana* process to be make hairs black. We find the *Kāmasūtra* has discussed and supported the *Bṛhat Saṁhitā* (77.2-3) recommendations in this regard:

> Put into an iron vessel vinegar or the like sour liquor; put in it a quantity of the *kodrava* grain after removing the husk and iron dust; heat the mixture; grind it well on a stone; rub it over the hair of the head freed from oil; tie over the hair the moist leaves of the green juicy leaves; remain so for six hours.
>
> Then remove the mixture from the hair and rub over them the paste of the fruit of the *āmalaka* (*Emblic myrobalan*); cover them with moist leaves as before and remain so for another six hours; bathe as prescribed below; the hair will become black.

We find Vāgbhaṭa's *Aṣṭāṅga Hṛdayam* 6.24.44-45 talking about the sandalwood as a key ingredient of the medicine for baldness (Garde 1983: 427). It has further importance in the head-related diseases as well. Kāmaśāstra has used the same prescription and talks about applying the sandalwood coats on head regularly (Shastri 1992: 106; *KS* 1.4.5).

It is becoming compelling for me with acceptance of an error of digression to quote Kālidāsa (Kale 2015) in this regard:

जालोद्गीर्णैरुपचितवपुः केशसंस्कारधूपै-
र्बन्धुप्रीत्या भवनशिखिभिर्दत्तनृत्योपहारः ।

jālodgīrṇairupacitavapuḥ keśasaṁskāradhūpair-
bandhuprītyā bhavanaśikhibhirdattanṛtyopahāraḥ ।
– *Meghadūtam*, *śl* 32

We observe here the apparent usage of the term *keśa dhūpana* proving it was in vogue during ancient times in India. In fact, black hairs were an essential natural ornament of women. Ensuring its regular and proper maintenance has been emphasized by both Āyurveda and Kāmaśāstra coherently.

Kāmaśāstra describes *praharaṇa* process as a part of copulation (Shastri 1992: 327; *KS* 2.7.2). It literally means forceful striking on different parts of the body to create pleasure. On prima facia, this act looks very risky and painful, especially when delicate parts of body are concerned. However, as discussed earlier, Kāmaśāstra is cognizant about the *marma* concept of Āyurveda and very methodically uses the *praharaṇa* process while copulation. Kāmaśāstra recommends below special places for striking with passion:

- The shoulders
- The head
- The space between the breasts
- The back
- The (*jaghana*) middle part of the body
- The sides

Striking is of four kinds (ibid.: 328; *KS* 2.7.3):

- Striking with the back of the hand
- Striking with the expanded hand
- Striking with the fist
- Striking with the open palm of the hand

We could clearly observe here the Kāmaśāstra compliance with the Āyurveda *marma* theory.

Kāmaśāstra thinking goes beyond protecting Āyurveda-defined vital body points and ensures the safety and lower risking of health of the partners, while balancing the pleasure creation, during copulations by playing multiple techniques.

Kāmaśāstra clearly mentions that those techniques of striking are not prescribed for all the people but highly apt based on the regional customs and traditions (ibid.: 333; *KS* 2.7.24). The regional element is much conclusive and decisive than mere prescription of striking for pleasure generation. Kāmaśāstra believes in the regional influence on natural sexual power, diet, behavioural patterns and mental and physical balance. This thought process is itself a qualifier of an Āyurveda *cikitsā*.

Moreover, Kāmaśāstra clearly prohibits the striking when there is the possibility of serious injuries or death. In such cases, one should not perform the striking even if it is followed as regional custom (Shastri 1992: 335; *KS* 2.7.27). To strengthen this argument, Kāmaśāstra provides numerous examples of such historical incidents of deaths and injuries with detailed description of such episodes (ibid.: 335-36; *KS* 2.7.28-30). We could easily accept this approach as the prescription based on the medical clinical trials.

Kāmaśāstra exhibits its *nidāna* ability and provides root causes of striking mentality with multiple examples – primarily indicating the loss of control due to passion (ibid.: 336-37; *KS* 2.7.31-33).

We can conclude here that Kāmaśāstra is much aware of the destructive power of striking techniques and always suggests balancing its practice against compelling regional tendency of its use.

The entire approach of Kāmaśāstra in this regard clearly resembles with Āyurveda's stand on the *Agada Tantra*. The *Caraka Saṁhitā* described that the poison in the minute form of a dose can be used as *rasāyana* as well as *viṣa* (Mehar 2017: 215). Anything, when used by proper *yukti* (justification) can be converted to *bheṣaja* (medicine). Thus, even the poison, when used intelligently, improves the immunity and health of the person as opposed to the expected consequences of damaging the well-being and leading to death. Kāmaśāstra has picked up this concept while prescribing the *praharaṇa* process.

Kāmaśāstra describes the *ratāvasānika* technique which is a detailed step by step post-copulation pacification process. Burton Richard et al. (2009: 20) translated the same in very romantic words:

> At the end of the congress, the lovers with modesty and not looking at each other, should go separately to the washing-room. After this, sitting in their own places, they should eat some betel leaves and the citizen should apply with his own hand to the body of the woman some pure sandalwood ointment, or ointment of some other kind. He should then embrace her with his left arm and with agreeable words should cause her to drink from a cup held in his own hand, or he may give her water to drink. They can then eat sweetmeats, or anything else, according to their likings and may drink fresh juice, soup, gruel, extracts of meat, sherbet, the juice of mango fruits, the extract of the juice of the citron tree mixed with sugar, or anything that may be liked in different countries and known to be sweet, soft and pure. The lovers may also sit on the terrace of the palace or house and enjoy the moonlight and carry on an agreeable conversation. At this time, too, while the woman lies in his lap, with her face towards the moon, the citizen should show her the different planets, the morning star, the polar star and the seven r̥ṣis, or Great Bear.

The Kāmaśāstra *ratāvasānika* technique provides ideas for male partner to peacefully conclude the copulation process in five steps (Shastri 1992: 374-75, *KS* 2.10.6-9). This concept is very much Āyurveda influenced. Below is the review of those five steps:

- *Aligning to Prasannātmā Concept*: Kāmaśāstra says partners should slowly leave the passion and become "non-demanding" to each other. Like an Āyurvedic *satvāvajaya cikitsā*, partners should be calm, making all attempts to conquer the remnant desires with achieved satisfaction and end the congress happily.

- *Hygiene*: Like an Āyurveda medical professional, Kāmaśāstra recommends taking proper care of genitals post-sexual acts. Urination is a highly prescribed act post-copulation. Kāmaśāstra categorically mentions to use the separate washrooms for maintaining hygiene. Kāmaśāstra suggests using separate beds and space for copulation and sleeping. We are discussing these aspects in the next chapter.
- *Soothing*: Kāmaśāstra recommends performing massage to woman post above steps. It recommends usage of sandalwood and other seasonal compliant materials for the same. Male partner should use his own hands gently for massaging the exhausted female partner. It is not only for the physical recovery from the sexual fatigue but also for mental healing.
- *Consumption*: Kāmaśāstra further recommends consuming Āyurveda compliant food and juices. We have already discussed the significant role of sweet and milk-oriented recipes in sperm recovery and alleviation from post-sexual power loss. This consumption should lead to the quick and adequate physical recovery so that the partners can sleep peacefully. Very interestingly, Kāmaśāstra suggests using "romantic solicitation" for food consumption. Male partner should be beseechingly having a dialogue with his partner and make her feel special while this event of food consumption.
- *Sky Watching and Sleeping*: Lastly, if possible, partners should enjoy the sky watching and star watching together with full of romantic, sweet and love talks. Kāmaśāstra suggests the woman should lie on her man's lap and man should caress her gently. This romance will ensure with balancing (*susthira*) of body and mind before proceeding to peaceful sleep.

Let us examine now the above recommendations on Āyurveda prescriptions. We could apparently view the core principles of *satvāvajaya cikitsā* reflected in the format suggested by Kāmaśāstra for concluding the copulation process.

Satvāvajaya cikitsā is a unique non-pharmacological approach for treating the mental disorders (Bagali et al. 2016: 56). It not only prevents the impairments of *dhī*, *dhṛti* and *smṛti* but also brings them back to the normal state, playing a significant role in the maintenance of harmonious state between these three factors ultimately leading to happy, healthy state of an individual. The word *satva* refers to mind and *avajaya* refers to conquering or win over. Hence, *satvāvajaya* means to have control over the mind and thus abstaining from things that are not good for the health. The incompatible contact of organs is regarded as one of the principal causes of disease (physical or mental). Hence one should avoid the excessive, deficient and/or erroneous (*hīna*, *mithyā*, *ati-yoga*) usage of organs. Such a behaviour serves to cure the psychiatric disorders leading to healthy state.

Āyurveda emphasizes on the need of compassion and positive attitude towards the patient in administrating *satvavajaya*. It is said that the patient should be calmed down after establishing friendly doctor–patient relationship. We see the striking resemblance in Kāmaśāstra recommendations here wherein Kāmaśāstra advises to make partner calm slowly.

Āyurveda describes the other psycho-supportive techniques like assurance, consoling the patient by proper guidance and suggestion, preaching religious and moral statement, quoting well-known references and mythological stories with good moral, giving verbal, mental and physical shocks, replacing the emotions, entertaining the patient with recreational therapy and psycho-shock therapy, i.e. by creating fear and terror. We could see that Kāmaśāstra has picked up select techniques like assurance through soft talks, quoting mythological stories through sky watching and recreational therapy of massage. We could mark here a significant therapeutic coherence in the physical and psychological healing suggested by Āyurveda and Kāmaśāstra.

While we could see the essence of post-copulation process is highly influenced by Āyurveda, we could also see that *Suśruta Saṁhitā* 4.24.132 has very concisely put the theme of the entire *ratāvasānika* technique in one line (Bhishagratna 2018). In fact, we can accept (Madhavacharya 2008: 539) the hypothesis that Kāmaśāstra authors must have composed this text while keeping all Āyurveda recommendations in mind.

> Fatigue after coition should be removed by the enjoyment of a bath, a cool breeze, or a sound sleep. Food or milk, saturated with sugar and meat-juice, prove very refreshing after the act.

Kāmaśāstra categorically mentions body washing and cleaning of genitals post-sexual acts. We also observe the Āyurveda compliant food consumption prescribed by Kāmaśāstra here. Prescriptive Āyurveda influence on Kāmaśāstra is apparently proved here.

2.5.3.7 *Behavioural Aspects and Hygiene*

We find substantial parity between the Kāmaśāstra and Āyurveda prescriptions regarding the overall behaviours and hygiene management. The *Suśruta Saṁhitā* has devoted one entire chapter (*cikitsā*, chapter 24) on the subject with detailed discussions on the rules of hygiene and general conduct. Same is the case with Vāgbhaṭa's *Aṣṭāṅga Hṛdayam*. We could mark the importance of this subject from Āyurvedic perspective.

We have already dealt with the few related topics of this subject under routine management. Hence, I have discussed here only the key aspects related directly to the copulation act.

Kāmaśāstra provides detailed account on the unfit (*agamyā*) women and its reasoning. It recommends below types of women not to be enjoyed:

- A leper.
- A lunatic.
- A woman turned out of caste.
- A woman who reveals secrets.

- A woman who publicly expresses desire for sexual intercourse.
- A woman who is extremely white.
- A woman who is extremely black.
- A bad-smelling woman.
- A woman who is a near relation
- A woman who is wife's friend.
- A woman who leads the life of an ascetic.
- And, lastly, the wife of a relation, of a friend, of a learned brāhmaṇa and of the king.

Obviously, the above recommendations have emanated primarily for the health safety and social norms adherence. The style in which Kāmaśāstra has described this projects its authority on the subject and ability to interpret Āyurveda in detail.

It is interesting to cross review what the *Suśruta Saṁhitā* 4.24.132 has recommended for the unfit women:

> A woman in her menses, not amorously disposed, unclean in her habits, not sufficiently endeared and endearing and belonging to a higher social order, older than one's self, affected with any disease, wanting in any limbs, inimically disposed to one's self, in her period of gestation, suffering from any uterine disorder, belonging to his own blood (*gotra*), or leading the life of an anchorite, or who is his preceptor's wife, should not be gone unto by a man (seeking health and longevity). A woman should not be gone unto in the *sandhyās* (morning and evening), as well as on the *parva* days (prescribed in the Śāstras), early in the morning, at midday, or in the dead of night. Going unto a woman at an infamous, unwholesome, or exposed place is similarly forbidden. Sexual intercourse by a man who is hungry, or thirsty, or who may be suffering from any disease, or may be angry, or in a cheerless spirit, is strictly forbidden. A man should not go unto a woman by repressing a natural urging for *vāta* (flatus), stool or urine, or if he is in a weak state of health (as it would be highly injurious to his health). Incest with lower animals, unnatural sexual intercourse, obstruction of semen in its passage, as well as sexual intercourse

> with a woman having any vaginal disease are strictly forbidden even in respect of a strong person. – Bhishagratna 2018

The *Suśruta Saṁhitā* provides the detailed reasoning as well for restrictions on unfit woman:

> Visiting a woman in her menses results in the loss of sight, longevity and vital power and should be accordingly considered as a sinful act. The duration of a man's life is diminished by going unto a woman, older in age or higher in social status (*varṇa*), or unto the wife of his preceptor or superior, in the morning or the evening, or on the *parva* days (the interdicted days), or unto a woman belonging to the same blood, as he. A visit to a pregnant woman is extremely painful and injurious to the foetus confined in the womb. A visit to a diseased woman results in the loss of the man's vital power. A going unto a deformed, uncleanly, spiteful, non-amorous, or sterile woman, or at an unclean, infamous, or exposed place is detrimental to the semen and intellect of the visitor.

Further, the *Suśruta Saṁhitā* provides a detailed account of copulation hygiene and protocol:

> Similarly, sexual intercourse enjoyed by a man at noon time, or by one who is in an enfeebled, thirsty, or hungry state of the body, in a standing up posture, or in a cheerless mood, brings on an excessive loss of semen and aggravation of the bodily *vāyu*. Phthisis due to the loss of semen is the result of over-intemperance in sexual matters. Pain, enlargement of the spleen, epilepsy and even death may follow from sexual gratifications in a diseased state of health. The *vāyu* and the *pitta* become aggravated by the sexual intercourse enjoyed early in the morning or at midnight. An incest with lower animals, unnatural sexual intercourse, or that with a woman having a diseased vagina is attended with an excessive loss of semen and an aggravation of the bodily *vāyu* and is the cause of *upadaṁśa* (syphilitic virus). An act of coition enjoyed by holding the woman on one's bosom or by repressing the natural urgings towards urination or defecation, as well as a

> repressing of seminal discharge would help the early formation of seminal concretions in the bladder.
>
> It is highly injurious for a man to indulge excessively in sexual intercourse, or to enjoy it while standing, or while lying on his back, or to shake his head at the time; these should not be indulged in by an intelligent and judicious person even occasionally for pleasure's sake.

Vāgbhaṭa's *Aṣṭāṅga Hṛdayam* 6.33.2 uses the *agamyā* term as unfit women which is adopted by Kāmaśāstra (Garde 1983: 451). It provides the summarized view of the *Suśruta Saṁhitā* mentioned above on unfit woman.

Kāmaśāstra has adopted all these principles while theorizing the copulation recommendations. It does not stop there but puts a finer detail into it. For example, it says: a woman during her monthly courses, a woman who has been lately confined, who has recently delivered, one who is with a small vagina and a fat woman should not be made to the act the part of a man (Shastri 1992: 349, *KS* 2.8.41). Other instance could be bathing and washing genital post-sexual acts. We have already referred this point in the previous section.

Fascinatingly, we find absolute concurrence on the prescriptions on the nail maintenance by these two sciences. Āyurveda categorically restricts to grow nails beyond threshold to reduce chances of *guhya roga* (secret organ diseases) (Garde 1983: 451; VAYD 6.33.3).

Suśruta Saṁhitā 4.24 puts up a lucidly prescriptive approach:

> The first rule is that one should keep his nails and hair short.
>
> The shaving of hair and the paring of nails lead to the expiration of one's sins, make a man cheerful, tend to appease his fate, increase his energy and impart a lightness to the frame.
>
> – Bhishagratna 2018: 66

Acts using nails (*nakhavilekhanam*) is the key topic of interest for Kāmaśāstra. Like teeth description, we find Kāmaśāstra providing detailed qualitative recommendations on nails (Shastri 1992: 273; *KS* 2.4.8). The qualities of good nails are that they should be bright, well set, clean, entire, convex, soft and glossy in appearance. The special characteristic of softness is very crucial here from the Āyurveda standpoint.

While Kāmaśāstra does not provide absolute restriction on growing nails, it provides much appealing approach of hygiene-oriented maintenance and its romantic usage. It might be logical there to recommend beautiful designing on the body parts with longer scratches or markings using nails to enhance its usage as the arousing tool of building romance during copulation or as a memory mark. However, Kāmaśāstra does recognize the possible mishaps with long nails, especially during uncontrolled passionate practice of nail marking, pressing and scratching. Hence, we find Kāmaśāstra prescribes (ibid.: 275) to restrict the nail mark length in all cases. Nevertheless, it ensures that this prescription does not hinder or compromise the effectivity of the pleasure generation technique. Rather, it protects the partners from possible illness from long nails and its marks by advising proper maintenance of nails, ensuring its softness and mere restricting the marking length. Thus, there is complying of the Āyurveda-prescribed hygienic practice in a Kāmaśāstra style of romance.

Moreover, Kāmaśāstra recognizes the factor of regional taste and physiology and provides[41] the provincial preferences of Bengal, south India and Maharashtra-based citizens regarding nail properties and arts (Shastri 1992: 273-74; *KS* 2.4.9-11).

In this regard, we can review the *Suśruta Saṁhitā* (4.2) prescription as a summarized view of Āyurveda on overall copulation process:

> The injurious and harmful practices should be shunned by a man for his welfare in this life as well as for that in the next. On the contrary, repression of a natural and (legitimate) sexual desire,

---

41 सर्वस्थानेषु नातिदीर्घा लेखा (*sarvasthāneṣu nātidīrghā lekhā*) । – *KS* 2.4.17

> from a sense of unwise delicacy or shame, is a physical sin. Hence a healthy and passionate man possessed of the necessary fecundating element, under the course of a proper *vājīkaraṇa* (aphrodisiac) remedy, should cheerfully go unto and duly enjoy the pleasures of company with a girl, beautiful in looks, tender in years, modest, virtuous, equally passionate, cheerful, kindred to him both in physical and mental temperaments and well-decked with ornaments. – Bhishagratna 2018: 89

Thus, we can conclude that Kāmaśāstra has picked up the core theme of Āyurveda prescription and expanded its application in its own finer techniques of copulation. While doing so, it has taken the uncompromised clinical care of hygiene maintenance and still provided various avenues of pleasure generation to its follower and practitioner.

Moreover, Kāmaśāstra not only fine-tuned the Āyurveda prescriptions but added more irrefutable medical criteria to make the theory further scientific and its applications much practical. Hence, we see Kāmaśāstra lays its foundation based on Āyurveda's prescriptive influence of physiology and psychology, and then goes beyond it to connect those recommendations tightly with region–time continuum with socio-scientific and economic dimensions (Shastri 1992: 350; *KS* 2.8.41).

From all the above discussions through various topics, we have enough evidences of the overall Āyurveda impact on Kāmaśāstra to decisively accept the hypothesis that Kāmaśāstra theory of prescription is significantly influenced by Āyurveda theme.

2.5.4 SYMBOLIC INFLUENCE ON KĀMAŚĀSTRA PRACTICE

Under this section, I have reviewed different practices of Kāmaśāstra which are very specific in nature to the Kāmaśāstra subject; however, we could see the symbolic linking with Āyurveda concepts. These discussions span across varied topics like the *saṁkhyā* theory of Āyurveda and its symbolic connection with the Kāmaśāstra theory, grammatical symbolization between two sciences, psychology of

Āyurveda and symbolic domains of Kāmaśāstra, figurative disease management in Kāmaśāstra, Āyurveda messenger and her/his role and symbolic models in Kāmaśāstra.

2.5.4.1 *Symbolization through Baseline Philosophy*

Philosophical thinking strongly emphasizes clear formulation of ideas and problems, selection of relevant data and objective methods for assessing ideas and proposals. It also emphasizes development of a sense of the new directions suggested by new hypotheses and questions one encounters while doing research. Philosophers regularly build on both successes and failures of their predecessors. Such persons can readily learn any principle of any field.

In medical profession, philosophical thinking is essential to enhance professional ability to solve known and unknown problems, communication skills, persuasive powers and writing skills especially for composing texts and codifying knowledge for the future generations.

India has its six major philosophical systems viz. Nyāya, Vaiśeṣika, Sāṁkhya, Yoga, Mīmāṁsā and Vedānta. Each system typically deals with the topics like:

- Theory of causation.
- Views on evolution.
- Epistemology – sources of knowledge.
- Illustration, examples and explanations on rules of inductive and deductive logic.
- Views on Supreme Power and God.
- Theory of deeds, reincarnation, realization and liberation.

Here is the brief presentation of the core principles of each system.

Nyāya: This school is based on a system of logic that has been adopted by most of the Indian schools in parts or whole. Nyāya postulates that true knowledge is acquired through the sources of comparison, perception, testimony and inference. These are the only ways to achieve *nirvāṇa* (liberation).

Vaiśeṣika: Sage Kaṇāda founded this school. It is an atomist and pluralist in nature, i.e. it established the theory of atomic structure. The foundation of this school is the thought that in the physical universe all objects are reducible to a finite number of atoms. The fundamental force is *Brahman* which causes consciousness in all these atoms. This school's valid sources of knowledge are perception and inference.

Sāṁkhya: This philosophical school postulates that everything originates from *puruṣa* and *prakṛti*. *Puruṣa* is "self or soul or mind" and *prakṛti* is "matter, creative agency and energy". This philosophy is dualist in nature, which is between the self and matter. According to this school, the goal of life is liberation, i.e. soul's realization.

Yoga: The Yoga school is founded by Patañjali. It follows the Sāṁkhya psychology and metaphysics is more on theological side. This helps achieve the goal of calm mind and detachment.

Mīmāṁsā: The major objective of this school is to propagate the Vedas and establish their authority. The followers of this school require absolute faith in the Vedas and must do the regular ritual of the Vedic *havana*. Although this school agrees to the logical and philosophical prescriptions of the other schools, it emphasizes that liberation can only be attained through the teachings of the Vedas.

Vedānta: The focus of the philosophical teachings of this school is Upaniṣads, i.e. spiritual inspections within the Vedas. *Vedāntins* concentrate on the practical techniques of meditation, self-discipline and spiritual connectivity, more than any other traditional ritual. Advaita is the most popular branch of this school, which holds that the soul and *Brahman* are one and the same. They follow the ontology of illusion. Viśiṣṭādvaita, the other branch, teaches that the Supreme Being has a finite form and there is a combination of monism and dualism.

There are six means of acquiring knowledge in Indian philosophy, viz. *pratyakṣa, anumāna, upamāna, arthāpatti, anupalabdhi* and *śabda.*

Pratyakṣa (Perception): Two types of perceptions mentioned in Indian philosophical texts are external and internal. The perception which is empirical in nature is external; it gives us the knowledge coming from the interaction of five senses with the objects of the world. And the internal perception is described as that comes from the inner sense, means the mind.

Anumāna (Inference): When we find out new conclusions and truth using prior facts along with one or more observations plus by applying reason, it is called an inference, e.g. when we detect smoke and infer that there is some fire.

Upamāna (Comparison and Analogy): It is the knowledge which arises from the presence of some common factors in a thing, which was experienced previously in another thing.

Arthāpatti (Postulation, Derivation from Circumstances): In contemporary logic, this is like circumstantial implication. It is used to acquire conditional knowledge and acquire truths about an object and a subject in original or different grounds. One must rely on direct perception or proper inference instead to gather valid knowledge.

Anupalabdhi (Non-existence): Knowledge by which we immediately cognize the non-existence of an object is called *anupalabdhi.* For example, absence of rainfall indicates that the connection of cloud and wind has not happened.

Śabda (Authority of Word): This is statement of past or present trustworthy humans such as saints or sages. Knowledge depends on reliable authority and depends on a sentence or different sounds arising from musical instruments, bamboos, etc.

We find a close connection of Sāṁkhya, Yoga and Mīmāṁsā philosophy with the Āyurveda theory. We also see ample application of all six types of means of knowledge acquisition in Āyurveda texts. However, most of the modern Āyurveda professionals believe[42] that Āyurveda has its own philosophy.

Jaiswal and Williams (2017) unconditionally conclude that Āyurveda has its foundations laid by the Nyāya and Vaiśeṣika schools. It is also related to the manifestation framework, well known as Sāṁkhya. The Vaiśeṣika school preached about inferences and perceptions that should be obtained about a patient's pathological condition for treatment. Whereas, the Nyāya school propagated its teachings on the basis that one should have an extensive knowledge of the patient's condition and the disease condition before proceeding for treatment. Interestingly, both these schools of philosophy were merged in later years and brought glory to Āyurveda and helped in disseminating the knowledge about Āyurveda.

The school of Vaiśeṣika classifies the attributes of any object into six types: substance, particularity, activity, generality, inherence and quality called as *dravya*, *viśeṣa*, *karma*, *sāmānya*, *samavāya* and *guṇa* respectively. We find similar concepts in Āyurveda too.

In contrast to the above view, we find Āyurveda texts saying that its origin is divine and is from Brahmā who is called as the creator of the universe. It is believed that the creator of the universe passed on this holistic knowledge of healing onto the sages for the well-being of mankind. From the sages the knowledge of traditional medicines was passed on to the disciples and then to the common man by various writings and oral narrations. Again, we find the *R̥gveda* describing sixty-seven plants. The *Atharvaveda* and *Yajurveda* describe 293 and eighty-one medicinally useful plants respectively. The writings in the *R̥gveda* and *Atharvaveda* are attributed to "Ātreya" who is believed to have been conferred with this knowledge from Lord Indra, who initially received it from Lord

42 YouTube video by Dr Shreeprasad Bavadekar, Lecture on Philosophy, https://youtu.be/4HAaPsQO7kU

Brahmā. Agniveśa compiled the knowledge from the Vedas and it was edited by Caraka in the *Caraka Saṁhitā* and further texts of Āyurveda were flourished. Thus, one can conclude that the practice of Āyurveda is based upon the knowledge gained from these Vedas, which in turn indirectly linking to the Vedānta philosophy.

From the above discussions, one can conclude that the Āyurveda theory has its own strong ideological framework attached with all Indian schools of philosophy and we can draw parallel from each philosophical system in Āyurveda. Moreover, Āyurveda, being a divine creation, or even otherwise, from its technical, empirical, logical, methodical and systematic approach of dealing subject matter and narration, along with authoritative prescriptions and supported by its unique style of text composition, it can be concluded that Āyurveda has its own applied philosophy for medical sciences.

We see a symbolic social influence of Āyurveda baseline philosophy on Kāmaśāstra. The symbolic influence (Moscovici and Néve 1973: 462) affects the opinion or judgements of an individual to the extent that the opinions or judgements emitted by the source of influence are in this case considered as an indication of the source itself, i.e. of the source's intentions. We can interpret the symbolic social influence as psychological presence of Āyurveda's thought process especially on the socially connected matters, in the minds of Kāmaśāstra authors forming their mental representation. Thus, the Āyurveda philosophy influenced the behaviour and thoughts of Kāmaśāstra authors, which is reflected in the Kāmaśāstra texts, especially on the dimensions of the structural, conceptual and prescriptive narration.

Kāmaśāstra, like Āyurveda, claims its origination as divine and from the same preceptor, Brahmā. We have already discussed the structural, conceptual and prescriptive influence of Āyurveda on Kāmaśāstra texts and thought process. We clearly observe the empirical and logical deductions in the Kāmaśāstra theory. It shows high authority while describing various prescriptions and refers Āyurveda wherever applicable Kāmaśāstra uses the Yoga philosophy particularly in the *āsana* description and in general while describing the copulation process. We can conclude that symbolically Kāmaśāstra has its own applied philosophy influenced by Āyurveda.

2.5.4.2 *Symbolization through Grammatical Aspects*

Under structurally influential discussions, we have seen how Āyurveda has influenced Kāmaśāstra texts with reference to chapter sequencing, diction, style of expression and composition structure. We will review further the grammatical similarity between these two sciences.

The ancient Indian scholars maintained the learning and streamlined the flow of knowledge by rhythmic recitation for thousands of years even before the era of documentation.

A scholar of Āyurveda had adopted[43] three steps of learning, i.e. learning (*adhyayana*), teaching (*adhyāpana*) and discussions (*tadvidyāsambhāṣā*). The most preliminary stage of study was grasping and mastering of the text thoroughly. The texts were written mostly in a very concise style known as *sūtra*s and in combined form of both prose and verse. This prose is bound by some rules and the verses were mostly in simple form.

We see (Yerawar et al. 2019) that Vāgbhaṭa's *Aṣṭāṅga Hṛdayam* has used Anuṣṭup *chanda* in about 95.11 per cent of its *sūtras*. In fact, all the verses of Nidānasthāna and Kalpasthāna are in Anuṣṭup *chanda*. Maximum number of *chanda*s are used in Cikitsāsthāna, numbering thirty-two. Cikitsāsthāna and Sūtrasthāna are the chapters that used most varied types of *chanda*.

43 Vaidya Asit K. Panja, "A Critical Review of Meters in Aṣṭāṅga Hṛdaya", article published on Internet – http://www.ayurvedah.in/Articles/Chhanda_Articles/03_analysis_of_meter_in_astanga_hridaya.pdf

Unfortunately, I could not identify similar literature dealing with metrical analysis of Kāmaśāstra texts. I experienced that it is a mammoth work with significant expertise. Hence an approach of high-level symbolic comparison of both the sciences from their simplicity, conciseness, ability to balance poetic embellishment with required lucidity for technical subject matter (especially refraining from using words with multiple possible meanings) has been adopted.

We see both these sciences using very simple language and comprehensible terms. Memorization of *sūtras* is the prime objective. Interestingly, we find Āyurveda suddenly becomes more poetic textually when the topic is Kāmaśāstra oriented; and when a Kāmaśāstra text describes the therapeutic aspects, it becomes serious and secular leaving its primacy of romanticism and thus resembling the scientific text of medical science. This natural urge of changing text rhythm, exhibited by both sciences in their composition style, is symbolic of the interdependence between them. A few examples are cited below.

Āyurveda texts literally attain the altitude of Classical Sanskrit romance when compose *sūtra* on *vājīkaraṇa* or liquor consumption guidelines.

नामापि यस्या हृदयोत्सवाय
 यां पश्यतां तृप्तिरनाप्तपूर्वा ।
सर्वेन्द्रियाकर्षणपाषभूता
 कान्तानुवृत्तिव्रतदीक्षिताया ॥

nāmāpi yasyā hṛdayotsavāya
 yāṁ paśyatāṁ tṛptiranāptapūrvā ।
sarvendriyākarṣaṇapāṣabhūtā
 kantānuvṛttivratadīkṣitāyā ॥

कलाविलासङ्गयोवयोविभूषा
 शुचिः सलज्जा रहसि प्रगल्भा ।
प्रियंवदा तुल्यमनःशया या
सा स्त्री वृषत्वाय परं नरस्य ॥

kalāvilāsaṅgyovayovibhūṣā
śuciḥ salajjā rahasi pragalbhā ।
priyaṁvadā tulyamanaḥ śayā yā
sā strī vr̥ṣatvāya paraṁ narasya ॥
– VAYD 6.40.39-40

We see here the romantic poetry full of sentiments, emotions and imagination opposed the objectivity, which is maintained through verses otherwise. It is very difficult to believe that the above verses are drawn from a textbook of medical science.

Now we will review the Kāmaśāstra text. We find Kāmaśāstra assumes the Āyurveda tone to recommend authoritatively the therapeutic processes without any poetic embellishment.

देशसात्म्याच्च योषित उपचरेत ।
deśasātmyācca yoṣita upacaret ।

Kāmaśāstra suggests deploying the romantic moves as "treatment" based on regional specificity.

मेषवस्तमुष्कसिद्धस्य पयसः सशर्करस्य पानं वृषत्वयोगः ।
meṣavastamuṣkasiddhasya payasaḥ saśarkarasya pānaṁ vr̥ṣatvayogaḥ । – *KS* 2.5.20

Kāmaśāstra suggests here aphrodisiac medicine preparation process and its usage.

न प्रयुञ्जित संदिग्धान्न शरीरात्ययावहान् ।
न जीवघातसंबद्धान्नाशुचिद्रव्यसंयुतान् ॥

na prayuñjita sandigdhānna śarīrātyayāvahān ।
na jīvaghātasaṁbaddhānnāśucidravyasaṁyutān ॥ – *KS* 7.1.50

Kāmaśāstra prohibits here the usage of unhygienic, dangerous, lethal material medica and pharmacology to safeguard health.

We could locate many such examples in Āyurveda and Kāmaśāstra literatures. Interestingly, this transition in the tone happens significantly in the last section of both the sciences. As indicated earlier, this is obvious because in the last section, both these sciences are dealing with the topics which are primarily of other's domain. Moreover, a clear mention of each other is observed in the last section of these sciences. Kāmaśāstra mentions Āyurveda and vice versa. This strengthens the claim of significant symbolic relationships between these sciences.

2.5.4.3 *Symbolization through Figurative Disease Management*

Kāmaśāstra talks about the arousing and stimulating desires which were lost earlier due to physical or mental reasons. Such a mental condition would certainly cause psychological imbalance and implications on the overall health; hence this subject matter certainly needs medical treatment. However, we do not find this topic in Āyurveda texts. It is very interesting to interpret symbolically why this gap is observed in Āyurveda texts.

The author has proved the hypothesis here that Āyurveda texts have described the matter of sexual health and its maintenance (we see this predominantly under *vājīkaraṇa* section), however left the topic like recovery from psychosexual diseases through mind and instrument management for Kāmaśāstra to deal with. Moreover, Āyurveda, in its limited purview, dealt the sexual health topic in the generic medical way and passed the responsibility to Kāmaśāstra for detailing its practical and social implications. Hence, we find Kāmaśāstra has structured its theory around the sexual health maintenance as well as disease management in coherence with the Āyurveda theme of "स्वस्थस्य स्वास्थ्य रक्षणं, आतुरस्य विकार प्रशमनं (*svasthasya svāsthya rakṣaṇaṁ, āturasya vikāra praśamanaṁ*)".

Symbolically, the focus of Kāmaśāstra is well defined around filling the gaps that Āyurveda left in its own scope. Āyurveda might have chosen deliberately to avoid this subject discussion due to its remote relevance to main theme, or perceived digression, or to keep ethos of pure medical aspects leaving psychosocial elements. Nevertheless, Āyurveda did recognize the significance of the subject and placed a brief but separate chapter on it. From these facts, I put forth the argument that Āyurveda had played its role completely and left specialization-oriented discussions for Kāmaśāstra, which forms the core topic for Kāmaśāstra to deal with. Further, Kāmaśāstra while synthesizing and counselling on this topic, ensured the compliance with core Āyurveda principles and theorized the framework to address all opportunities (which were left by Āyurveda) that needed attention from therapeutic perspective.

In the second chapter seventh Adhikarana titled, "revamping lost desires", the *Kāmasūtra* has detailed the topic with clinical approach providing causes, symptoms, therapies, medicines and even surgery mechanisms. Vātsyāyana assumes here the role of an Āyurveda *vaidya* and surgeon, and recommends different *cikitsās* in a step by step manner. It provides therapeutic approach ranging from easy and natural cure to customized and fabricated treatment.

The central theme of this chapter is to guide the male partner by proving techniques of counselling to arouse the desires of a sexually disappointed woman and make her satisfied using instruments. Vaidya Vātsyāyana begins with explaining simple physiological methods of exciting women by inserting and fingering into her secret organ, followed by using artificial penis-like instruments made from different materials, keeping hygiene and utility in mind. Further, he provides a detailed account on specific techniques of mesmerism and intoxicants.

It is very apparent that Āyurveda Vaidyas would always prefer initially to treat the patient with simple and natural healing-oriented therapy and would deploy complex surgeries at later point in time, if imperative. We observe the Vaidya Vātsyāyana following the same philosophy while prescribing the overall therapeutic flow. It starts from standard physiological prescriptions and progresses towards surgical and specialty-oriented treatments. The diagnostic elements that are considered during the initial investigations are clinical based, for example, anatomy and physiological aspects. Later, it scopes psychological and homeostasis elements which are primarily pathognomonic.

We see a strong correlation here with Āyurveda pharmacology and therapeutic approach, and even with the surgical principles. Interestingly, we find Kāmaśāstra coherence with Āyurveda's Dysphoria Treatment using surgical ways, recommended pre-operative and post-operative care, hygiene of surgical instruments and their applications, usage of different medications in penis surgery and care for lowering the risk of infections.

We observe here the undoubtful command of the Kāmaśāstra author over the medical language and domain. Below is the description of penis surgery observed in the *Kāmasūtra* (Richard et al. 2009: 129):

> Now, when a young man perforates his penis, he should pierce it with a sharp instrument and then stand in water so long as the blood continues to flow. At night he should engage in sexual intercourse, even with vigour, to clean the hole. After this he should continue to wash the hole with decoctions and increase the size by putting into it small pieces of cane and the wrightia antidysenterica and thus gradually enlarging the orifice. It may also be washed with liquorice mixed with honey and the size of the hole increased by the fruit stalks of the *simā-patrā* plant. The hole should be anointed with a small quantity of oil.
>
> In the hole made in the penis a man may put *apadravyas* of various forms, such as the "round", the "round on one side", the "wooden mortar", the "flower", the "armlet", the "bone of the heron", the "goad of the elephant", the "collection of eight balls", the "lock of hair", the "place where four roads meet", and other things named according to their forms and means of using them. All these *apadravyas* should be rough on the outside according to their requirements.
>
> The ways of enlarging the penis must be now related.
>
> When a man wishes to enlarge his penis, he should rub it with the bristles of certain insects that live in trees and then, after rubbing it for ten nights with oils, he should again rub it with the bristles as before. By continuing to do this a swelling will

> be gradually produced in the penis and he should then lie on a cot and cause his penis to hang down through a hole in the cot. After this he should take away all the pain from the swelling by using cool concoctions. The swelling, which is called *śuka,* and is often brought about among the people of the Draviḍa country, lasts for life. If the penis is rubbed with the following things, viz. the plant *Physalis flexuosa*, the *śavara-kandaka* plant, the *jalasuka* plant, the fruit of the egg plant, the butter of a she buffalo, the *hasti-carma* plant and the juice of the *vajra-rasa* plant, a swelling lasting for one month will be produced.
>
> By rubbing it with oil boiled in the concoctions of the above things, the same effect will be produced, but lasting for six months.
>
> The enlargement of the penis is also effected by rubbing it or moistening it with oil boiled on a moderate fire along with the seeds of the pomegranate and the cucumber, the juices of the *valuka* plant, the *hasti-carma* plant and the egg plant.

We find Āyurvedic surgical processes like *vyadhana*, *chedana*, *bandhana*, *śodhana* are recommended by the *Kāmasūtra* (Madhavacharya 2008: 1129-31; *KS* 7.2.15-19).

In this context, it is very interesting to understand Āyurveda's view on overall surgery aspects. The *Suśruta Saṁhitā* describes over 300 various surgical procedures, viz. cosmetic, ophthalmic, dental, orthopaedic and abdominal operations. It describes eight types of surgical procedures which are explained below (Joshi et al. 2016):

Chedana (*surgical excision*): It is a procedure to excise a diseased or damaged part by using scalpel, circular surgical knife, bone saw.

Bhedana (*incision and exploration*): It is a procedure to be made to expose underlying structures and to let out the content by using scalpel and single-edged knife.

Lekhana (*scraping*): Scraping or scooping is carried out to remove undesired tissues like hyper granulations, epithelized tissue and sequestrum.

Vedhana (puncturing): It is a procedure to pierce the epithelial surface, superficial veins, etc.

Eṣaṇa (probing): The *eṣaṇa* process should be practised using holes in pieces of wood eaten by moths, bamboos and mouth of a dried gourd.

Āharaṇa (extraction): It is an act of removal of a foreign body by pulling out.

Viśravaṇa (drainage/removal of vitiated doṣa): This method is used to remove the abnormal collection of fluids in body cavities and to let out the vitiated blood.

Sīvana (suturing) and application of kṣāra (alkaline substance), agni (cautery) bandhana (bandaging): This technique is defined for approximation of cut margins of wound, which are produced by surgical or non-surgical process. A suitable *bandhana* helps for early healing of crushed, lacerated wound and to stabilize the fracture, dislocation, etc. so that a wounded person can sleep well, able to walk and sit comfortably. These include para-surgical tools and miscellaneous processes like enema therapy, wound cleaning and irrigation.

Based on the above discussions, we could accept the hypothesis that Kāmaśāstra is highly influenced symbolically by the surgery processes that the *Suśruta Saṁhitā* has described.

Further, Āyurveda has provided highly detailed recommendations on pre-operative and post-operative surgery care. The *suśruta Saṁhitā* has classified (Neelam et al. 2018) the entire surgery procedures as *pūrva-karma* (pre-operative), *pradhāna karma* (operative) and *paścāt karma* (post-operative). Pre-operative procedures include *laṅghana* to *virecana karma*, operative or main procedures contain eight surgical procedures, *sandhāna*, *pīḍana*, *śonita-sthāpana*, etc. and post-operative includes *āhāra*, *vihāra*, care of the wound and *rakṣā vidhāna*. The post-operative wound or the ulcer gets eroded by aggravation of *doṣa*, exercise, injury, indigestion and too much of emotions, i.e. joy or anger. For the avoidance of post-operative complications these factors should be avoided by the patient. It is controlled by proper conduct of *paścāt karma*. The need of post-operative measures is for restoration of patient's physical as well as mental strength, complexion and digestive power, maintaining the equilibrium of *doṣa* and management of post-operative complications.

We could see the strong symbolic influence of the *Suśruta Saṁhitā* on the *Kāmasūtra* especially with the aspects of wound care and deployment of *satvāvajaya cikitsā*.

The *Suśruta Saṁhitā* prescribed the following actions for managing wound care:

1. The bandage should be removed on the third day, tied again with bandage of clothes. The dressing should not be removed in haste on the second day itself. The wound should not be made to heal in a hurry when the vitiated *doṣas* are still inside.
2. In Hemanta (dewy), Śiśira (winter) and Vasanta (spring) seasons, bandaging of the wound should be removed after three days, while in Śarada (autumn), Grīṣma (summer) and Varṣā (rainy) seasons after two days.

The *Suśruta Saṁhitā* prescribes aspects of *satvāvajaya cikitsā*:

1. In house the wounded person resides should be served by affectionate friends and relatives who talk pleasingly.
2. He should avoid, even at distance, seeing, talking and touching the woman. By these activities, the semen gets dislodged and flows out.
3. The patient should be clean and wear white dress and always remain devoid of undesirable nails and hairs.
4. The patient should reside in a house decorated with lights, water, weapons, garland, flowers, etc. and spend his time, listening to stories which are benevolent, auspicious and pleasing to the mind.

We could see the significant parity between the *Suśruta Saṁhitā* recommendations and the post-operative care suggested by Kāmaśāstra after penis surgery. Moreover, it is very interesting to note that Kāmaśāstra has adopted all the best practices prescribed across Āyurveda literature ranging from physical aspects, medication, various therapies to surgical aspects.

Figure 2.2 depicts the entire flow of Kāmaśāstra prescription. We could clearly observe here that the therapeutic approach of Āyurveda is symbolically deployed in the Kāmaśāstra theory.

2.5.4.4 *Psychology of Āyurveda and Symbolic Domains of Kāmaśāstra*

The framework of Āyurveda is wide enough to include all that is very essential to make the humans healthy and happy (Chandramouleeswaran and Govadhan 2012). It includes the study of the desire which is very essential for producing the healthy progeny which in turn produces a healthy society. Further, it deals with the philosophical aspect of life, the knowledge of which greatly contributes to the comfort and happiness of all humans. Āyurveda believes that the sexual activity is not only about the physical intercourse but the sum of man's existential presence in the world. Based on his sense of sexual identity with which he identifies his sex roles and modulates his interaction with the society around him. A person recognizes his sex role through three means – his family ties, his social standing and codes of behaviour, his sexual values and priorities. It can be generally said that the climax aims at the bodily activity brought about by coordinated functioning of the autonomous nervous system, hormones and muscle groups is procreation. Further, Āyurveda deploys the super specialty practice which deals with diagnosis and management of defective spermatogenesis in accordance with *vājīkaraṇa*. The role of psychology in entire sex activity is crucial as per above description.

Āyurveda's *tridoṣa* theory believes that each constituent gives certain characteristic qualities to the person. It recognizes seven types or categories into which people can be classified,

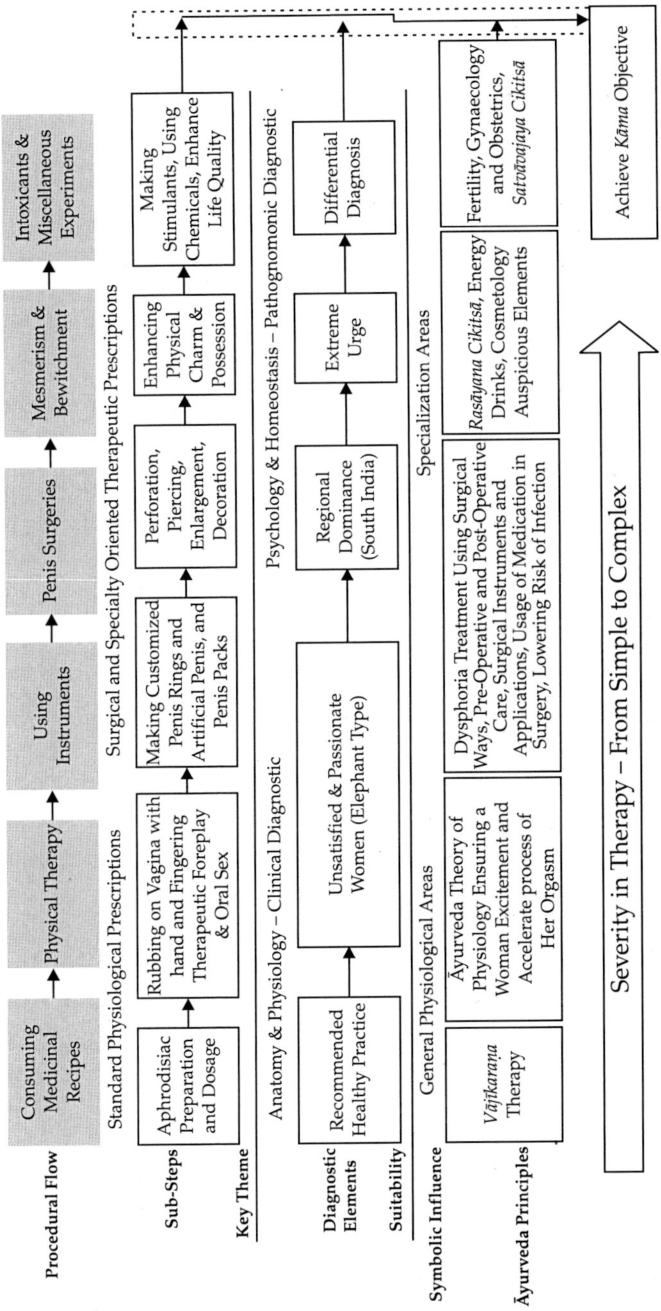

fig. 2.2: Arousing Lost Desires: Vaidya Vātsyāyana's Prescriptive Flow

depending on the dominance of the *doṣa* in their body. Moreover, Āyurveda propounds (Shilpa et al. 2011) the most applied aspect of philosophical concept of *triguṇa* in the field of science and medicine. One of the invaluable deduction Āyurveda provides that the behaviour exhibited by individuals depend on the dominance of one or the other *doṣa* or *guṇa* that is constitutionally present in the person from conception, which is referred to as the particular *prakṛti-guṇa* combination that a person exhibits. This combination is unique to every individual and is not changeable during their lifetime. The classification gives a good indication of physiologic strengths and weaknesses, mental tendencies and susceptibility to illnesses of different kinds.

Kāmaśāstra is completely aligned with this theory of Āyurveda and provided the classification logic of male and female with twenty-seven permutations. We have already discussed the same in conceptual influence section. Further, we see Kāmaśāstra describes the best fit techniques of pre/post and during copulation like nailing acts and teething acts, usage of different instruments, medicines, food consumption and even hugging and kissing. Kāmaśāstra always aims to suit the individual and pair harmony while suggesting these acts. Symbolically, we can conclude here that Kāmaśāstra has considered the significance of the *prakṛti-guṇa* combination on individual and partner behaviour and prescribed the copulation techniques to ensure the prime objective of Āyurveda is met in all possibilities. Thus, Kāmaśāstra practices have pre-packaged benefits of Āyurveda therapy which provides enhancement of sexual vigour, desire, libido, penile erectile capacity, sexual substance power, modulation of ejaculation, repeated sexual performance.

2.5.4.5 *Role of Messenger in Āyurveda and Symbolic Models in Kāmaśāstra*

Role of messenger is very crucial in Āyurveda and we have already discussed the same in previous section of precision aspects.

Symbolically, Āyurveda model of messenger is very much in line with the Kāmaśāstra model of messenger positioning.

Figure 2.3 explains the same.

In Āyurveda, patient calls the messenger and asks to reach out to the *vaidya* to bring him for treatment. Messenger goes for the task and ensures the visit of *vaidya* at patient's place and apt treatment with medicines and patient recovers.

In Kāmaśāstra, *nāyaka* (symbolically a patient), deploys messenger to reach out to *nāyikā*, to bring her for the therapeutic romance. She (*nāyikā*) pays visit to patient's place and treats him with *rati-rāga* medicine and *nāyaka* recovers.

It is very interesting to observe the symbolic model of messenger used with Āyurveda ethos in Kāmaśāstra theory, when Kāmaśāstra describes the adultery. *Figure* 2.3 shows the flow.

Kāmaśāstra suggests deploying messenger as an expert envoy for the specialized job of adultery. Messenger plays a vital role and applies primarily reverse and forward *satvāvajaya cikitsā* to create required emotions in the mind of *nāyikā.*

To start with, messenger intelligently observes the mindset of *nāyikā* (a married woman here) and decides if she is in highly balanced state. Such *nāyikā* is regarding as *satī* and should not be persuaded any more. The women who is in the tentative mindset and has already shown signs of interest should be persuaded (Shastri 1992: 552; *KS* 5.4.1). Messenger then creates the adverse feelings and distance from her husband by certain set well defined narrative (ibid.: 553; *KS* 5.4.4). In fact, messenger deploys reverse and forward *satvāvajaya cikitsā* to create multiple emotions in her mind. One side, she creates a significant mental distance from her husband and on other side, makes her mind susceptible to *bhaya jvara* and *śoka jvara*. While messenger does her job in stage 2 (refer *fig*. 2.3), *nāyaka* advances with having pleasant conversations with *nāyikā* and gifts her memorable objects.

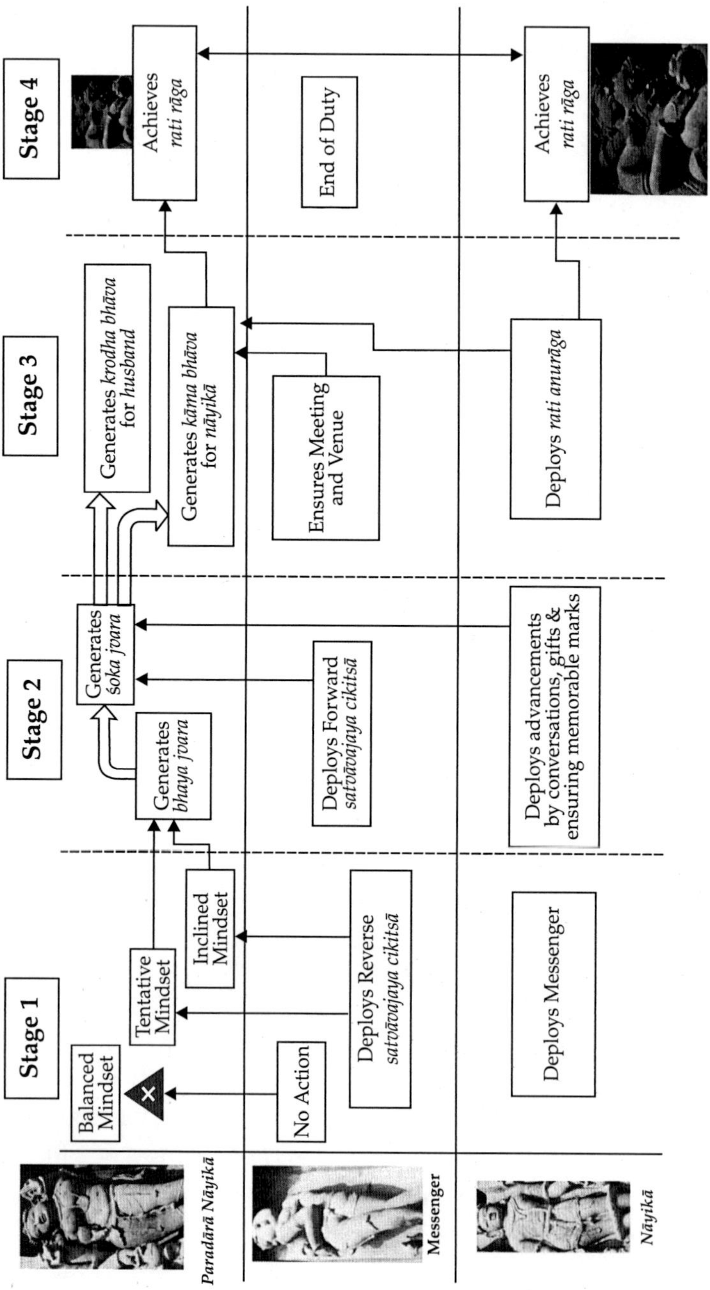

fig. 2.3: Symbolic model of role of messenger in Kāmaśāstra

In the next stage, Kāmaśāstra suggests (ibid.: 553-54; *KS* 5.4.7-8) the different ideas to the messenger to engage the narration with *nāyikā* and recommends pointing out the "misfit" candidature of her husband. This impression will create (Shastri 1992: 554-56; *KS* 5.4.10, 12, 15) *krodha bhāva* for husband and *kāma bhāva* for *nāyaka*. The messenger arouses these emotions in the mind of *nāyikā* through very adaptive and rightly paced conversions (ibid.: 554-55; *KS* 5.4.11, 13-14) to ensure successful seeding of such feelings.

Like a typical medical treatment, Kāmaśāstra suggests *ākāraṁ cāsyā lakṣayet* (ibid.: 556, *KS* 5.4.16) monitoring and minute observations of the *nāyikā* on the continuous basis and appropriately manage her therapy. It further enlists all the possible symptoms (ibid.: 556-58; *KS* 5.4.17-29) in the form of responses, gestures and reactions expressed by *nāyikā* and tweak her treatment accordingly, ensuring the increase in the *kāma bhāva* for *nāyaka*.

Finally, the messenger should succeed in getting acceptance from the *nāyikā* on meeting and venue. Thus, based on the messenger's expertise, *nāyaka* can be cured from the *kāma jvara*.

2.5.4.6 *Symbolic Concept of Kāma Vaidya*

From the above discussions, Vātsyāyana appears to be an Āyurveda *vaidya* than a Kāmaśāstra author. There is an interesting symbolic concept I have identified from Kāmaśāstra and Āyurveda comparison and termed as *kāma vaidya*.

Kāmaśāstra has positioned the courtesan especially chaste (*ekacariṇī*) as *kāma vaidya*. Hence, we find the entire Āyurveda framework symbolically fitting to the Kāmaśāstra theory of prescription here. Below are the points of discussion in this regard.

2.5.4.7 *Objective of the Profession: Kāma Therapy* (ibid.: 616, *KS* 6.2.2-29)

Kāma therapy can be defined as the romantic treatment by a chaste courtesan to her *nāyaka*, wherein she assumes the role of his wife and ensures his complete pleasure without any attachment to him; however never makes him realize the same. Like, an Āyurveda

Table 2.11: Cikitsā Catuṣṭaya in Kāmaśāstra

Āyurveda Cikitsā Catuṣṭaya	*Kāmaśāstra Cikitsā Catuṣṭaya*
Patient	*Nāyaka*
Vaidya	*Kāma vaidya*
Messenger	Messenger
Medicine	*Rati karma*

vaidya, who makes his patient comfortable and treats with utmost care, without any attachment, but never makes patient feel about it.

The intimacy, ultimate pleasure, artistic copulation, satisfaction through realization of fantasies, respect, devotion and loyalty are the key characteristics exhibited during the *kāma* therapy.

2.5.4.8 *Critical Components of the Profession: Cikitsā Catuṣṭaya*

Like Āyurveda's components, Kāmaśāstra also has its four critical components to be compared with the former (Table 2.11).

Kāmaśāstra describes in detail the qualification and selection process of a *nāyaka*. It further provides a thorough account on the role and qualities of *kāma vaidya*. She should understand and follow the *trisūtrī* of Kāmaśāstra which is based on the Āyurveda theory.

Kāmaśāstra talks about the objectives (*hetu*), symptoms (*lakṣaṇa*) and remedy (*samprāpti*) that the *kāma vaidya* should analyse for her patient who is nothing but her *nāyaka*. It is very interesting to note how Kāmaśāstra has conceptualized the *trisūtrī* here.

Kāmaśāstra mentions the main reasons or objectives of a *nāyaka* to approach a *kāma vaidya* as love, fear, money, pleasure, returning some act of enmity, curiosity, sorrow, constant intercourse, religious influence, compassion, the desire of having a friend, shame, the getting rid of the love of somebody else, living in the same place, constancy. Vātsyāyana decides that desire of wealth, freedom from misfortune and love are the only causes that affect the union of a courtesan with her *nāyaka* (Shastri 1992: 607-08-56; *KS* 6.1.17-18).

Kāmaśāstra further advises (Shastri 1992: 608; *KS* 6.1.20) that the testing of the symptom in the *nāyaka* before proceeding further in relationship building (treatment). In fact, Kāmaśāstra cautions (ibid.: 608; *KS* 6.1.21) about the popping up of the possible errors in the *cikitsā* (treatment) if this diagnostic has not done properly.

Kāmaśāstra, like a pathological help, recommends (ibid., 609; *KS* 6.1.22) deploying external services from rigthtly skilled partners to determine first level diagnosis of *bhāva*. The list of partners include the maid servants, singers and jesters, who may be in her service. The prime objective of their engagement is to conduct dipstick test of the *nāyaka*'s true inclination behind the relationship building. It further advocates the second level of diagnosis using the skills of *viṭa* (middleman). *Viṭa* should help diagnosing and qualifying the *nāyaka* from physical and psychological disorders standpoint. He should also help in assessing the *nāyaka* for the chronic conditions, if any, and financial instabilities.

Symbolically, we can compare this with the initial pathological testing to determine the treatment direction. Burton (Richards 2009: 104) has described this as:

> On such occasions she should first send the shampooers and the singers and the jesters, who may be in her service, or, in their absence the *pīṭhamardas*, or confidants and others, to find out the state of his feelings and the condition of his mind. By means of these persons she should ascertain whether the man is pure or impure, affected, or the reverse, capable of attachment, or indifferent, liberal or niggardly.

Once properly qualified, the *kāma vaidya* starts her *bhāvanirmiti cikitsā* on *nāyaka* by arousing his curiosities, tendering soft, sweet and long conversations, entertaining his wills and fancies, dramatizing the reality with her behaviour, performing various arts, romantically respecting him, gifting him the precious objects. This will gradually lead to the establishing, building and nurturing of the relationship with soft feelings (*rasa*) attached. This will also create a strong foundation of long-lasting mental bonds.

A *kāma vaidya*, then proceeds with the next level of *kāma* therapy wherein she continuously attempts to provide personalized treatment to her *nāyaka* by always welcoming and greeting him with a mixture of betel leaves and betel nut, garlands of flowers of his choice and perfumed ointments that make him delightful and excited. This marks her second milestone of therapy, i.e. the *bhāva* creation in his mind.

Moving ahead, a *kāma vaidya*, will now start advancing with pre-copulation techniques of making compelling ambience, intense physical traces, wild but suitable foreplay and indicative conversations followed with direct sexual talks. This will lead to the emanation of the *rati-anurāga* and finally the Āyurveda *samprāpti* in the form of Kāmaśāstra *rati-rāga*. While she progresses through these steps, she ensures the critical ingredient of unattached mindset with proficient and empathetic behaviour thus focusing on the innovating and sustaining physical, mental and even economic stability in the entire game of association and assimilation. As if like an Āyurveda *vaidya* ultimately succeeds in establishing through his therapy the balanced and homeostasis state in the patient. Moreover, like the Āyurveda recommended routine equips the person with the immunity against the diseases, Kāmaśāstra *kāma* therapy arms the *nāyaka* with immense power to contest against any odds that harms his mental health. Kāmaśāstra not only symbolically but categorically advises,[44] like an authoritative text of medicine, to the *kāma vaidya* about maintaining her external looks and internal body health by adopting balanced diet.

We could conclude from here the significant symbolic influence of Āyurveda on the theory of Kāmaśāstra.

---

[44] नित्यमलङ्कायोगः परिमितः अभ्यवहारः (*nityamalaṅkāyoga parimitaḥ abhyavahāraḥ*)। – *KS* 6.2.41 (Shastri 1992: 552)

3

Reinterpreting Kāmaśāstra Theory

3.1 Introduction

We have seen in the last chapters that the Āyurveda is one of the most renowned traditional systems of medicine that has survived and flourished from ages till date. We could see therein enormous knowledge of nature-based medicine, deep thoughts on the relationship of human body constitution and function to nature and unique perception of the elements of the universe that act in coordination and affect the living beings.

In practice, Āyurveda has eight disciplines called "Aṣṭāṅga Āyurveda". They are *kāya-cikitsā* (internal medicine treatment), *bhūta-vidyā* (treatment of psychological disorders), *kaumāra-bhṛtya* (paediatric treatment), *rasāyana* (study of geriatrics), *vājīkaraṇa* (treatment through aphrodisiacs and eugenics), *śalya* (surgical treatment), *śālākya* (otorhinolaryngological and ophthalmological treatment) and *agada tantra* (toxicological studies). We could see here a very careful approach to chisel out to meet specific needs in the process of maintaining health and preventing diseases.

In this section, I have attempted to analyse the technical strengths of Kāmaśāstra and presented the concept of Aṣṭāṅga Kāmaśāstra, which can be regarded as the logical mechanism to comprehend the whole idea of Kāmaśāstra, which was evolved and culminated in our country. These elements of Kāmaśāstra are necessary and sufficient to understand all the aspects of Kāmaśāstra. Their nomenclature and scope are described below.

3.2 Concept of Aṣṭāṅga Kāmaśāstra

Aṣṭāṅga Kāmaśāstra has the following eight elements:

- *Nāyaka* (*Male*): Here various characteristics of the males are discussed including their classification based on physical attributes and skills. It further discusses aspects of horoscope, caste, education, skills, behaviour, character and its impact on their overall performance of satisfaction creation.
- *Nāyikā* (*Female*): This aspect of Aṣṭāṅga Kāmaśāstra describes female types based on physical attributes, skills, relationship with males and even profession. The topic further discusses the role and responsibilities of females in their satisfaction creation.
- *Vāstu* (*Venue*): Right from the theory of hygiene for copulation up to the selection of proper place, interior, designer furniture, various utility arrangements, etc. are discussed here.
- *Kāmadeva* (*Rituals*): This aspect of Aṣṭāṅga Kāmaśāstra supplies details on all types of required rituals like various sacrifices, *homa*, *yāga*, *śānti* and chanting, which are performed by the *nāyaka* to yield progeny, prosperity, protection and happiness from the divinity of Kāmadeva.
- *Rasa and Bhāva* (*Morale and Feeling*): This aspect of Aṣṭāṅga Kāmaśāstra determines the rules of morale, taboos, best and preferred match of *nāyaka* and *nāyikā*, impacts of the external factors on the mind orientation of both male and female. It discusses the significance of the right copulation mood and energy on progeny and pleasure.
- *Āsana* (*Postures*): Here we find the best possible body postures for a highest probability of conceiving and pleasure

simultaneously. It describes the recommended positions and its benefits.

- *Bhojya* (*Consumption Rules*): This deals with the different ingredients including food and medicinal materials that *nāyaka* and *nāyikā* should consume for better performance. It also deals with the regular and specific process of consumption leading to desired effects. The term consumption is used in its wider meaning. It suggests the acceptance of tangibles or non-tangibles by body across senses including oral consumption (using different methods), application of medicines on body parts, inhalation of spray, consumption via viewing of different colour schemes and even listening to music. The ultimate impact of *bhojya* is seen in creation of right mood, feelings and necessary physical strength.
- *Upakaraṇa* (*Instruments*): This aspect of Aṣṭāṅga Kāmaśāstra suggests the usage of different instruments made from select materials that are used during copulation. It further discusses the fabrication of these instruments and most important is their regular maintenance.

We can mark in *Aṣṭāṅga Kāmaśāstra* the timeless truths, which were explored and practised in ancient India, are clubbed with logical and convenient manner.

Aṣṭāṅga Kāmaśāstra deals in detail with all the aspects of Kāmaśāstra: male–female matching, emphasis on sanitation, sacrament and symbolization, morale and feelings, various types of body positions, consumption of food and medicinal ingredients, space, furniture and overall ambience, application and necessary hygiene of artificial instruments, etc.

I have proved here that all the topics related to Kāmaśāstra are covered in this framework of *Aṣṭāṅga Kāmaśāstra* scoped with eight elements discussed above. Further, this logic can be used to treat or rectify any imbalance or abnormality in the combinatory behavioural pattern of *nāyaka*, *nāyikā* and other related aspects.

3.3 The Nāyaka

3.3.1 CLASSIFICATION OF THE NĀYAKA

Kāmaśāstra classifies all the males based on multiple criteria. Primarily, it includes organ size, passion, stamina and even regional elements. Kāmaśāstra classifies (Shastri 1992: 183; *KS* 2.1.1) males as hare, bull or stallion according to the size of their sexual organ. It further classifies (ibid. 191; *KS* 2.1.5) males based on passion as low, middling and intense. This classification also calibrates the low, medium and high ejaculation amount and physical strength of male vis-à-vis different aggressive pleasure techniques. The third classification (ibid. 192; *KS* 2.1.8) is based on the stamina of male to enjoy and remain active in the copulation over a period. It denotes three types – short, moderate and lasting. It also indicates how fast a male ejaculates and retires from the union mentally and physically.

Upadhyaya (1965: 34) presented the pictorial views of various types of *nāyakas*.

Interestingly, Kāmaśāstra does not blame, ridicule or praise any type of male, but provides the guidelines on proper partnering based on the classification. We are discussing these aspects under *rasa-bhāva* section.

I have presented below pictorially all the permutations conceptualized by Kāmaśāstra for the types of *nāyakas*. Appendix 3 (*Pls* 8 and 9) displays the physical proportions of *nāyakas* and *nāyikās* from Khajurāho sculptures.

We could see above the nine possible permutation within the Hare type of *nāyaka*.

Similarly, *figs* 3.3 and 3.4 indicate all possible permutations within bull and stallion types of *nāyakas*.

Kāmaśāstra suggests one important criterion for classification of males based on the regional characteristics. There are basically two types of dwellers based on their living regions – one is a citizen (*nāgaraka*) and the other is a villager (*grāmavāsī*) (Shastri 1992: 151; *KS* 1.4.36).

fig. 3.1: Nāyaka Types

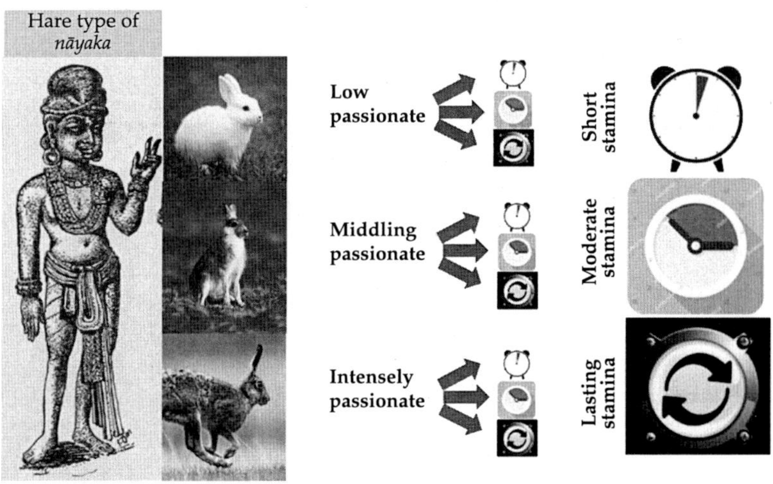

fig. 3.2: Permutations within Hare Nāyaka Type

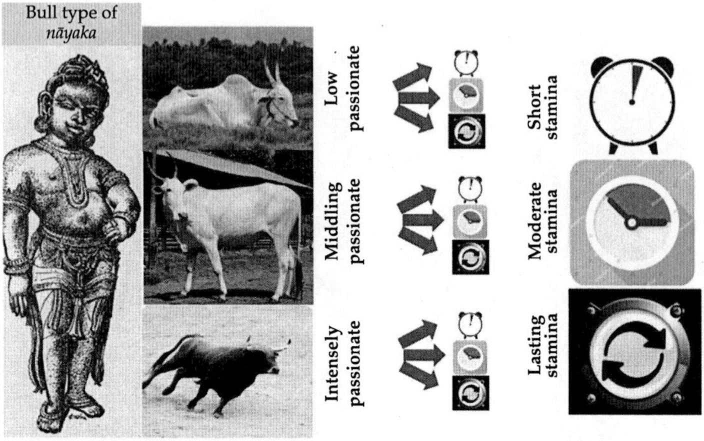

fig. 3.3: Permutations within Bull Nāyaka Type

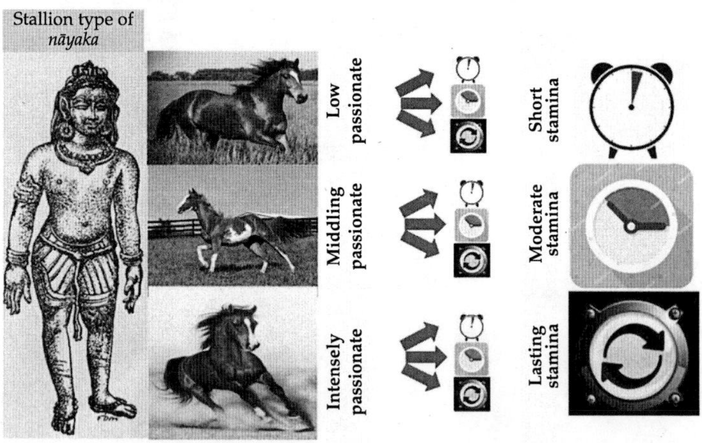

fig. 3.4: Permutations within Stallion Nāyaka Type

Moreover, Kāmaśāstra also suggests (Madhavacharya 2008: 161; *KS* 1.4.34) a typical class of *nāyaka* as *upanāgaraka* (second citizen). There are three categories mentioned within them. They are: the *pīṭhamarda*, the *viṭa* and the *vidūṣaka*. Burton Richard et al. (2009: 22) describe them as:

> A *pīṭhamarda* is a man without wealth, alone in the world, whose only property consists of his *mallikā*, some lathering substance and a red cloth, who comes from a good country and who is skilled in all the arts; and by teaching these arts is received in the company of citizens and in the abode of public women.
>
> A *viṭa* is a man who has enjoyed the pleasures of fortune, who is a compatriot of the citizens with whom he associates, who is possessed of the qualities of a householder, who has his wife with him and who is honoured in the assembly of citizens and in the abodes of public women and lives on their means and on them.
>
> A *vidūṣaka* (also called a *vaihāsaka*, i.e. one who provokes laughter) is a person only acquainted with some of the arts who is a jester and who is trusted by all.
>
> These persons are employed in matters of quarrels and reconciliations between citizens and public women.

Kāmaśāstra also describes one specific type of *nāyaka*, i.e. the king himself. Technically, a king might be qualified as one of the earlier classified *nāyakas*, however, the special role (Shastri 1992: 506; *KS* 4.2.70-71) which he supposed to play to satisfy multiple wives makes him a different and unique among others. In fact, this responsibility element of ensuring pleasure of wives makes the king a unique type of *nāyaka*.

One of the best examples of social inclusivity and scientific approach adopted by Kāmaśāstra can be seen in its unique proposition of classifying *nāyakas* in the category of customers of prostitutes. Kāmaśāstra provides (ibid.: 667; *KS* 6.4.9) description of three types of such *nāyakas* and provides with behavioural recommendations as well. *Figure* 3.5 shows this classification. Kāmaśāstra classifies customers primarily into three clusters based on the mental traits of the *nāyaka*, viz. his romantic nature, generous attitude and gratefulness. Further, Kāmaśāstra provides one more dimension to classify *nāyaka* based on his social and physical attributes like his economic status (richness and poverty),

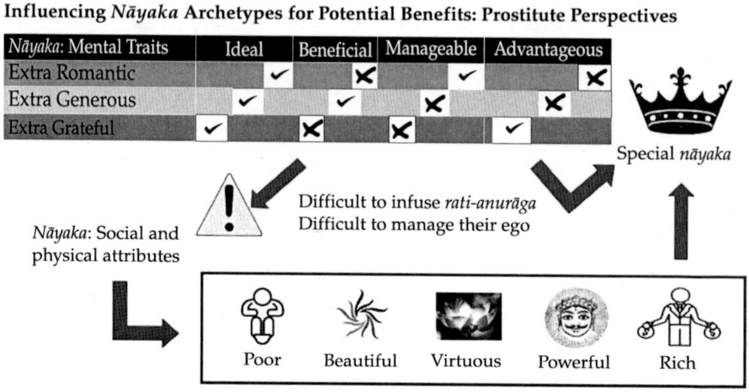

fig. 3.5: Nāyaka Types from Customer Perspective

physical attributes like beauty and virtuousness and his powerful social status due to his political nexus and influencing position. Kāmaśāstra, very interestingly, details the potential benefits to the prostitute from each possible combination of *nāyaka* attributes. The specialty in the males described by Kāmaśāstra within this framework is the richness to spend wealth on the prostitute or gratefulness to help her in all odd situations.

3.3.2 GENERAL CHARACTERISTICS OF THE NĀYAKA

The *Anaṅga Raṅga* describes (Arbuthnot and Burton 1907: 80) twenty-one characteritstics of the best-fit *nāyaka*. It says that the man should be tried like the gold is tested in four ways: by the touchstone, by cutting, by heating and by hammering. Similarly, we should take into consideration learning, disposition, qualities and action of a man to judge him. The first characteristic of a man is courage, with endurance; if he attempts any deed, great or small, he should do it with the spirit of a lion. Second is prudence: time and place must be determined and opportunity devised, like the black-heron, that stands intently eyeing its prey in the pool below. The third is early rising and causing others to do the same. The fourth is hardihood in war. The fifth is a generous distribution and division of food and property amongst family and friends. The sixth is duly attending to the wants of his wife. The seventh is circumspection in love matters. The eighth is secrecy and privacy in the venereal act. The ninth is patience and perseverance in all the business of life. The tenth is judgement in collecting and in storing up what may be necessary. The eleventh is not to allow wealth and worldly success to engender pride and vanity, magnificence and ostentation. The twelfth is never aspiring to the unattainable. The thirteenth is contentment with what the man has, if he can get no more. The fourteenth is plainness of diet. The fifteenth is to avoid oversleep. The sixteenth is to be diligent in the service of employers. The seventeenth is not to fly when attacked by robbers and villains. The eighteenth is working willingly, for instance, not taking into consideration the sun and shade if the labourer be obliged to carry a parcel. The nineteenth is the patient endurance of trouble. The twentieth is to keep the eye fixed upon a great business; and the twenty-first is to study the proper means for success.

We could see the depth of physical, psychological, social, economic and even moral framework suggested by Kāmaśāstra for a *nāyaka*.

Further, the *Anaṅga Raṅga* suggests (Arbuthnot and Burton 1907: 81) the criteria on which son-in-law should be selected. We are discussing that below:

- *While choosing a son-in-law, the following characteristics should be aimed at*: He must come from a large·family, which has never known sin and poverty. He must be young, handsome, wealthy, brave and influential; diligent in business, moderate in enjoying riches, sweet of speech, well versed in discharging his own duties, known to the world as a mine of virtues, steadfast in mind and a treasury of mercy, who gives alms and makes charities as far as his means permit. Such a man is described by celebrated poets as a fit person to whom the daughter should be given in marriage.
- *The defects and blemishes of a son-in-law*: The man who is born

in a low family, who is vicious, a libertine, pitiless and ever sickly with dangerous disease, sinful and very wicked, poor and miserly, impotent, prone to conceal the virtues and to divulge the vices of others, a constant traveller, an absentee, one ever away from his home and residing abroad, a debtor, a beggar, a man who has no friendship with the good or who, if he have it, breaks into quarrel upon trifling things – such a person the wise will not accept as a son-in-law.

3.3.3 CHIROMANTIC CHARACTERISTICS OF THE NĀYAKA

The *Anaṅga Raṅga* provides a detailed account of the horoscopic and palmistry characteristics of the *nāyaka*. While introducing the topic it says (Arbuthnot and Burton 1907: 82) – Every perfect hand and foot consists of five members, viz. the *aṅguṣṭha* (thumb), *tarjanī* (forefinger), *madhyamā* (middle-finger), *anāmikā* (ring-finger) and *kaniṣṭhikā* (little finger). Now, if an unbroken line in the palm run from the "mount" or base of the little finger, to that of the forefinger, it is a sign that the bearer will live a hundred years. But the man in whose palm an unbroken line runs from the ball or cushion of the little finger to that of the middle-finger, should be considered as likely to live for a period of sixty years. Moreover, the man upon whose thumb or chest there is a figure shaped like a barley grain, the same will eat bread earned by his own exertions and he will ever remain happy. As a rule, if the lines in the palms be few, men are poor and penniless; if there be four, they are happy; and if more than four, they are threatened with mean and wretched fortunes; moreover, the much streaked palm shows a quarrelsome nature.

The man whose eyes are red, whose body is fair and of good complexion like gold, whose trunk is fleshy and whose arms reach his knees, the same will always remain rich and enjoy grandeur, opulence, lordship and supremacy. The man whose thighs are large, will win great wealth; the man whose waist is broad, will be blessed in his wife and many children; the man whose feet is long and whose hands are very delicate, will always enjoy happiness; and the man whose head is large and lengthy, will rise to be a prince. The man whose penis is very long will be wretchedly poor. The man whose penis is very thick, will ever be in distress. The man whose penis is thin and lean, will be very lucky; and the man whose penis is short, will be a king.

3.3.4 PRESCRIBED BEHAVIOUR OF THE NĀYAKA

A nāyaka must follow the day and night routine prescribed by Kāmaśāstra. We have already discussed this matter in the last chapter. The summary of the same is presented below:

The householder should wake up early in the morning and perform his necessary activities like teeth wash, application of a limited quantity of ointments and perfumes to his body. Then he should wear some ornaments and put collyrium on his eyelids and below his eyes, colour his lips with alacktaka. Then he should consume betel leaves, with other things that give fragrance to the mouth and start his usual business.

He should bathe daily, anoint his body with oil every other day, apply a lathering substance to his body every three days, get his head (including face) shaved every four days and the other parts of his body every five or ten days. All these things should be done without fail and the sweat of the armpits should be well taken care of. Meals should be taken in the forenoon, in the afternoon and again at night. After breakfast, he should spend time with pet animals like parrots and other birds like cocks. A limited time should be devoted to diversions with *pīṭhamardas*, *viṭas* and *vidūṣakas* and then should be taken the midday sleep. In the late afternoon, he should put on his clothes and ornaments and spend time with his friends on conversations. In the evening he should be enjoying the singing and other entertaining options. In the later evening, along with his friend, he should decorate the room and make it further romantic by spraying the perfume. He should then wait or arrange the arrival of the *nāyikā*. After her arrival at his house, he and his friend should welcome her and entertain her with a loving and agreeable conversation. The *nāyaka* should enjoy his time and achieve *kāma* objectives. Thus end the duties of the day.

Kāmaśāstra categorically provides some behavioural restrictions on the *nāyaka* to ensure his overall well-being and health. On the other hand, Kāmaśāstra encourages the *nāyaka* to adopt a few ways to make life meaningfully happy. Thus, we find various taboos and prescriptions as messenger management (*dūtī-karma* or *dhātreyikā karma*), restricted usage of adultery and prostitution, prohibition on mingling with *agamyā* type of *nāyikā*, prescriptive behaviour with wife, religious comportment and recommended socialization, celebrations and outing and playing amusement games (Shastri 1992: 124; *KS* 1.4.14).

3.4 The Nāyikā

3.4.1 CLASSIFICATION OF THE NĀYIKĀ

Like the *nāyaka*, the *Kāmasūtra* classifies (ibid. 183) women into multiple types based on different criteria. According to the depth of her genital, the *nāyikā* is classified as a female deer, a mare or a female elephant. Further, like the *nāyaka* men classification, Kāmaśāstra puts forth the criteria of passion intensity and stamina to differentiate the categories of *nāyikās*. Thus, we can see twenty-seven permutations of the *nāyikā* described in the *Kāmasūtra*.

Interestingly, the *Anaṅga Raṅga* classifies (Arbuthnot and Burton 1907: 80) women into four basic categories (orders) based on the four classes of temperaments. These are: Padminī, Citriṇī, Śaṅkhinī and Hastinī. We find very lucid description of the physical peculiarities of all these four types. We are discussing the same below:

Padminī (*Lotus Woman*): Her face is pleasing as the full moon; her body, well clothed with flesh, is soft as the mustard-flower; her skin is fine, tender and fair as the yellow lotus, never dark-coloured, though resembling, in the effervescence and purple light of her youth, the cloud about to burst. Her eyes are bright and beautiful as the orbs of the fawn, well-cut and with reddish corners. Her bosom is hard, full and high; her neck is good shaped as the conch-shell, so delicate that the saliva can be seen through it; her nose is straight and lovely, and three folds or wrinkles cross her middle, about the umbilical region. Her vagina resembles the opening lotus-bud and her love-seed is perfumed like the lily which has newly burst. She walks with swan-like gait and her voice is low and musical as the note of the *kokilā*-bird; she delights in white raiment, in fine jewels and in rich dresses. She eats little, sleeps lightly and, being as respectful and religious as she is clever and courteous, she is ever anxious to worship the gods and to enjoy the conversation of brāhmaṇas.

Citriṇī (*Art Woman*): She is of the middle size, neither short nor tall, with bee-black hair, thin, round, shell-like neck, tender body; waist lean-girthed as the lion's; hard, full breasts; well-turned thighs and heavily made hips. The hair is thin about the vagina, the Mons Veneris being soft, raised and round. The love-seed is hot and has the perfume of honey, producing from its abundance a sound during the venereal rite. Her eyes roll and her walk is coquettish, like the swing of an elephant, whilst her voice is that of the peacock. She is fond of pleasure and variety; she delights in singing and in every kind of accomplishment, especially the arts manual; her carnal desires are not strong and she loves her pets – parrots, hen (*mainā*) and other birds.

Śaṅkhinī (Conch Woman): She is of bilious temperament, her skin being always hot and tawny, or dark yellow brown; her body is large, her waist thick and her breasts small; her head, hands and feet are thin and long and she looks out of the corners of her eyes. Her vagina is ever moist with love-seeds, which is distinctly salty and the cleft is covered with thick hair. Her voice is hoarse and harsh, of the bass or contralto type; her gait is precipitate; she eats moderately and she delights in clothes, flowers and ornaments of red colour. She is subject to fits of amorous passion, which make her head hot and her brain confused and now of enjoyment, she thrusts her nails into her husband's flesh. She is of choleric constitution, hard-hearted, insolent and vicious; irascible, rude and ever addicted to finding fault.

Hastinī (Elephant Woman): She is short of stature and has a stout, coarse body. Her skin, if fair, is of a dead white. Her hair is tawny, her lips are large and her voice is harsh, choked and throaty and her neck is bent. Her gait is slow and she walks in a slouching manner; often the toes of one foot are crooked. Her love seeds have the savour of the juice which flows in spring from the elephant's temples. She is tardy in the art of love and can be satisfied only by prolonged congress, in fact, the longer the better, but it will never suffice her. She is gluttonous, shameless and grumpy.

The *Anaṅga Raṅga* assumes the three types of women mentioned by the *Kāmasūtra* are the sub-types within the four orders of the *nāyikā*s described above. Thus, the *Anaṅga Raṅga* propounds (Arbuthnot and Burton 1907: 25) that *Padminī*, *Citriṇī*, *Śaṅkhinī* and *Hastinī* are further subdivided based on their vagina size and depth as – deer, mare and elephant. Thus, we get nine combinations here. Further, when we add passion and stamina, it will amount to eighty-one types of *nāyikā*s.

Upadhyaya (1965: 33) presents the pictorial views of various types of *nāyikā*s.

Upadhyay (1965: 33) presented the pictorial views of various types of *nāyikā*. These are reproduced in *fig*. 3.6.

The *Anaṅga Raṅga* further defines different types of *nāyika*s based on the age factor (Arbuthnot and Burton 1907: 25). In fact, it further provides ideas of congress based on the age. Table 3.1 provides the details.

The *Anaṅga Raṅga* emphasizes on the different *nāyika* types based on the Āyurveda concept of *prakṛti*, which we have already discussed in the last chapter.

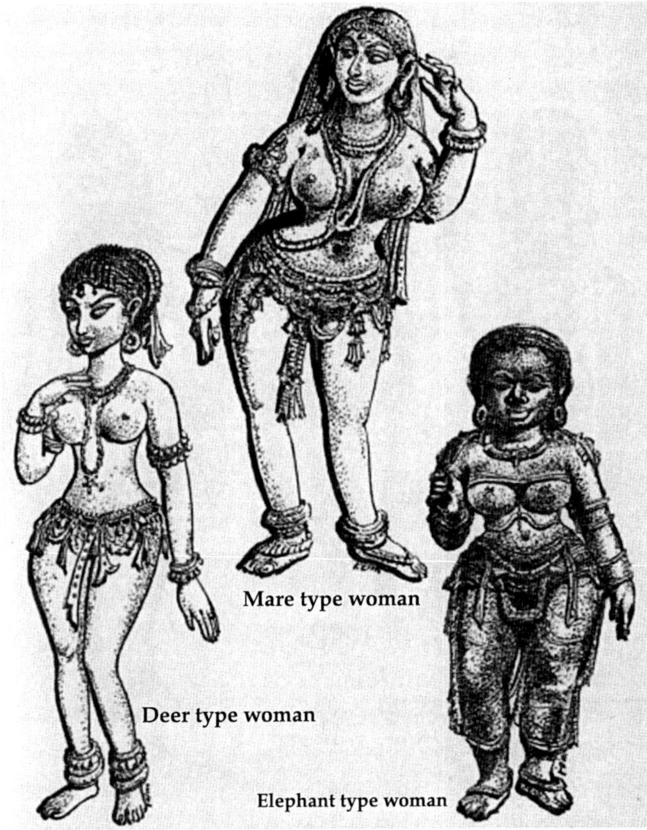

fig. 3.6: Nāyikā Types

Table 3.1: Nāyikā Types Based on Life Cycle

Age (Years)	*Name*	*Fitness to Love Making*	*Preference to Congress*	*How Subjected*
11-16	*Bālā*	Fit	Darkness	By flowers, small presents, gift of betel and so forth.
16-30	*Taruṇī*	Fit	In light	By gift of dresses, pearls and ornaments
30-55	*Prauḍhā*	Fitness doubtful	Both in darkness and light	By attention, politeness, kindness and love
Above 55	*Vṛddhā*	Unfit	Becomes sick and infirm	By flattery

We find a detailed classification of a *nāyika* based on her previous state of existence, the *sattva* or disposition inherited from a former life and which influences her worldly natures. This classification is presented in the *Anaṅga Raṅga* (Arbuthnot and Burton 1907: 26).

Deva sattva: She belongs to the gods, is cheerful and lively, pure-bodied and clean, with perspiration perfumed like the lotus-flower; she is clever, wealthy and industrious, of sweet speech and benevolent, always delighting in good works; her mind is sound as her body, nor is she ever tired of or displeased by her friends.

Gāndharva sattva: She derives this name from the heavenly minstrels. She has beautiful shape, patient in mind, delighting in purity; wholly given to perfumes, fragrant substances and flowers, to singing and playing, to rich dress and fair ornaments, to sport and amorous play, especially to the romance and make-ups, one of the classes of feminine actions which indicates the passion of love.

Yakṣa sattva: She derives this name from the demigod presiding over the gardens and treasures of Kubera. She has large and fleshy breasts, with a skin fair as the white *campā* (*Plumeria alba*) flower. She is fond of flesh and liquor; devoid of shame and decency; passionate and irascible and at all hours greedy for congress.

Manuṣya sattva: She belongs essentially to humanity, delights in the pleasures of friendship and hospitality. She is respectable and honest; her mind is free from guile and she is never wearied of religious actions, vows and penances.

Piśāca sattva: She relates to the class of demons. She has a short body, very dark and hot, with a forehead ever wrinkled; she is unclean in her person, greedy, fond of flesh and forbidden things and, however much enjoyed, she is ever eager of congress, like a harlot.

Nāga sattva: She is a snake-woman. She is always in hurry and confusion; her eyes look drowsy; she yawns repeatedly and she sighs with deep-drawn respiration; her mind is forgetful and she lives in doubt and suspicion.

Kāka sattva: She retains the characteristics of the crow, ever rolls her eyes about as if in pain; throughout the day she wants food; she is silly, unhappy and unreasonable, spoiling everything that she touches.

Vānara sattva: She is a monkey-woman, who rubs her eyes throughout the day, grinds and chatters with her teeth and is very lively, active and mercurial.

Khara sattva: She preserves the characteristics of the ass. She is unclean in her person and avoids bathing, washing and pure raiment; she cannot give a direct answer and she speaks awkwardly and without reason, because her mind is crooked. Therefore, she pleases no one.

The *Anaṅga Raṅga* clearly concludes that the identification of a *nāyika* within the above classification is very tough and a skilful job. Hence, it should be carried out only by an expert and experienced.

The *Anaṅga Raṅga* further provides (Arbuthnot and Burton 1907: 28) the sexual inclinations of different *nāyikās* based on the physical attributes and habits.

The woman whose bosom is hard and fleshy, who appears short from the fullness of her frame and looks bright and light-coloured, such a one is known to enjoy daily congress with her husband.

The woman who, being thin, appears very tall and somewhat dark, whose limbs and body are unenergetic and languid, the effect of involuntary chastity, such a one is Virahinī, who suffers from long separation from her husband and from the want of conjugal embraces.

A woman who eats twice as much as a man is four times more reckless and wicked, six times more resolute and obstinate and eight times more violent in carnal desire. She can hardly control her lust of congress, despite the shame which is natural to the sex.

Table 3.2: Sub-types of Nāyikās with Married Status

Type of Nāyikā	*Sub-types*			
	Ekacāriṇī			*Radnyā*
		Sapatnikā	Punarbhu	
		• *Jeṣṭhā*	• *Vidhavā*	
Bhāryā		• *Kaniṣṭhā*	• *Svecchayā*	
		• *Navapariṇitā*	• *Saukyārthinī*	
			• *Durbhagā*	

Kāmaśāstra provides a detailed classification framework of wives. The arrow Table 3.2 signifies the level of social recognition is as per the appearance of the description of the *nāyikā* types. For example, *punarbhu* is the lowest significant wife than the other types.

Kāmaśāstra classifies *paradārā nāyikā* into three types, viz. Satī, Vyabhicāriṇī and Carṣiṇī. Relationships cannot be established with Satī. Vyābhicāriṇī can be seduced and loved as per the restricted code of conduct. Carṣiṇī type of *nāyikā* is ready to mingle primarily due to high status of the *nāyaka* and she is typically belonging to a small village.

Kāmaśāstra classifies prostitutes on various criteria. Importantly, we can observe the detailing Kāmaśāstra provides to respect and extend the compassion to this class of human beings.

The arrow in Table 3.3 signifies the level of social recognition is as per the appearance of the description of the *nāyikā* types. For example, Kumbhadāsī is the lower significant prostitute than the Madhyamā.

Kāmaśāstra also signifies the third gender person as *nāyikā*. It recommends the oral sexual technique for her satisfaction.

The *Anaṅga Raṅga* provides a detailed account on the regional influence on the nature and characteristics of the *nāyikā*.

Table 3.3: Sub-types of Nāyikā within Prostitute Status

Type of Nāyikā	*Sub-types*				
Prostitute	*Aparigrahā*				
		Ekaparigrahā			
			Anekaparigrahā →		
	Gaṇikā (*Uttamā*)				
		Kāmavaidyā			
			Madhyamā		
				Adhamā	
					Laghu
			• *Rupājivā* • *Prakāśaviniṣṭā*	• *Kumbhadāsī* • *Śilpakārikā* • *Naṭī*	• *Svairiṇī* • *Kulaṭā* • *Paricārikā*

3.4.2 SIGNS AND DRIVERS OF THE NĀYIKĀ PSYCHOLOGY

The *Anaṅga Raṅga* provides a detailed account on the signs that qualify a woman as amorous (Arbuthnot and Burton 1907: 28). Those are discussed below: She rubs and repeatedly makes her hair (so that it may look well). She scratches her head (that notice may be drawn to it). She strokes her own cheeks (to entice her husband). She draws her dress over her bosom, apparently to readjust it, but leaves her breasts partly exposed. She bites her lower lip, chewing it, as it were. At times she looks ashamed without a cause (the result of her own warm fancies) and she sits quietly in the corner (engrossed by concupiscence). She embraces her female friends, laughing loudly and speaking sweet words, with jokes and jests, to which she desires a return in kind. She kisses and hugs young children, especially boys. She smiles with one cheek, loiters in her gait and unnecessarily stretches herself under some pretense or other. At times she looks at her shoulders and under her arms. She stammers and does not speak clearly or distinctly. She sighs and sobs without reason and she yawns whenever she wants tobacco, food, or sleep. She even throws herself in her husband's way and will not readily get out of his path.

The *Anaṅga Raṅga* further talks about the eight signs of indifference to be noted in womankind: When worldly passion begins to subside, the wife does not look straight between her husband's eyes. If anything, be asked of her, she shows unwillingness to reply. If the man draws near her and look happy, she feels pained. If he departs from her, she shows symptoms of satisfaction. When seated upon the bedstead, she avoids amatory blandishments and lies down quietly to sleep. When kissed or toyed with she jerks away her face or her form. She cherishes malicious feelings towards her husband's friends; and, finally, she has no respect nor reverence for his family. When these signs are seen, let it be known that the wife is already weaned from conjugal desires.

The *Anaṅga Raṅga* also discusses the principal causes which drive the *nāyikā* to deviate from the right way and to fall into the society of profligates. These are:

- Remaining, when grown up, in her mother's house, as opposed to that of her husband's parents.
- Evil communication with the depraved of her own sex.
- The prolonged absence of her husband.
- Living in the society of vile and licentious men.
- Poverty and the want of good food and dress.
- Mental trouble, affliction and unhappiness, causing her to become discontented and reckless.

The *Anaṅga Raṅga* provides the fifteen principal causes which make a *nāyikā* unhappy. These are:

- The parsimony of parents and husband, because the young are naturally generous.
- Receiving too much respect or reverence when they are lighthearted; also, being kept in awe by those with whom they would be familiar and a too strict restraint as regards orderly and guarded deportment.

- Trouble of disease and sickness.
- Separation from the husband and the want of natural enjoyment.
- Being made to work too hard.
- Violence, inhumanity and cruelty, such as beating.
- Rough language and abuse.
- Suspicion that they are inclined to evil.
- Intimidation and threats of punishment for going astray.
- Calumny, accusing of ill deeds and using evil words about them.
- Want of cleanliness in person or dress.
- Poverty.
- Grief and sorrow.
- Impotence of the husband.
- Disregard of time and place in the act of love.

3.4.3 PRESCRIBED BEHAVIOUR OF THE NĀYIKĀ

Kāmaśāstra categorically emphasizes on women education and empowerment. It strongly recommends (Shastri 1992: 75; *KS* 1.3.2) all *nāyikās* must take proper education and master various arts – not only in her father's home but after marriage as well. Moreover, to avoid unreasonable delays, the *Kāmasūtra* strongly recommends (ibid.: 451; *KS* 3.4.26) to the eligible woman that she should manage her marriage by herself without being depending upon anyone including parents. It goes further and suggests (ibid.: 451-54; *KS* 3.4.37, 48-49) how to find a bridegroom. He could be her childhood friend, or a virtuous, or rich or powerful *nāyaka*.

While Kāmaśāstra advocates the rights and freedom of a *nāyikā*, it suggests a framework of responsible behaviour as a wife, lover and even as a prostitute.

3.5 The Vāstu

Aṣṭāṅga Kāmaśāstra includes a very critical element as an abode or a place of pleasure (*vāstu*). It is a significant consideration from the overall scope of the Kāmaśāstra theory. We could see a lot of requirements and specifications mentioned in Kāmaśāstra on this topic. It has been taken (Altekar et al. 2020: 15) as recommendations by Vāstusāstra while developing the home-building programme. The major recommendations include the following:

- Separate room (*ratigṛha*) for copulation.
- Separate beds for sleeping and conjugal arts.
- Artistic and useful designs of interior and exteriors of the home.
- Harems in the royal palaces should be thoughtfully constructed.

Kāmaśāstra recommends below arts to deploy in *vāstu*:

- Art of decorating home with flowers.
- Art of arranging the bed.
- Art of building homes.

Shastri (1992: 93) interpreted the word *kalā* referred in Kāmaśāstra as the skills that is used to attract males or females. It also creates aesthetic value (*rasa*) in the mind of performer. This interpretation helps us in understanding the applications of Vāstusāstra principles in Kāmaśāstra perspective.

While describing the best place to stay, Kāmaśāstra suggests (ibid.: 99)[1] one should live in a city, capital, district place where luxuries, amenities and facilities are available in abundance. Even Kāmaśāstra does not hesitate to advise people to stay abroad locations, where they can enjoy their life better.

The place should be picturesquely located between rivers,

---

[1] नगरे पत्तने खर्वटे महति वा सज्जनाश्रये स्थानम् (*nagare pattane kharvaṭe mahati vā sajjanāśraye sthānam*) । –*KS* 1.4.2

mountains and trees. It is further emphasized that the home should be constructed near water reservoirs and gardens (or both may be created later near the home) and should have two parts called the inside house (*antaḥ prakoṣṭha*) and the outside house (*bāhya prakoṣṭha*) (ibid.: 101; *KS* 1.44).

Kāmaśāstra introduces the concept called *goṣṭhī vihāra*, where the people in the late afternoon assemble for gossiping, discussions, etc. Later in the evening, they used to go to *saṅgīta goṣṭhī* where various musical programmes were arranged. From this description we may conclude that the concept like pub or hotel must have prevailed in those periods. Kāmaśāstra recommends the usages of these pleasure creation spaces.

The idea of *ratigṛha* in Vāstusāstra is imported from Kāmaśāstra. We find references of decorated conjugal room forming the major part of the house. Second, we find the significance of terrace home clearly mentioned, where couples should enjoy their nights. One more point is to be noted regarding the lighting in the *ratigṛha*. Kāmaśāstra says darkness is necessary in case of copulation with novice and unknown girl, whereas lights are required in case of a previously known girl.

Kāmaśāstra recommends the exteriors of the home should be green. A garden (*vāṭikā*) is necessary to be cultivated with a lot of useful medicinal plants. We observe a detailed list of such trees and plants suggested by Kāmaśāstra that includes rose, lotus of different types, jasmine, various vegetables, teak wood, etc. The verse *Kāmasūtra* 4.1.29 gives further a detailed list of all medicinal plants. Kāmaśāstra strongly recommends constructing a decorated well, fountain or a big square tank at the midst of the garden.

Regarding the orientations, Kāmaśāstra suggests that the kitchen should be in such a way so that an outsider or alien will not able to observe anything inside easily. It suggests that the kitchen should be properly cleaned, well equipped and decorated with paintings. We could see a meticulous approach of home design here.

While describing the royal palaces Kāmaśāstra recommends that the harem should be placed at the safest location of the house. Its centre place was reserved for the married girls, outer house was allocated for mistresses, the next row for prostitutes and the last row was allocated for the actresses and dancers. One point is to be noted here is that normally no outsider could enter the harem; similarly, no insider could go out of the palace. Rather, the construction of the harem was made in such a way that the gate crasher would confuse after entry and easily got caught. On the contrary, Kāmaśāstra further narrates about the typical secret apertures from harem to the main road called *suraṅgī* to meet the woman in the harem. These narrations show the spacious, huge and the secure construction requirements of the royal palaces.

While addressing the issues of seducing a woman, Kāmaśāstra points out that the woman standing in the door, as well as the wife of the newly-married man staying alone in the home, are easily get seduced. It also describes other cases of seducing the woman, which are related to the type of home constructions. Hence, the laying out of the home must be based on the above considerations. And hence we get some recommendations like no harem should be constructed facing roads, or with such windows that open towards roads. In fact, as mentioned earlier, the harem is placed at the centre of the home.

We get a few references in Kāmaśāstra regarding the secret places for love meetings. One of the best places as suggested by Kāmaśāstra is the home of *viṭa*. The other places mentioned are fields, gardens, ruined temples, cemeteries, riverbanks and caves. Kāmaśāstra had discussed this issue in detail and concluded that the courtyard of *viṭa* to be the best place for secret love meetings. It is further added that *viṭa*'s home should be equipped with secret doors, windows and other types of apertures.

Kāmaśāstra mentions the storerooms in the home required to store grains, cotton, grass, fibres, yarns, etc. The use of such storeroom can also be made to spend time with female servants.

Kāmaśāstra introduces the concept of specially made love chambers and pleasure rooms in the royal palaces where women from other towns and cities come, meet and play with the wives of the dweller. Normally such celebrations are made on *aṣṭamī* or *kaumudī* days. It further describes the interior and the exterior of the love chambers like all the floors are decorated with pearls and other precious stones, outside the home beautiful gardens with fountains and plants full of fruits should be cultivated, *samudra gṛha*, i.e. a salon with walls on which water is flowing should be constructed, a *citraśālā* is to be maintained, separate place should be allocated for the cages of the animals, artificial animals, i.e. toys, etc. This shows the aesthetic requirements of interiors suggested by Kāmaśāstra.

We find in Kāmaśāstra a social and generous approach followed by *gaṇikā* in those periods. It supplies the strong evidences of the donations given by *gaṇikā* community for all civil works like temples, bridges, lakes, water reservoirs, gardens, *ghāṭs*, altars, small homes for rituals, etc. This proves that in those periods, apart from the kings, a *gaṇikā* community used to provide the necessary funds for all above-mentioned structures. We also get a few references (Shastri 1992: 637) [2] of typical technique followed by *gaṇikā*, where the costly artistic works were done from craftsmen and the bills recovered from the customers (*nāyakas*).

We find in Kāmaśāstra a few precautions were mentioned, which were to be taken by the prostitutes regarding the cleaning and daily maintenance of the home. It says prostitutes should artistically decorate their homes. They should buy high-quality commodities and arrange them properly; for example, various utensils, curtains, furniture, etc. should be bought and placed them in a manner to improve the "look" of the home. Similarly, the doors and windows should be made with beautiful designs and cleaned daily. The cloths used in the home like curtains, bed sheets, wall cloths, etc. should be washed regularly to create shining effects.

---

2 नायकार्थं च शिल्पिषु कार्यम् (*nāyakārthaṁ ca śilpiṣu kāryam*) । – *KS* 6.3.14

Interestingly, Kāmaśāstra mentions a term called *gandharvaśālā*, the place or the building where prince, sons of rich people, even kings, come to learn arts from the courtesans. This building is either a part of courtesan's huge palace (as observed in the *Mṛcchakaṭikam*) or the extension of royal palace of the king, where the courtesans come to teach. The minute detailing of this structure makes us feel that the entire narration is done as if by an architect.

3.6 The Kāmadeva

The astrological, religious and spiritual influence is reflected as the Kāmadeva concept in the Kāmaśāstra theory. We can trace this back to the *Ṛgveda* and find many relevant references around progeny and affluence (to be interpreted as wealth of offspring including daughters). *Ṛgveda* X.184 mentions:

विष्णुर्योनिं कल्पयतु त्वष्टा रूपाणि पिंशतु ।
आ सिञ्चतु प्रजापतिर्धाता गर्भं दधातु ते ॥ १॥

गर्भं धेहि सिनीवालि गर्भं धेहि सरस्वति ।
गर्भं ते अश्विनौ देवावा धत्तां पुष्करस्रजा ॥ २॥

हिरण्ययी अरणी यं निर्मन्थतो अश्विना ।
तं ते गर्भं हवामहे दशमे मासि सूतवे ॥ ३॥

viṣṇuryoniṁ kalpayatu tvaṣṭā rūpāṇi piṁśatu ।
ā siñcatu prajāpatirdhātā garbhaṁ dadhātu te ॥ 1 ॥

garbhaṁ dhehi sinīvāli garbhaṁ dhehi sarasvati ।
garbhaṁ te aśvinau devāvā dhattāṁ puṣkarasrajā ॥ 2 ॥

hiraṇyayī araṇī yaṁ nirmanthato aśvinā ।
taṁ te garbhaṁ havamahe daśame māsi sūtave ॥ 3 ॥

May Viṣṇu construct the womb, may Tvaṣṭā fabricate the member, may Prajāpati sprinkle the seed, may Dhātrī cherish thy embryo;

Sustain the embryo Sinīvāli, sustain the embryo Sarasvatī, may the divine Aśvins, garlanded with lotuses, sustain thy embryo;

> We invoke thy embryo which the Aśvins have churned with the golden pieces of *araṇi* (firewood), that thou mayest bring it forth in the tenth month. – tr. Wilson 1888: 410-11

Although, the hymn talks about the conceptual origination of the entire universe, it resembles very well with the conception of the human babies as well.

The Vedic texts have many passages, where the hymn solemnizes the desire for having a child, without specifying the gender of the child. These elements must have formed the foundation of the Kāmaśāstra theory in the later periods.

Since the *R̥gveda* periods, the auspicious and divine perspective in the human copulation process seems to be established. This is further evolved into the fine framework of the Kāmaśāstra theory encompassing the mental mechanics and physical techniques. The basic instinct of all the ancient Indian sciences is seen in its natural tendency to explain, theorize and prescribe the value-based principles in the practice. The perfection and the human centricity are always the part of this practice. We should remember the famous quote here – to err is human. The toughest problem in front of any social science is to balance smoothly the human tendencies which are inclined largely towards the errors and deviations, from the required scientific and perfect behaviour. To ensure the easy, convincing and precise adoption of the core and natural but tough prescriptions by the society, ancient Indian sciences, especially social sciences, deploy the unique approach of interweaving the theory of divinity, astrology and rituals with the expected methodical behaviour from humans. It provides them with the necessary scientific reasoning, motivation and even compulsion without pains, to follow the perfect behaviour. This approach, due to its own logical virtue, ensures the experience of precision, success, happiness and sense of fulfilment within the followers.

धर्मार्थकामेभ्यो नमः।
(*dharmārthakāmebhyo namaḥ*)

Image of Kāmadeva and Rati in the Cennakeśava Temple, Beḷūr

fig. 3.7: Kāmadeva

ॐ शंखं चक्रं जलौकां दधदमृतघटं चारुदोर्भिश्चतुर्मिः।
सूक्ष्मस्वच्छातिहृद्यांशुक परिविलसन्मौलिमंभोजनेत्रम॥
कालाम्भोदोज ज्वलांगं कटितटविलसच्चारूपीतांबराढ्यम।
वन्दे धन्वंतरिं तं निखिलगदवनप्रौढदावाग्निलीलम॥
oṁ śaṅkhaṁ cakraṁ jalaukāṁ dadha-
damṛtaghaṭaṁ cārudorbhiścaturmiḥ।
sūkṣmasvacchātihṛdyāṁśuka parivila-
sanmaulimaṁbhojanetrama॥
kālāmbhodojjvalāṅgaṁ kaṭitaṭavilasac-
cārūpītāṁbaraḍhyama।
vande dhanvantariṁ taṁ nikhilagada-
vanaprandhadavagnilīlama॥

fig. 3.8: Dhanavantari

Thus, the prescribed model sustains over ages within the society and achieves the status of a benchmark or a standard, generations after generations. We should see and interpret the concept of Kāmadeva exactly in the similar sense.

The immense respect and ardent followership of an ethical marriage system, linking copulation to a grade of ritual (and not a sinful act), ensuring the compulsory rest to the women during her monthly cycle, celebration and reverence to the pregnancy, consumption of aphrodisiac, daily routine management, are the few examples of this models developed by Kāmaśāstra theory. Investigator has classified all these elements under the concept of Kāmadeva.

The *Kāmasūtra* starts its first verse with saluting the deities of objectives of life. Symbolically, we can say Kāmadeva is propitiated in the first verse itself. Same is the case of Āyurveda. We find that Vāgbhaṭa's *Aṣṭāṅga Hṛdayam* starts with saluting the supreme deity of medicines.

The copulation is seen as sacred activity and we have seen that the *Ṛgveda* provides the foundation for the same. Kāmaśāstra recommends the complete celibacy post-marriage for three days including diet rules. We have already discussed these aspects in the last chapter. The scientific idea behind the strict observation of celibacy is to provide enough time to evolve the trusted relationship and mental assimilation between the unknown partners before their journey of the physical union. Kāmaśāstra mentions the same (Upadhyaya 1965: chap. 8, p. 44). To facilitate this penance of patience, probably, in the later periods, *garbhadhāraṇa vidhi* has been included as post-nuptial conduct for these three days.

Kāmaśāstra uses the special machinery of *mantra* concept for attracting and satisfying the women. The *Rati Rahasya* provides the Kāmeśvara Mantra for exciting and hypnotizing the women (ibid.: chap. 14.4-5, p. 82). In fact, the *Rati Rahasya* mentions that Kāmadeva resides amid the jewel-like beauty of love-play between man and woman; since the man and woman belong to different sexes, there springs a twofold difference in love. This *mantra* should be recited with the offering of *kiṁśuka* flowers to fire, one lakh times, then it becomes unfailingly efficacious. Thereafter, the *mantra* is directly exhaled into the vagina of the lady and resplendent like flame of lamp, it reaches the lotus-bud within her, releases the nectar like fluid and rapidly climaxing her emotions, so that she is utterly subjugated by the lover. The *Rati Rahasya* further deals with the multiple versions of the chanting and its administrations to achieve various objectives.

Anaṅga Raṅga 1.3 provides the listing of the best days of the month and even timing in a day for the copulation with a *nāyikā* type (Arbuthnot and Burton 1907: 6). This is as good as *pañcāṅga* for copulation, which provides the auspicious and restricted days and hours for copulation, based on the state of the moon and the hour of the day or night.

Table 3.4 explains the same. It recommends the *tithi* (day in a lunar month) in which each order derives the greatest amount of pleasure from the venereal rite.

Tables 3.5 and 3.6 explain the day and night hours where particular type of *nāyikā* derives the maximum satisfaction.

Table 3.4: Tithi and Recommended Focus on Nāyikā Types

Preference for Copulation – Tithi/Days of Month				*Nāyikā Type*
1	2	4	5	Padminī
6	8	10	12	Citriṇī
3	7	11	13	Śaṅkhiṇī
9	14	Full Moon	New Moon	Hastinī

Table 3.5: Regulating Night Hours and Recommended Focus on Nāyikā Types

Night Hours				*Nāyikā Type*
1st *Prahara*	2nd *Prahara*	3rd *Prahara*	4th *Prahara*	
6 p.m. to 9 p.m.	9 p.m. to 12 p.m.	0 a.m. to 3 a.m.	3 a.m. to 6 a.m.	
✗	✗	✗	✓	Padminī
✓	✗	✗	✗	Citriṇī
✗	✗	✓	✗	Śaṅkhiṇī
✓	✓	✓	✓	Hastinī

Table 3.6: Regulating Day Hours and Recommended Focus on Nāyikā Types

Day Hours				*Nāyikā Type*
1st *Prahara*	2nd *Prahara*	3rd *Prahara*	4th *Prahara*	
6 a.m. to 9 a.m.	9 a.m. to 12 noon	12 p.m. to 3 p.m.	3 p.m. to 6 p.m.	
✓	✓	✓	✓	Padminī
✗	✗	✗	✗	Citriṇī
✗	✗	✗	✗	Śaṅkhiṇī
✗	✗	✓	✓	Hastinī

It is very interesting to note *Anaṅga Raṅga* 1.4 theory. It says:

> Women, be it observed, differ greatly in the seasons which they prefer for enjoyment, according to their classes and temperaments. The Padminī, for instance, takes no satisfaction in night congress; indeed, she is thoroughly averse to it. Like the sunflower (day-lotus) which opens its eyes to the sunlight, so she is satisfied even by a boy-husband in the bright hours. The Citriṇī and the Śaṅkhinī are like the moon flower (night-lotus), that expands to the rays of the moon; and the Hastinī, who is the coarsest, ignores all these delicate distinctions.
>
> – Arbuthnot and Burton 1907: 6

It is very interesting to note *Anaṅga Raṅga* 2 theory. It says:

> Women, be it observed, differ greatly in the seasons which they prefer for enjoyment, according to their classes and temperaments. The Padminī, for instance, takes no satisfaction in night congress; indeed, she is thoroughly averse to it. Like the sunflower (day-lotus) which opens its eyes to the sunlight, so she is satisfied even by a boy-husband in the bright hours. The Citriṇī and the Śaṅkhiṇī are like the moon flower (night-lotus), that expands to the rays of the moon; and the Hastinī, who is the coarsest, ignores all these delicate distinctions.
>
> – Ibid. 1907: 8-10

Anaṅga Raṅga 2 believes that the passion resides in different parts and members of the woman and that by applying to these the necessary *candrakalā* (it is properly a digit, or one-sixteenth of the lunar orb), or preparatory touching, great comfort and pleasure are experienced by both husband and wife (ibid.: 11-14). It recommends the proper process of touching based on the days in month. It further says that if the recommended process is not performed, neither sex will be thoroughly satisfied; indeed, both will be disposed to lust after strange embraces and thus they will be led by adultery into quarrels, murders and other deadly sins, all of which may be avoided by studying and bearing in mind the *candrakalā*.

Passion resides in the woman's right side during the *śuklapakṣa*, the first or light fortnight of the lunar month, from new moon to full, including the fifteenth day. The reverse is the case on the dark fortnight, including its first day and lasting from the full to the new moon. The shifting is supposed to take place by the action of light and darkness, otherwise the site of passion would be one and the same.

The *Anaṅga Raṅga* further recommends the specific techniques of satisfying different types of *nāyikās*. It begins with the Padminī and discusses – in what limb or member passion resides; and, second, by what process it can be satisfied. The husband must continue his action till he sees the body-hair bristle and hears the *śītkāra* – the inarticulate sound produced by drawing in the air between the closed teeth. Thus, he will know that the paroxysm has taken place and the beloved one is thoroughly satisfied. Below tables provide the details.

Tables 3.7-3.9 explain the manipulations of the various *nāyikās*.

The *Kāmasūtra* mentions (Shastri 1992: 627) proper Kāmadeva Pūjā to be performed (even) by prostitute (*kāma-vaidyā*). In fact, it describes the details of *śānti karma* (ibid.; *KS* 6.2.66), *manauti* (ibid.; *KS* 6.2.68), *pūrṇapātra vidhi* (ibid.; *KS* 6.2.69), *vāyas pūjā* (ibid.; *KS* 6.2.670). It recommends (ibid.; *KS* 6.2.65) strongly to think

Table 3.7: The Recommended Touches per Days of Month

Śuklapakṣa or Light Fortnight; Right Side		*The Touches by which Passion is Satisfied*	*Kṛṣṇapakṣa or Dark Fortnight; Left Side*	
Day	*Place*		*Place*	*Day*
15th	Head and hair	Hold hair and caress the head with finger tips	Head and hair	1st
14th	Right eye	Kiss and fondle	Left eye	2nd
13th	Lower lip	Kiss, bite and chew softly	Upper lip	3rd
12th	Right chest	Do	Left chest	4th
11th	Throat	Scratch gently with nails	Throat	5th
10th	Side	Do	Side	6th
9th	Breasts	Hold in hands and gently knead	Breasts	7th
8th	All bosom	Tap softly with base of fist	All the bosom	8th
7th	Navel	Pat softly with open palm	Navel	9th
6th	Nates	Hold, squeeze and tap with fist	Nates	10th
5th	*Yoni*	Work with friction of *liṅga*	*Yoni*	11th
4th	Knee	Press with application of knee and fillip with finger	Knee	12th
3rd	Calf of leg	Press with application of calf and fillip with finger	Calf of leg	13th
2nd	Foot	Press with toe and thrust with latter	Foot	14th
1st	Big toe	Do	Big toe	15th

positively and dream positively (*iṣṭa svapna darśana*). There were classic celebrations and festivals like spring festival (*suvasantaka*), Kaumudī, Madana Mahotsava (ibid. 696; *KS* 6.6.46). Appendix 4 shows the select moments of Kāmadeva Pūjan celebrations in India and its tradition.

3.7 Rasa and Bhāva

It is a critical element of Aṣṭāṅga Kāmaśāstra that determines the achievement of ultimate objective of Kāmaśāstra – which is far more and beyond the mere bodily pleasure and happiness from the union. These two elements drive the entire action programme of *nāyaka* and *nāyikā*. It is with the absolute clarity that Kāmaśāstra states that the best union results out of the strong moral foundation and total respect to the partner. These basics can be further embellished with the romantic therapy and techniques to achieve the next level of joy, fulfilment, conservation of physical health and mental peace with the systematic acceleration towards the salvation. The morality and ethics play a vital role here. The otherwise situation will not warrant the quality of pleasure and overall sustainable fulfilment expected from the physical union.

Interestingly, we find the roots of this theory in the *R̥gveda*. Many hymns there provide the moral framework for copulation and overall rules for the ethical union. Hence, we find the *R̥gveda* restricts union with *guru*'s wife (Trivedi 1954: 1215; *R̥V* X.5.6), proposes a meticulous approach to select husband (not just based on wealth) (ibid.: 1249; *R̥V* X.5.12), compares behaviour of wife with husband as holy sacrifice (ibid.: 125; *R̥V* X.5.5), advocates permanency in relationship (ibid.: 1344; *R̥V* X.5.24), advises enjoying life with all amenities and intimacy (ibid.: 1346; *R̥V* X.5.42) and also warns about the fluctuating (ibid.: 1370; *R̥V* X.5.15) mood swings of women nature.

Kāmaśāstra has used all these principles in prescribing the matching of *nāyaka* and *nāyikā* not only on the grounds of physical and mental parameters but also on moral compliance. Thus, the concept of *rasa* and *bhāva* is core to Kāmaśāstra theory.

The words, *rasa* and *bhāva* are used in multiple sense in the Sanskrit literature. Much from subject relevance, investigator is reviewing the reference of these terms from classical Sanskrit literature and Āyurveda perspective and categorically leaning towards the Āyurveda side.

Sage Bharata presented a *rasa* formula in the context to drama and later it became the touchstone for all the poetics. The aim of a

Table 3.8: The Manipulation of the Padminī and Citriṇī Type of Nāyikās

Member	*Pratipadā (1st Day)*	*Dvitiyā (2nd Day)*	*Caturthī (4th Day)*	*Pañcamī (5th Day)*
Throat	Huge with force	"	"	"
Cheek	Kiss and scratch	Kiss and scratch	"	"
Hair	"	"	"	Stroke slowly with right hand
Waist	Apply nails and scratch	"	"	"
Breast	"	"	Scratch gently	"
Back	Scratch and tap with fist	"	"	"
Bosom	"	Press with nails	Squeeze and knead	Press and rub
Side	Scratch and press with nails	"	"	"
Thigh	"	Scratch and press with nails	"	"
Belly	Scratch and press with nails	"	"	"
Arm	"	"	Jerk suddenly and twitch	"
Lip	Bite softly and kiss	Kiss	Bite softly and suck	Bite softly
Nipple	"	"	"	Kiss, pinch softly and rub with thumb and forefinger
Space between eyes	Kiss	"	"	"
Foot	"	Scratch and press with nails	"	"

Member	*Ṣaṣṭhī (6th Day)*	*Aṣṭamī (8th Day)*	*Daśmī (10th Day)*	*Dvādaśī (12th Day)*
Yoni	"	Insert *linga.*	Rub and scratch with left hand	"
Lower lip	Kiss	"	"	Bite very gently
Throat	Embrace	Clasp firmly with hands	Scratch and pass fingers over it	Embrace firmly
Waist	Scratch and press with nails	"	Pass left hand over it and rub	"
Navel	"	Pinch with nails and fingers	"	"
Lip	"	Bite quickly and repeatedly	"	"
Breast	"	Hold in hand	Pass left hand over it and rub	"
Ear	"	"	Caress with left hand	Set nails upon it
Thigh	"	"	Rub with left hand	"
Middle of body	"	"	Pass left hand over it and rub	"
Back	"	"	Rub with left hand and tap with fist	"
Nates	"	"	"	"
Forehead	"	"	Kiss strongly	"
Chest	"	"	"	Kiss and pat
Eye	"	"	"	Do something that will make the eyes close rapidly
Hair	"	"	"	Pull gently

Table 3.9: The Manipulation of the Śaṅkhiṇī and Hastinī Type of Nāyikā

Member	*Tṛtiyā (3rd Day)*	*Saptamī (7th Day)*	*Ekādaśī (11th Day)*	*Trayodaśī (13th Day)*
Body generally	Twist it about	Embrace firmly	Clasp with force	"
Lower lip	Bite	"	"	"
Arm	?	"	"	"
Breasts	Scratch roughly till marks are left	"	"	Squeeze till she makes the sound of *śītkāra*
Belly	"	Scratch and press with nails	"	"
Chest	"	Press with nails and caress	"	"
Throat	"	Scratch and press with nails	"	"
Ear	"	Press with nails	"	"
Foot	"	Press so as to leave nail marks	"	"
Mouth or face	"	Kiss	"	"
Yoni	"	Apply *liṅga* with force	Apply *liṅga* as it were with a blow	"
Lip	"	"	Kiss and suck	"
Inch below head	"	"	"	Write upon it, as it were, with nails
Lower edge of *yoni*	?	"	"	"

Member	*Navamī (9th Day)*	*Caturdaśī (14th Day)*	*Pūrṇimā (Full Moon)*	*Amāvasyā (New Moon)*
Yoni	Thrust violently with *liṅga* or even rub hard with hand	Scratch press in member till her waist bends	"	Manipulate and pull open like a flower
Navel	Rub and frequently pass hand over	"	"	"
Lip	Kiss and suck	"	Kiss in various ways	Kiss in various ways
Side	Press with fingers and scratch very softly	"	"	"
Breast	Rub, squeeze, twist and make it very small	"	Pull hard	Scratch till it bears nail marks
Chest	"	"	Scratch and leave marks	Scratch and leave marks
Nipple	"	"	Kiss and rub with thumb and forefinger	Pass hand over it and rub with thumb and forefinger
Body generally	"	"	Embrace in various ways	Embrace in various ways and press
Eye	"	Kiss	Kiss	Kiss
Armpit	"	"	Scratch and tickle	Scratch and tickle

dramatic performance is to evoke sentiment or (*rasa*) in the mind of the *sahṛdaya* (learned audience) (Shridevi 2020: 31). According to the theory, the major purpose of dance, drama, ritual and poetry is catalytic in that aesthetic performance should provoke an emotion that is already present in members of the audience.

The word *rasa* is derived from the root *rasaḥ* meaning juice, taste or flavour or savour or relish. The extract of a fruit is referred to as *rasa*, which itself is the essence of it, the ultimate flavour of it. In a metaphorical sense, it refers to the emotional experience of beauty in poetry and drama. The goal and purpose of writing, presenting and viewing a play are to experience *rasa* realization. It is associated with palate and it is delight afforded by all forms of art; and the pleasure that people derive from their art experience. It is literally the activity of savouring an emotion in its full flavour.

Further, a member of the audience who has cultivated his or her own aesthetic response may experience a transformation of his own emotion into a purely aesthetic, transcendental feeling – an experience of divine bliss. This is the transformation of *bhāva* (mood) into its essence – *rasa*. According to Bharata, *rasa* is the mental condition of delectation produced in the spectator of a play or in the hearer or the reader of poem, as the inevitable reaction of the *bhāva* (emotions) manifested by the characters.

It has been found (ibid.: 32) that no one word or phrase is adequate to convey the total meaning of *rasa*. *Rasa* is the impression created in the mind of the sympathetic audience by the expression of *bhāva* and is an experience the individual is subjected to on account of this expression. *Bhāva* is the emotion that creates a sense of enjoyment or experience which is an entity and that enjoyment or experience is *rasa*.

Sage Bharata gives a detailed account of the eight different *rasas*, viz. Śṛṅgāra (erotic), Vīra (heroic), Karuṇa (pathetic), Hāsya (comic), Raudra (furious), Bhayānaka (terrible), Bībhatsa (odious) and Adbhuta (marvellous).

Bhāva, literally, means existence and mental state. In aesthetic contexts, it has been translated as feelings, psychological states and emotions. Bharata explains that there are three types of *bhāva*:

- *Sthāyī bhāva* (static emotions).
- *Sañcārī bhāva* or also called *vyabhicārī bhāva* (transitory emotions).
- *Sāttvika bhāva* (responsive emotions).

The static emotions are eight in number and they correspond to the eight sentiments and they are: *rati* (love), *hāsa* (mirth), *śoka* (grief), *krodha* (anger), *utsāha* (enthusiasm), *bhaya* (fear), *jugupsā* (aversion) and *vismaya* (wonder).

The transitory emotions are thirty-three in number. They are: *nirveda* (dejection), *glāni* (depression), *śaṅkā* (suspicion), *asūyā* (jealousy), *mada* (intoxication), *śrama* (weariness), *ālasya* (laziness), *dainya* (helplessness), *cintā* (anxiety), *moha* (passion), *smṛti* (recollection), *dhṛti* (boldness), *vrīḍā* (shame), *capalatā* (fickleness), *harṣya* (joy), *āvega* (agitation), *jaḍatā* (stupor), *garva* (arrogance), *viṣāda* (despair), *autsukya* (inquisitiveness), *nidrā* (sleep), *apasmāra* (epilepsy), *supta* (dream), *vibodha* (awakening), *amarṣa* (intolerance), *avahittham* (concealment), *ugratā* (ferocity), *mati* (knowledge), *vyādhi* (sickness), *unmāda* (insanity), *maraṇam* (death), *trāsa* (fright) and *vitarka* (doubt).

The responsive emotions are also eight. They are *stambha* (stunned), *sveda* (sweating), *romāñca* (thrill), *svarabheda* (break in voice), *vepathu* (trembling), *vaivarṇya* (pallor), *aśru* (tears) and *pralaya* (swoon).

The realization of *rasa* is said to result from the union of three interrelated elements – determinants (*vibhāva*), consequents (*anubhāva*) and complementary psychological states (*vyābhicārī bhāva*).

The root-cause or the excitant that creates the emotion is called *vibhāva* (determinant). So, *vibhāva* is the cause and *bhāva* is the effect. The voluntary expression following the emotions caused by the determinant is called *anubhāva* (consequent). *Vibhāva*, *anubhāva* and *bhāva* are thus intimately connected with one another.

Further, if *rasa* is the purpose of Sanskrit drama then the tool, which is utilized to bring about *rasa*, is *abhinaya* (acting). The word *abhinaya* means that which brings the thing to the spectator. There are four types of acting – *āṅgika* (physical), *vācika* (verbal), *sāttvika* (emotional) and *āhārya* (make-up and costumes or material).

Kāmaśāstra theory has used many terms and concepts from classical *rasa* theory described above.

Let us now examine the terms *rasa* and *bhāva* from Āyurveda perspective. Āyurveda uses the term *rasa* mainly in three ways. One, it demotes the tissue fluids (one of the seven tissues), the second in the sense of tastes (six types of sensory knowledge through taste buds and the trigeminal senses as well) and the third in the sense of mercury (or metal materials). We have already discussed the first two concepts in detail in the previous chapters.

The word *rasaśāstra* literally means the "Science of Mercury", which is a specialized branch of Āyurveda dealing mainly with materials which are known as *rasa dravya*. They have the following three characteristic attributes: instant effectiveness, requirement of very small doses and extensive therapeutic utility irrespective of constitutional variation.

Pharmacopoeia of Āyurveda comprises of drugs derived not only from herbs but also from minerals, metals and animal products (Savrikar et al. 2011). The therapeutic properties of plants, animal products and minerals were extensively described in Āyurveda. In therapeutics, emphasis was given on the use of medicinal plants, being more familiar and assimilable in the human body. Minerals were used, but their use was very much limited compared to the use of plants. Most of the times the minerals were used in combination with plants (herbo-mineral drugs) but use of independent mineral drugs was also not uncommon. The minerals were subjected to intensive processing for giving them a form of drug.

Nāgārjuna, the father of Rasaśāstra, is known for his extraordinary acumen in processing mercury with respect to its alchemic and therapeutic use. With the advent of mercury, a miracle substance in those days, a new class of drugs termed as *rasauṣadhi* with a new science termed as "Rasaśāstra" appeared on the horizon of Āyurveda system of medicine. Rasaśāstra can be defined as a science of study of mineral and metallic substances with respect to their therapeutic utility including processing of these substances to prepare a drug. In today's scientific parlance "Rasaśāstra" can be equated with "Iatrochemistry". Although Rasaśāstra deals with therapeutic processing and use of all minerals and metals, the study is dominated by knowledge about mercury and techniques of its processing. The science is named after mercury – *rasa* being a synonym of "mercury". Physicians using *rasauṣadhi* in the management of disease are known as *rasa-vaidya*. These professionals were supposed to be superior to their professional counterparts using surgical procedures and plants drugs for treating diseases.

Āyurveda uses the term *bhāvanā* in the sense of a typical pharmacological process. Grinding of the material, completely soaked in prescribed liquid media, till the liquid is completely evaporated and the material is dried, is termed as *bhāvana* (Savrikar et al. 2011: 76). Sometimes the material may be soaked and left for drying on its own without grinding. This basic raw material is subjected to wet grinding in the juices or decoctions of prescribed plant material. The wet grinding is stopped when the contents in the grinder are converted into dough. The dough is then cut into pellets of required size. The pellets are preferably air dried and then subjected to further processing of incineration.

There is one more dimension in Āyurveda about *rasāyana cikitsā*. It is considered as rejuvenation therapy (Gupta 2013: 1). The person, who gets treated according to the prescribed procedure, not merely enjoys long life in this world, but also after death enjoys the auspicious life of the *devas* and *ṛṣis*, and gets submerged in immutable cosmos. The term *ūrjā* is applied in the context of prolongation and promotion of life, augmentation of strength, energy, enthusiasm, etc. The substances or drugs, which are meant for longevity and enhanced efficiency of the immune system by fighting against all diseases or reducing the recurrences in episodic diseases, are known as *ūrjaskara* (*rasāyana* and *vājīkaraṇa*). It provides optimum quality of the body tissues due to which it provides both physical and mental health, prevents ageing and disease thus enables to live for a longer period of youthfulness and ensures the powerful physical stamina for copulation.

It is very fascinating to understand how Kāmaśāstra theory has deployed the concept of *rasa*, which is more inclined towards Āyurveda; however, the *bhāva* concept shows high parity with classical literature. Interestingly, Kāmaśāstra connects both these concepts tightly and connotes strong affiliation.

Rasa means interest and physical compellation towards the pleasure-generating activities. Basically, it amounts to arousing the desire and urge for physical pleasure. *Rasa* triggers physiological and physical responses that make sexual activity enjoyable and even possible. Medically, it triggers a release of oxytocin, dopamine and serotonin. This chemical cocktail lowers cortisol (stress hormone) levels and increases feelings of affection, bonding and euphoria. *Rasa* creation literally gets the juices flowing by increasing sexual arousal.

These arousal causes several physical responses in human body, including an increase in heart rate, pulse and blood pressure, dilation of blood vessels, including more blood flow to the genitals, which causes the labia, clitoris and penis to swell and even swelling of the breasts and erect nipples, lubricating of the vagina, which can make intercourse more enjoyable and prevent pains. This in a nutshell amounts to the erotic stimulation preceding intercourse.

Prima facie, one might relate this *rasa* concept to the contemporary term – sexual foreplay, which is widely used among society. However, Kāmaśāstra concept of *rasa* creation is much more than the mere sexual foreplay. It does have those essential ingredients to arouse desires (like foreplay), but it is more about slowly leading to building the emotional intimacy that can make *nāyikā* and *nāyaka* feel more connected to each other in and out of the bedroom. And that is the *bhāva* concept of Kāmaśāstra theory.

While *rasa* is focused more on the "individualism" and lays down foundation for arousal and compels towards efforts to fulfil self-desire; *bhāva* leads to the craving and strong attempts to get fulfilled from that particular person. Thus, *rasa* is more physical phenomenon and *bhāva* is more emotional and psychological aspect.

Kāmaśāstra proposes tight integration between *rasa* and *bhāva* to prepare for the *rati-anurāga* followed by *rati-rāga* creation. The *āsanādi vidhi* will ensure the last two creations. Kāmaśāstra believes in the scientific and systematic evolution of romantic feelings on moral grounds and then achievement of pleasure through numerous techniques.

Figure 3.9 explains the various elements in the *rasa* and *bhāva* model. There are five stages of achieving complete accomplishment as shown in *fig*. 3.9. Each stage has a well-defined objective and an expected outcome. Kāmaśāstra provides different techniques to achieve these outcomes and compliance on objectives. For example, the journey should start aiming at the fear removal and interest creation. The technique used for this is *ratāvasthāpana vidhi*. The output from this stage is *rasa* creation. This is very essential and foundation step for the accomplishment and immaculate pleasure experience in later stages. Below paragraphs explain the mechanics of each technique suggested by Kāmaśāstra.

3.7.1 RATĀVASTHĀPANA VIDHI

In this phase Kāmaśāstra recommends very interesting analysis and provides a step by step process to create *rasa*. The idea here is to create awareness in the mind of partners and also eliminate any distress. We have to understand here that all these techniques are

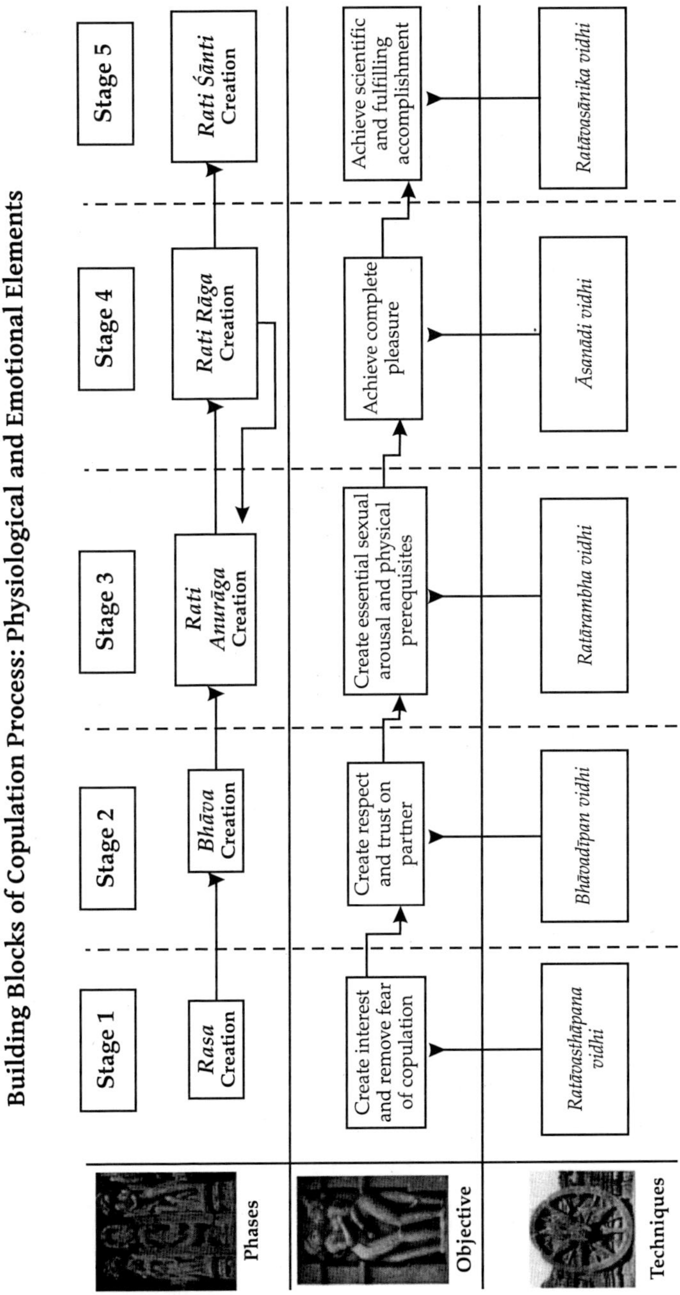

fig. 3.9: The Dynamics of Rasa and Bhāva Model

mainly suggested for married couple; however can be used in case of adultration and with prostitute.

Table 3.10 details the scope of techniques Kāmaśāstra suggests. Kāmaśāstra advocates differential approaches for creating interest within *nāyikā*. It suggests (Shastri 1992: 439; *KS* 3.3.32) the above-mentioned approaches should be deployed diligently with different aged *nāyikās* and ensure proper administration to create required *rasa*. It further suggests[3] touch technique to create a deeper feeling (ibid.: 444). The various ideas of showing erotic pictures has been suggested (ibid.: 444; *KS* 3.4.4). *Nāyaka* should trickily and meaningfully touch during water sports (ibid.: 445; *KS* 3.4.6).

Table 3.10: Rasa Creation Model

Sensing Medium	*Sensualizing Element*	*Techniques*
Eyes	Visualizing impacts	• Gestures and gift, showing erotics • Leave marks on body • Arousing dressing and costume
Nose	Fragrance impacts	• Togetherness • Usage of cologne and arousing scents
Tongue	Flavour impacts	• Aphrodisiac consumption • Betel recipe consumption
Body	Touching impacts	• Leaking • Eating • Bting • Kissing • Holding • Hugging
Ear	Conversational impact	• Direct romantic • Indirect and indicative

---

[3] द्यूते क्रीडेनेषु च विवदमानः साकारमस्याः पाणिमवलम्बेत (*dyūte krīḍeneṣu ca vivadamānaḥ sākāramasyāḥ pāṇimavalambeta*)। – *KS* 3.4.2

Primarily, *rasa* is created in significant amount by kissing and hugging. Kāmaśāstra suggests various ways and details of the same. Burton Richard has described (2009: 35) the same in very lucid words.

In the case of a young girl, the *nāyaka* should use three sort of kisses: the nominal, the throbbing and the touching kiss.

- When a girl only touches the mouth of her lover with her own, but does not herself do anything, it is called the "nominal kiss".
- When a girl, setting aside her bashfulness a little, wishes to touch the lip that is pressed into her mouth and with that object moves her lower lip, but not the upper one, it is called the "throbbing kiss".
- When a girl touches her lover's lip with her tongue and having shut her eyes, places her hands on those of her lover, it is called the "touching kiss".

Other authors describe four other kinds of kisses: the straight kiss, the bent kiss, the turned kiss, the pressed kiss.

- When the lips of two lovers are brought into direct contact with each other, it is called a "straight kiss".
- When the heads of two lovers are bent towards each other and when so bent kissing takes place, it is called a "bent kiss".
- When one of them turns up the face of the other by holding the head and chin and then kissing, it is called a "turned kiss".
- Lastly, when the lower lip is pressed with much force, it is called a "pressed kiss".
- There is also a fifth kind of kiss called the "greatly pressed kiss", which is effected by taking hold of the lower lip between two fingers and then after touching it with the tongue, pressing it with great force with the lip.

As regards kissing, a wager may be laid as to which will get hold of the lips of the other first. If the woman loses, she should pretend to cry, should keep her lover off by shaking her hands and turn away from him and dispute with him, saying "let another wager be laid". If she loses this a second time, she should appear doubly distressed and when her lover is off his guard or asleep, she should get hold of his lower lip and hold it in her teeth, so that it should not slip away and then she should laugh, make a loud noise, deride him, dance about and say whatever she likes in a joking way, moving her eyebrows and rolling her eyes.

When a man kisses the upper lip of a woman, while she in return kisses his lower lip, it is called the "kiss of the upper lip". When one of them takes both the lips of the other between his or her own, it is called "a clasping kiss". A woman, however, only takes this kind of kiss from a man who has no moustache. And on the occasion of this kiss, if one of them touches the teeth, the tongue and the palate of the other, with his or her tongue, it is called the "fighting of the tongue". In the same way, the pressing of the teeth of the one against the mouth of the other is to be practised.

Further, kissing can be classified in four kinds: moderate, contracted, pressed and soft, according to the different parts of the body which are kissed, for different kinds of kisses are appropriate for different parts of the body.

- When a woman looks at the face of her lover while he is asleep and kisses it to show her intention or desire, it is called a "kiss that kindles love".
- When a woman kisses her lover while he is engaged in business, or while he is quarrelling with her, or while he is looking at something else, so that his mind may be turned away, it is called a "kiss that turns away".
- When a lover coming home late at night kisses his beloved, who is asleep or in bed, in order to show her his desire, it is called a "kiss that awakens". On such an occasion the woman may pretend to be asleep at the time of her lover's arrival,

so that she may know his intention and obtain respect from him.

- When a person kisses the reflection of the person he loves in a mirror, in water, or on a wall, it is called a "kiss showing the intention".
- When a person kisses a child sitting on his lap, or a picture, or an image, or figure, in the presence of the person beloved by him, it is called a "transferred kiss".
- When at night at a theatre, or in an assembly of caste men, a man coming up to a woman kisses a finger of her hand if she be standing, or a toe of her foot if she be sitting, or when a woman is shampooing her lover's body, places her face on his thigh (as if she was sleepy) so as to inflame his passion and kisses his thigh or great toe, it is called a "demonstrative kiss".

We find similar discussions on the other techniques as well to create *rasa.*

3.7.2 BHĀVADĪPANA VIDHI

The key objective behind this action is to create a strong binding between partners and strong urge to get satisfied from each other, especially from the *nāyikā* standpoint.

Typically, Kāmaśāstra suggests two key processes, nail pressing and teeth biting for creating and enhancing *bhāva*. This leads to the better handling of the strong passion and creating immense trust on the partner as unique element of orgasm and pleasure patron. This creates a solid respect and enormous feelings about the partner.

Richard Burton has described (2009: 35) the detailed mechanics of the processes. Pressing with the nails is of the eight following kinds, according to the forms of the marks which are produced:

- When a person presses the chin, the breasts, the lower lip or the *jaghana* of another so softly that no scratch or mark is left, but only the hair on the body becomes erect from the touch of the nails and the nails themselves make a sound, it is called a "sounding or pressing with the nails". This pressing is used in the case of a young girl when her lover shampoos her, scratches her head and wants to trouble or frighten her.

- The curved mark with the nails, which is impressed on the neck and the breasts is called the "half-moon". When the half-moons are impressed opposite to each other, it is called a "circle". This mark with the nails is generally made on the navel, the small cavities about the buttocks and on the joints of the thigh.
- A mark in the form of a small line and which can be made on any part of the body, is called a "line".
- This same line, when it is curved and made on the breast, is called a "tiger's nail".
- When a curved mark is made on the breast by means of the five nails, it is called a "peacock's foot". This mark is made with the object of being praised, for it requires a great deal of skill to make it properly.
- When five marks with the nails are made close to one another near the nipple of the breast, it is called "the jump of a hare".
- A mark made on the breast or on the hips in the form of a leaf of the blue lotus, it is called the "leaf of a blue lotus".
- When a person is going on a journey and makes a mark on the thighs, or on the breast, it is called a "token of remembrance". On such an occasion three or four lines are impressed close to one another with the nails.

The places that are to be pressed with the nails are: the armpit, the breasts, the throat, the backside of the body, the lower belly area (lower abdomen), and the thighs.

All the places that can be kissed, are also the places that can be bitten, except the upper lip, the interior of the mouth and the eyes. The following are the different kinds of biting:

- The biting, which is shown only by the excessive redness of the skin that is bitten, is called the "hidden bite".
- When the skin is pressed down on both sides, it is called the "swollen bite".
- When a small portion of the skin is bitten with two teeth only, it is called the "point".
- When such small portions of the skin are bitten with all the teeth, it is called the "line of points".
- The biting which is done by bringing together the teeth and the lips, is called the "coral and the jewel". The lip is the coral and the teeth the jewel.
- When biting is done with all the teeth, it is called the "line of jewels".
- The biting, which consists of unequal risings in a circle and which comes from the space between the teeth, is called the "broken cloud". This is impressed on the breasts.
- The biting, which consists of many broad rows of marks near to one another and with red intervals, is called the "biting of a boar". This is impressed on the breasts and the shoulders; and these two last modes of biting are peculiar to persons of intense passion.

The lower lip is the place on which the "hidden bite", the "swollen bite" and the "point" are made; again the "swollen bite" and the "coral and the jewel" bite are done on the cheek. Both the "line of points" and the "line of jewels" are to be impressed on throat, armpit and joints of the thighs; but the "line of points" alone is to be impressed on the forehead and the thighs.

While explaining the dynamics of these actions, Kāmaśāstra advocates that when a man bites a woman forcibly, she should angrily do the same to him with double force. Thus a "point" should be returned with a "line of points," and a "line of points" with a "broken cloud," and if she be excessively chafed, she should at once begin a love quarrel with him. At such a time she should take hold of her lover by the hair and bend his head down and kiss his lower lip and then, being intoxicated with love, she should shut her eyes and bite him in various places. Even by day and in a place of public resort, when her lover shows her any mark that she may have inflicted on his body, she should smile at the sight of it and turning her face as if she were going to chide him, she should show him with an angry look the marks on her own body that have been made by him.

This technique of *bhāvadīpana vidhi*, wherein men and women act according to each other's liking, their love for each other will not be lessened even in one hundred years (Shastri 1992: 294; *KS* 2.5.43).

3.8 Āsanas (Postures)

As shown in *fig.* 3.12 this element of Aṣṭāṅga Kāmaśāstra includes primarily three processes: *ratārambha vidhi*, *āsanādi vidhi* and *ratāvasānika vidhi.*

3.8.1 RATĀRAMBHA VIDHI

This step is very important. Kāmaśāstra suggests a systematic way of creating conducive environment for copulation. Richard Burton (2009: 55) explained it.

In the pleasure-room, decorated with flowers and fragrant with perfumes, attended by his friends and servants, the citizen should receive the woman, who will come bathed and dressed, and will invite her to take refreshment and to drink freely. He should then seat her on his left side and holding her hair and touching also the end and knot of her garment, he should gently embrace her with his right arm. They should then carry on an amusing conversation on various subjects and may also talk suggestively of things which would be considered as coarse, or not to be mentioned generally in society. They may then sing, either with or without gesticulations and play on musical instruments, talk about the arts and persuade each other to drink. At last when the woman is overcome with love and desire, the citizen should dismiss the people that may be with him, giving them flowers, ointment and betel leaves, and then when the two are left alone, they should proceed.

These steps will ensure the necessary physical prerequisite of secretion from physiological standpoint eliminating the painful penetration and accelerated enjoyment. From process point view, it leads to *rati-anurāga* which is necessary before physical union.

3.8.2 ĀSANĀDI VIDHI

This is the main celebration the *nāyaka* and *nāyikā* do, and achieve the supreme pleasure what Kāmaśāstra defines as achieving *rati-rāga*. This process includes many sub-steps and not just the penetration. Kāmaśāstra suggests apt deployment of below techniques during this entire process:

- Striking
- Sound Making
- Pressing and penetration positioning
- Acting male role
- Oral sex

Kāmaśāstra deals with very detailed treatment on this subject and investigator has summarized the same below. Kāmaśāstra also takes care of specificity of the *nāyaka* and *nāyikā* physiology here.

Burton Richard (2009: 47) mentions that the place of striking with passion is the body and on the body the special places are shoulders, head, the space between the breasts, back, the *jaghana*, or middle part of the body and the sides.

The striking is of four types:

- Striking with the back of the hand
- Striking with the fingers a little contracted
- Striking with the fist
- Striking with the open palm of the hand.

On account of its causing pain, striking gives rise to the hissing sound, which is of the eight types:

- The sound *hin*
- The thundering sound
- The cooing sounds
- The weeping sounds
- The sound *phuṭ*
- The sound *phāṭ*
- The sound *sūṭ*
- The sound *plāṭ*

Besides these, there are also words having a meaning, such as "mother" and those that are expressive of prohibition, sufficiency, desire of liberation, pain or praise and to which may be added sounds like those of the dove, the cuckoo, the green pigeon, the parrot, the bee, the sparrow, the flamingo, the duck and the quail, which are all occasionally made use of.

For the occasion of a penetration position, Kāmaśāstra recommends (Richard 2009: 43) specifics. For example, the deer woman should lie down in such a way as to widen her vagina, while the elephant woman should lie down to contract hers. For an "equal congress" they should lie down in the natural position. Further, the deer woman has the following three ways of lying down:

- When she lowers her head and raises her middle parts, it is called the "widely opened position". At such a time the man should apply some unguent, to make the entrance easy.
- When she raises her thighs and keeps them wide apart and engages in congress, it is called the "yawning position".
- When she places her thighs with her legs doubled on them upon her sides and thus engages in congress, it is called the position of Indrāṇī and this is learnt only by practice.

The other positions are clasping position, pressing position, twining position, mare's position, rising position, pressed position, half-pressed position, splitting of a bamboo, fixing of a nail, crab's position, packed position, lotus-like position, turning position, supported congress, suspended congress, congress of a cow, united congress and congress of a herd of cows.

In the same way can be carried on the congress of a dog, the congress of a goat, the congress of a deer, the forcible mounting of an ass, the congress of a cat, the jump of a tiger, the pressing of an elephant, the rubbing of a boar and the mounting of a horse. And in all these cases the characteristics of these different animals should be manifested by acting like them.

The following kinds of congress, viz. sporting in water, or the congress of an elephant with many female elephants, which is said to take place only in the water, the congress of a collection of goats, the congress of a collection of deer, take place in imitation of these animals.

The concluding verse (Richard et al. 2009: 46) of Kāmaśāstra is very much clear on the overall outcome of the penetration process:

> An ingenious person should multiply the kinds of congress after the fashion of the different kinds of beasts and of birds. For these different kinds of congress, performed according to the usage of each country and the liking of everyone, generate love, friendship and respect in the hearts of women.

Kāmaśāstra further suggests the reverse role of women wherein she behaves like a man. While proving the reason behind this Kāmaśāstra mentions (ibid.: 49) – when a woman sees that her lover is fatigued by constant congress, without having his desire satisfied, she should, with his permission, lay him down upon his back and give him assistance by acting his part. She may also do this to satisfy the curiosity of her lover or her own desire of novelty.

There are two ways of doing this, the first is when during congress she turns round and gets on the top of her lover, in such a manner as to continue the congress, without obstructing the pleasure of it; and the other is when she acts the man's part from the beginning. At such a time, with flowers in her hair hanging loose and her smiles broken by hard breathings, she should press upon her lover's bosom with her own breasts and lowering her head frequently, should do in return the same actions which he used to do before, returning his blows and chaffing him, should say, "I was laid down by you and fatigued with hard congress, I shall now therefore lay you down in return". She should then again manifest her own bashfulness, her fatigue and her desire of stopping the congress. In this way she should do the work of a man, which we shall presently relate.

When a woman acts the part of a man, she has the following things to do in addition to the nine things normally man does:

- When the woman holds the penis in her vagina, draws it in, presses it and keeps it thus in her for a long time, it is called the "pair of tongs".
- When, while engaged in congress, she turns around like a wheel, it is called the "top".
- When, on such an occasion, the man lifts the middle part of his body and the woman turns around her middle part, it is called the "swing".

When the woman is tired, she should place her forehead on that of her lover and should thus take rest without disturbing the union of the organs and when the woman has rested herself the man should turn round and begin the congress again.

On this, Kāmaśāstra concludes (Richards et al. 2009: 52) with a verse saying:

> Though a woman is reserved and keeps her feelings concealed, yet when she gets on the top of a man, she then shows all her love and desire. A man should gather from the actions of the woman of what disposition she is and in what way she likes to be enjoyed. A woman during her monthly courses, a woman who has been lately confined and a fat woman should not be made to act the part of a man.

Kāmaśāstra has a specific view about oral congress. It is

recommended primarily for the eunuchs. These eunuchs derive their imaginable pleasure and their livelihood from this kind of congress and they lead the life of courtesans (Richards et al. 2009: 52). There are two kinds of eunuchs, those that are disguised as males and those that are disguised as females. Eunuchs disguised as females imitate their dress, speech, gestures, tenderness, timidity, simplicity, softness and bashfulness.

A few Kāmaśāstra authors suggest (ibid.: 54) that the *auparișṭaka* (oral congress) is practised only by unchaste and wanton women, female attendants and serving maids, i.e. those who are not married to anybody, but who live by shampooing. But the *Kāmasūtra* author says that the law prohibits this practice with married women only.

While mentioning the vogue practices, Kāmaśāstra says – the male servants of some men carry on the mouth congress with their masters. It is also practised by some citizens, who know each other well, among themselves. Some women of the harem, when they are amorous, do the acts of the mouth on the vagina of one another and some men do the same thing with women. The way of doing this should be known from kissing the mouth. When a man and woman lie down in an inverted order, i.e. with the head of the one towards the feet of the other and carry on this congress, it is called the "congress of a crow".

The mouth congress should never be done by a learned brāhmaṇa, by a minister that carries on the business of a state or by a man of good reputation, because though the practice is allowed by the law, there is no reason why it should be carried on and need only be practised in particular cases.

Kāmaśāstra describes six different types of *rati-rāga* that can be achieved based on the relationship dimensions between the *nāyaka* and *nāyikā*. We could see the different mental status of the *nāyaka* and *nāyikā* considered here (Richard et al. 2009: 377). Table 3.11 explains these configurations.

Table 3.11: Types of Rati Rāga and Recommended Steps from Rasa-Bhāva Model

Rati Rāga Type	*Relationship Dimension between Nāyaka and Nāyikā*	*Prescription for Rati Rāga Creation*
Rāgavat (Natural)	Mostly legal and moral	Follow four-stage process and automatically achieve pleasure
Āhārya Rāga (Developed)	Mostly legal and moral Partners have learned Kāmaśāstra techniques	Adopt 64 arts and follow four-stage process to achieve pleasure
Kṛtrima Rāga (Artificial)	Both love someone else but come together for a purpose	Try following four-stage process to achieve pleasure
Vyavahita Rāga (Moral equivalence)	Both dream their own different lovers and wish to be extend adultery relationship sincerely	Follow four-stage process and achieve pleasure
Potārata Rāga (Sensuality driven)	The *nāyaka* establishes relationship with low-grade *nāyikā* with compelling urge	Can skip stages 1 and 2 and directly follow stages 3 and 4
Khalarata Rāga (Unjustified and maniac driven)	This happens when an earnest relationship developed between a couple, which is a socially unaccepted partnership. For example, a serious relationship between a Prostitute and her Rural *nāyaka*, or a prostitute with her *nāgaraka* customer or a *nāgaraka* with a socially high grade *nāyikā*.	No recommendations from Kāmaśāstra
Ayantritaratam	Due to constant interactions, trust and suitability, opportunistic relationship gets established between the *nāyaka* and *nāyikā*	No recommendations from Kāmaśāstra

We could judge here that very matured, scientifc and value-based recommendations are described in Kāmaśāstra.

3.8.3 RATĀVASĀNIKA VIDHI

After multiple rounds of unions and complete pleasure, the *nāyaka* and *nāyikā* should progress for complete accomplishment and peaceful fulfilment and the end of copulation leading to *rati śānti*.

Kāmaśāstra describes the scientific ending – At the end of the congress, the lovers with modesty and not looking at each other, should go separately to the washing room (Richard et al. 2009: 56). After this, sitting in their own places, they should eat some betel leaves and the citizen should apply with his own hand to the body of the woman some pure sandalwood ointment or ointment of some other kind. He should then embrace her with his left arm and with agreeable words should cause her to drink from a cup held in his own hand or he may give her water to drink. They can then eat sweetmeats, or anything else, according to their likings and may drink fresh juice, soup, gruel, extracts of meat, sherbet, the juice of mango fruits, the extract of the juice of the citron tree mixed with sugar, or anything that may be liked in different countries and known to be sweet, soft and pure. The lovers may also sit on the terrace of the palace or house and enjoy the moonlight and carry on an agreeable conversation. At this time, too, while the woman lies in his lap, with her face towards the moon, the citizen should show her the different planets, the morning star, the polar star and the seven R̥ṣis or Great Bear.

3.9 Bhojya

We see very evidently Kāmaśāstra advocates the food consumption rules as per Āyurveda. These aspects are already discussed in the earlier chapter.

Kāmaśāstra suggests wife should be like *āhārvaidyā*. She should take care (Shastri 1992: 474, *KS* 4.1.10) of her husband by providing him food with healthy and medicinal elements. Food has very significant role in providing necessary strength to partners for copulation. Primarily, the term food is used here inclusive of diet, medicines (including applications) and aphrodisiac recipes along with liquor and betel leaves recipes. Moreover, Kāmaśāstra also recommends the timing, quality, quantity and even the arrangement of food for consumption.

Burton Richard (2009: 124) explains lucidly the Kāmaśāstra recommendations for aphrodisiac recipes.

- An ointment made of the *Tabernaemontana coronaria*, the *Costus speciosus* or *arabicus* and the *Flacourtia cataphracta* can be used as an unguent of adornment.
- If a fine powder is made of the above plants and applied to the wick of a lamp, which is made to burn with the oil of blue vitriol, the black pigment or lamp black produced therefrom, when applied to the eyelashes, has the effect of making a person look lovely.
- The oil of the hog weed, the *Echites putescens*, the *sarina* plant, the yellow amaranth and the leaf of the nymphae, if applied to the body, has the same effect.
- A black pigment from the same plants produces a similar effect.
- By eating the powder of the *Nelumbrium speciosum*, the blue lotus and the *Mesna roxburghii*, with ghee and honey, a man becomes lovely in the eyes of others.
- The above things, together with the *Tabernaemontana coronaria* and the *Xanthochymus pictorius*, if used as an ointment, produce the same results.
- If the bone of a peacock or of a hyena be covered with gold and tied on the right hand, it makes a man lovely in the eyes of other people.
- In the same way, if a bead, made of the seed of the jujube, or of the conch shell, be enchanted by the incantations mentioned in the Āyurveda, or by the incantations of those well skilled in the science of magic and tied on the hand, it produces the same result as described above.

Additionally, Kāmaśāstra recommends that when a female attendant arrives at the age of puberty, her master should keep her secluded and when men ardently desire her on account of her seclusion and on account of the difficulty of approaching her, he should then bestow her hand on such a person as may endow her with wealth and happiness.

Kāmaśāstra suggests a specific medicinal consumption and application (Richard et al. 2009: 126). Different ways described by Kāmaśāstra for subjugating a partner are:

- If a man, after anointing his penis with a mixture of the powders of the white thorn apple, the long pepper and the black pepper and honey, engages in sexual union with a woman, he makes her subject to his will.
- The application of a mixture of the leaf of the plant *vatodbhrānta*, of the flowers thrown on a human corpse when carried out to be burnt and the powder of the bones of the peacock and of the *jivāñjivā* bird, produces the same effect.
- The remains of a kite who has died a natural death, ground into powder and mixed with honey give the same effect.
- Anointing oneself with an ointment made of the plant *Emblic myrobalan* has the power of subjecting women to one's will.
- If a man cuts into small pieces the sprouts of the *vajñāsunhi* plant and dips them into a mixture of red arsenic and sulphur, and then dries them seven times and applies this powder mixed with honey to his penis, he can subjugate a woman to his will directly that he has had sexual union with her, or, if, by burning these very sprouts at night and looking at the smoke, he sees a golden moon behind, he will then be successful with any woman; or if he throws some of the powder of these same sprouts mixed with the excrement of a monkey upon a maiden, she will not be given in marriage to anybody else.
- If pieces of the *arris* root are dressed with the oil of the mango and placed for six months in a hole made in the trunk of the *śisū* tree and are then taken out and made up into an ointment

and applied to the penis, this is said to serve as the means of subjugating women.

- If the bone of a camel is dipped into the juice of the plant *Eclipta prostata* and then burnt and the black pigment produced from its ashes is placed in a box also made of the bone of a camel and applied together with antimony to the eyelashes with a pencil also made of the bone of a camel, then that pigment is said to be very pure and wholesome for the eyes and serves as a means of subjugating others to the person who uses it. The same effect can be produced by black pigment made of the bones of hawks, vultures and peacocks.

Kāmaśāstra fuṛther suggests aphrodisiac recipes and its consumption for increasing the sexual vigour their as follows:

- A man obtains sexual vigour by drinking milk mixed with sugar, the root of the *ucchāta* plant, the piper chaba and liquorice.
- Drinking milk mixed with sugar and having the testicle of a ram or a goat boiled in it is also productive of vigour.
- The drinking of the juice of the *Hedysarum gangeticum*, the *kuili* and the *kṣīrikā* plant mixed with milk produces the same effect.
- The seed of the long pepper along with the seeds of the *Sanseviera roxburghiana* and the *Hedysarum gangeticum* plant, all pounded together and mixed with milk is productive of a similar result.
- If a man pounds the seeds or roots of the *Trapa bispinosa*, the *kasurikā*, the *Tuscan jasmine* and liquorice, together with the *kṣīrākapoli* (a kind of onion) and puts the powder into milk mixed with sugar and ghee, and having boiled the whole mixture on a moderate fire, drinks the paste so formed, he will be able to enjoy innumerable women.
- In the same way, if a man mixes rice with the eggs of the sparrow and having boiled this in milk, adds to it ghee and

honey, and drinks as much of it as necessary, this will produce the same effect.

- If a man takes the outer covering of sesamum seeds and soaks them with the eggs of sparrows and then, having boiled them in milk, mixed with sugar and ghee, along with the fruits of the *Trapa bispinosa* and the *kasurikā* plant and adding to it the flour of wheat and beans, and then drinks this composition, he is said to be able to enjoy many women.
- If ghee, honey, sugar and liquorice in equal quantities, the juice of the fennel plant and milk are mixed together, this nectar-like composition is said to be holy and provocative of sexual vigour, a preservative of life and sweet to the taste.
- The drinking of a paste composed of the *Asparagus racemosus*, the *śvādāustra* plant, the *guḍucī* plant, the long pepper and liquorice, boiled in milk, honey and ghee, in the spring, is said to have the same effect as the above.
- Boiling the *Asparagus racemosus* and the *śvādāustra* plant, along with the pounded fruits of the *Premna spinosa* in water and drinking the same, is said to act in the same way.
- Drinking boiled ghee or clarified butter in the morning during the spring season is said to be beneficial to health and strength, and agreeable to the taste.
- If the powder of the seed of the *śvādāustra* plant and the flower of barley are mixed together in equal parts and a portion of it, i.e. two *palāśa* in weight, is eaten every morning on getting up, it has the same effect as the preceding recipe.

As a conclusive remark, Kāmaśāstra cautions to use all these techniques diligently and by a learned and skilled person.

3.10 Upakaraṇa

Kāmaśāstra has presented a very interesting topic and framework of usages of artificial sexual instruments. It not only deals with the usage but also about it design, fabrication and maintenance.

The *Nāyaka*, when finds difficult to satisfy his *nāyikā* due to many reasons including the size of the penis, can use artificial instruments to ensure the process compliance as per the *rasa-bhāva* model discussed earlier.

The *Nāyaka* makes use of certain *apadravya*, or things which are put on or around the penis to supplement its length or its thickness, to fit it to the vagina. These instruments should be made of gold, silver, copper, iron, ivory, buffalo's horn, various kinds of wood, tin or lead and should be soft, cool, provocative of sexual vigour and well fitted to serve the intended purpose. The *Kāmasūtra* specifically says that they may be made according to the natural liking of everyone (Richard 2009: 128).

The following are the different kinds of instruments:

- "The armlet" should be of the same size as the penis and should have its outer surface made rough with globules.
- "The couple" is formed of two armlets.
- "The bracelet" is made by joining three or more armlets, until they come up to the required length of the penis.
- "The single bracelet" is formed by wrapping a single wire around the penis, according to its dimensions.
- The *kantuka* or *jālaka* is a tube open at both ends, with a hole through it, outwardly rough and studded with soft globules and made to fit the side of the vagina and tied to the waist.
- When such a thing cannot be obtained, then a tube made of the wood apple, or tubular stalk of the bottle gourd, or a reed made soft with oil and extracts of plants and tied to the waist with strings, may be made use of, as also a row of soft pieces of wood tied together.

The above instruments can be used in connection with or in the place of the penis.

Kāmaśāstra further describes (Richard 2009: 129) about the perforation of penis. Some *nāyakas* think that true sexual pleasure cannot be obtained without perforating the penis and hence they pierce it like the lobes of the ears of an infant pierced for earrings.

Kāmaśāstra advises the systematic process for the same. The *nāyaka* should perforate his penis and pierce it with a sharp instrument and then stand in water so long as the blood continues to flow. At night he should engage in sexual intercourse, even with vigour, to clean the hole. After this he should continue to wash the hole with decoctions and increase the size by putting into it small pieces of cane and the *Wrightia antidysenterica*, and thus gradually enlarging the orifice. It may also be washed with liquorice mixed with honey and the size of the hole increased by the fruit stalks of the *simā-patrā* plant. The hole should be anointed with a small quantity of oil.

In the hole made in the penis, *nāyaka* may put instruments of various forms, such as "round", "round on one side", "wooden mortar", "flower", "armlet", "bone of heron", "goad of elephant", "collection of eight balls", "lock of hair", "place where four roads meet" and other things named according to their forms and means of using them. All these instruments should be rough on the outside according to their requirements.

Appendix 6 lists the technical glossary terms used in Kāmaśāstra especially in Aṣṭāṅga Kāmaśāstra context.

4

Prospects of Kāmaśāstra

4.1 Introduction

WE HAVE seen in the earlier chapters the growth and further decline of the Kāmaśāstra concept. In the previous chapter we have seen the Aṣṭāṅga Kāmaśāstra and its technical analysis. In this chapter we are looking into current plight of Kāmaśāstra and its potential applications vis-à-vis the modern trends in eugenics, sex psychology, social behavioural sciences and medical sciences including Āyurveda. I have tried in this chapter to spell out exactly which are the areas where we can learn from Kāmaśāstra to refine our present Āyurveda positioning and regard Kāmaśāstra as a special branch of Āyurveda dealing with eugenics for better future.

The course of action consists of the following steps:

1. Designing the thematic questionnaire, and collection of data and response from information sources like professional universities, Āyurveda practitioners, Sanskrit scholars, Internet content and other relevant entities.
2. Analysis of data collected in the form of feedback from above-mentioned sources and estimation of the degree of understanding of Kāmaśāstra concept.
3. Exploring the areas of prospective learning, where the

timeless principles of Kāmaśāstra are described with their present and modern relevance.

4. Finally, the summary and conclusions are presented.

4.2 Data Collection and Analysis

Efforts are made here to present collected opinions and views of authorities in educating bodies, government institutions, autonomous bodies and Āyurveda practitioners. About fourteen Sanskrit scholars, more than thirty sex consultants or institutions across the globe, more than twenty Āyurveda practitioners, faculties of major Āyurveda colleges and more than 200 people from society have been contacted for this data collection. This data has been collected in a questionnaire format and validated before drawing any inferences. Most of the time, the Internet technology has been used to accelerate the data collection process. The format of the questionnaire is provided in Appendix 1.

In the data collection phase, basically, attempts were made to gauge the Kāmaśāstra-related subject knowledge of the respondent and its source. The Āyurveda practitioners, without interest and knowledge of Kāmaśāstra, have been eliminated. The choices for the source of Kāmaśāstra knowledge were given like formal or informal education, or experience, or by intuition. Most of the respondents replied that the source of Kāmaśāstra knowledge as informal education through books, research papers and through experience, a very few said through formal education and very less from intuition. To substantiate the statistical significance, a rough-cut questionnaire reliability analysis is carried out; however, no questions have been eliminated due to lack of lower Cronbach alpha value. The primal argument here is to less applicability of true validation in case of the social science domain; moreover, in the virgin area of Kāmaśāstra and Āyurveda influence.

Regarding the opinions about prospects of Kāmaśāstra, a few hints were given like availability of authentic Kāmaśāstra literature and its modern interpretation, case studies known, awareness in society and trend, situation and approach of sex consultants, art community (cinemas, Internet content), role of government, academic institutes, consumer protection act and Āyurveda practitioners, etc. While answering this question 60 per cent of the respondents replied positively about Kāmaśāstra. Most of the Āyurveda practitioners had shown their concerns about Kāmaśāstra, mainly because of the "sex commercials" involved and a few others had shown their incompetence to comment just because they did not have sufficient knowledge regarding the subject. Most of the Sanskrit scholars hardly knew about the scientific Kāmaśāstra concept and its close connection with Āyurveda; though they view Kāmaśāstra more as a part of the classical Sanskrit literature and are neutral about the prospective use of Kāmaśāstra. One of the sex consultants supplied valuable information about the Kāmaśāstra considerations of the aphrodisiac recipe. He reported his view as most of the patients do ask for the similar tonics and there is a huge potential for research and untapped business value. This was not yet completely licence-controlled and many illegal recipes are recommended and supplied. The hard-core scientific diagnosis is many a time missing. Many sex consultants refused initially even to respond but later after being convinced about the approach they showed slight interest. But most of them answered vaguely and concentrated on the basic Āyurveda aspects leaving the concept of therapeutic romance.

It is found from the data that the term Kāmaśāstra is being used loosely even by Sanskrit scholars, the sex consultants, governments, universities, colleges, Āyurveda practitioners, art fraternity and in general by the entire society including foreign residents. Sometimes, it is used to denote the text of sexual postures, or sometimes used in the similar sense of ancient Indian pornography. We also find confusion around Kāmaśāstra and the *Kāmasūtra* or total interchangeability of each other. Many people attached to the subject are not aware of distinctions between *śāstra*, *vidyā* and *kalā*, and hence a lot of conceptual errors are floating around

Kāmaśāstra. This unfortunate ignorance is prevailing all over basically due to the lack of initiative evinced by society, educating bodies, governments and Sanskrit scholars. We can see that most of PhD or postdoctoral researches in Sanskrit are typically related either to poetic literature or Vedānta. A few deals with grammar as a science and hardly anything in connection with areas associated with *śāstra*. This aversion about Sanskrit literature other than poetics is aggravating the contemporary pathetic plight of Sanskrit language towards *śāstra*.

Today, the Kāmaśāstra concept is receiving keen attention from all strata of society including professional sex consultants, foreign academic world, common man, etc. and we find the following myths in the society:

- There is one prescription, philosophy or text called Kāmaśāstra.
- Kāmaśāstra is the *Kāmasūtra*.
- Kāmaśāstra is pornography.
- Kāmaśāstra only deals with the technique of copulation gymnastics (only about the sexual positions and postures).
- Kāmaśāstra was relevant in the ancient India, but now it has become an outdated concept.
- Kāmaśāstra is basically relevant to the sex psychology.
- Kāmaśāstra is not a science, but an unexplained religious text that deals as an intercourse guide.
- Kāmaśāstra has one branch, called Yoga Kāmaśāstra.
- Kāmaśāstra deals with physical and sensual phenomenon especially without any legal/moral qualification of partners.
- Kāmaśāstra if used will shower pleasure and satisfaction; in short, Kāmaśāstra is a panacea to all sexual problems.
- There is nothing in Kāmaśāstra, it is only a way to cheat people.

We can thus see the width of misunderstanding regarding

this science ranging from black magic to total omnipotence. The scenario can be narrated metaphorically "water, water everywhere and no water to drink" and can be summarized into:

1. Original texts written in Sanskrit are not easily understood.
2. Even all the Sanskrit texts are not available with apt translation.
3. Most of the works that are available in English are in discrete and history form.
4. No integral work linking all texts, clearly stating all principles, scientific notions, experimentation and practising hints, i.e. in the form of handbook, is readily available.
5. Most of the present-day sexual therapies (by Āyurveda practitioners) are done with the scant regards to Kāmaśāstra, due to many reasons including no formal inclusion of Kāmaśāstra in Āyurveda curriculum.
6. On one side we see abundance of newly written non-research commercial (NRC) literature, which is revolving around sexual positioning aspects, whereas modern academician's view is against Kāmaśāstra disparaging it as not being in the purview of science.
7. Total ignorance regarding the well-developed social and behavioural science dealing with the anatomy of males and females, scientific routine management compliant with Āyurveda, guidelines on maintaining body hygiene, caring body organs, apt consumption of food and its quality, the regional significance on human behaviour and pleasure preferences, deep views and analysis on sex psychology, *rasa-bhāva* model, permitted prostitution and guidelines, sexual power increase techniques, usage of instruments and medicines, overall guidelines for successful and fruitful married life, cognizance of sexual crimes erupted out of starvation or aberrant tendencies, lawful design of practical

behavioural prescriptions including deviations from idealism, and most important is the integration of Āyurveda principles in recommendations.

8. Āyurveda practitioners, sex consultants and overall society are not getting the due benefit of our ancient knowledge and wisdom presented in Kāmaśāstra, which may have potential to reduce social, family related and health problems in this country.
9. No special efforts observed yet have been made to explore the strength, relevance and prospects of Kāmaśāstra in contemporary and future lifestyles of the society.

It is interesting to note the coherence of the above findings with the observations made by V.K. Hampiholi about two decades ago. Unfortunately, it means the perception about Kāmaśāstra in contemporary Indian society has not much changed from what we could note from below ones compiled by Hampiholi (1988: 1-57):

- Sex is an instinct; it should not be taught.
- Sex is against *dharma.*
- Sex is obscene.
- Sex-sport is a heinous act.
- Sex is an enemy.
- Unfavourable attitude towards women.

4.3 Internet and Entertainment Content and NRC Literature

Television, films and print media play a vital role on society's perceptions and awareness about any topic. We find today more than 200 Internet websites in the world talking of Kāmaśāstra as term and phrase, and branded mostly near to the pornography. Interestingly, Wikipedia expresses[1] the right fact of the *Kāmasūtra* like:

---

[1] https://en.wikipedia.org/wiki/Kama_Sutra

> The *Kāmasūtra* is neither exclusively nor predominantly a sex manual on sex positions, but written as a guide to the art of living well, the nature of love, finding a life partner, maintaining one's love life and other aspects pertaining to pleasure-oriented faculties of human life. Indira Kapoor, a director of the International Planned Parenthood Foundation, states that the *Kāmasūtra* is a treatise on human sexual behaviour and an ancient attempt to seriously study sexuality among other things. According to Kapoor, quotes Jyoti Puri, the attitude of contemporary Indians is markedly different, with misconceptions and expressions of embarrassment, rather than curiosity and pride, when faced with texts such as the *Kāmasūtra* and amorous and erotic arts found in Hindu temples. The *Kāmasūtra*, states Kapoor, must be viewed to discover and improve the "self-confidence and understanding of their bodies and feelings.

Although the difference between Kāmaśāstra and the *Kāmasūtra* is not discussed even in Wikipedia. There are more than four full commercial English movies on the subject and many YouTube video contents are available. However, nothing is strictly based on Kāmaśāstra but just the superficial theme has been used for commercial entertainment purposes.

4.4 Trends in Academia

In precise and short words, we can say that no formal and certified education on Kāmaśāstra is available across any global institutes or universities. Unfortunately, no subject or a course is available on Kāmaśāstra in any degree or similar programme including basic Sanskrit courses. Regrettably, the Indian Faculties of Sanskrit Education is completely indifferent on the scenario.

The situation with Āyurveda is better compared to Kāmaśāstra. As already discussed in Chapter 1, cancer therapy is the latest interest in Āyurveda studies these days. There are many avenues of Āyurveda still to be explored by the researchers, practitioners and experts in the field to contribute towards global human health and overall social development in the future. However, we still find adverse situation even with Āyurveda like:[2]

> The rift between the Indian Medical Association (IMA) and the Ayush Ministry has intensified. IMA is against the government's decision to allow the Āyurveda doctors to perform medical surgery. In the latest statement, IMA has termed the government's decision to allow Āyurveda doctors to perform surgery "Khichdification of medical education". The medical body went on to say that the entire medical profession feels betrayed. The IMA has stated that government's clarification is a deceptive camouflage and has called it a blatant attempt at mixopathy. It further said that we are prepared for ensuing long drawn struggle and has demanded the withdrawal of government notification.

While the government is trying to promote Āyurveda, it resulted in a very high degree of agitation in the Indian allopathy fraternity.

Āyurveda has the ability (Chauhan et al. 2015) to treat many chronic diseases such as cancer, diabetes, arthritis and asthma, which are untreatable or difficult to treat even in modern medicine. Unfortunately, due to lack of scientific validation in various concepts, this precious gift from our ancestors is trailing. Hence, evidence-based research is highly needed for global recognition and acceptance of Āyurveda, which needs further advancements in the research methodology. The different avenues of Āyurveda including literary, fundamental, drug, pharmaceutical and clinical research are much essential to regain the coveted glamour back to this ancient Indian medical science. I feel the same approach must be adopted to improve the Kāmaśāstra positioning among the social science and medical faculties with main emphasis on the fundamental research and application areas.

---

2 https://www.timesnownews.com/videos/mirror-now/society/ima-condemns-ayush-ministrys-move-demands-withdrawal-of-government-notification/81985

4.5 Prospect of Kāmaśāstra

Kāmaśāstra identifies its root in the *Ṛgveda* as does Āyurveda. Thus, the key theme of Vedic philosophy is percolated in Kāmaśāstra naturally like in Āyurveda. Interestingly, the *Ṛgveda* describes *Urvaśī* mentioning about the inconsistent and vulnerable tendency in women. Kāmaśāstra acknowledges the same and provides the ethical and romantic framework of behaviour for a *nāyaka*, which not only alleviates the agony due to the natural women tendency but its scientific reduction or elimination as well. The courage to embrace the worldly (physical) truth alongside the non-tangible timeless human values is the essence of most of the Indian philosophical systems. Kāmaśāstra is not an exception. It provides the fundamental hypothesis that the physical pleasure is the essential ingredient of human fulfilment, however, the journey should be aimed at psychological in the broad sense, wherein the mental evolution should be the final objective, which leads to the liberalization. Kāmaśāstra should be positioned as the specialized extension of Indian Medical Systems, the Āyurveda. It specializes in Āyurveda driven therapeutical approach for treating the disorders classified into sex psychology, behavioural science, and related physiology. The key aspects Kāmaśāstra deals with are, the specialized therapy of romance (not just sex), copulation techniques for pleasure and fertilization with high probability, remedies on sex psychological related diseases, and ensures the mental health of individuals and society.

I strongly recommend that Kāmaśāstra should be considered as an extension of Āyurveda texts dealing specifically on sex psychology and behavioural therapy and can be considered as Āyurvedic branch of eugenics and therapeutic romance. Any medical science provides two basic approaches of counselling for the therapy: behavioural and psychodynamic. Kāmaśāstra should be considered as the Āyurveda's methodology for the behavioural counselling. In earlier chapters, we have seen the strong interdisciplinary approach both these sciences reflect from their prime texts. For example, the minute details Kāmaśāstra talks about ensuring the adherence to the etiquette of food consumption and behavioural habits are the part of the role of a wife. Those prescriptions are Āyurveda-compliant routine and form the premise of first objective, that is to retain health.

Kāmaśāstra strongly prohibits multiple relationships and strictly recommends the *rasa-bhāva* model-based marriages to ensure the harmony and continuity in connubial relationships with strong trust. It also addressed the scenarios of polygamy and prostitution. The concept of prostitution reflected in Kāmaśāstra is unlike the contemporary one. Today's prostitution is more as business (or industry) focusing on creating the so-called happiness by way of male ejaculation wherein services are paid off. Kāmaśāstra, while recognizing the need of the prostitution, provides a respectable structure and basic rights to the prostitutes of selecting her *nāẏaka*. It suggests the guideline of qualifying and accepting based on the current well-being and future of herself and not just business for money. I have already proved the maturity Kāmaśāstra expects in this unsolicited topic, which has huge social and health-related implications. In fact, we have already discussed that a few prostitutes are like *kāma-vaidyā*.

Lastly, Kāmaśāstra looks at *saṁbhoga* as *yoga* (art and science) and not less than that.

Thus, Kāmaśāstra should not be considered as a handbook describing the pleasure ideas; but Āyurveda-compliant rule book which details the techniques and taboos for sustainability of healthy and ethical pleasure maximization for well-defined *nāyaka* and *nāyikā*.

In this regard, it is worthwhile to note the findings on the future of Indian sexuality (Chakraborty and Guha Thakurata 2013). The famous Indian sensuality quoted incessantly in the world, mentioning Tāntric lifestyles, the *Kāmasūtra* and erotic arts will change the face of the world again in coming decades when Indian people find themselves again. A cross-section of Indian people who are adjusted in the less dogmatic and prosperous Western societies and their behavioural patterns and views reflect that a healthier sexual approach to our lives is eventually healthier for our well-being, our overall progress and of course a new awakening on personal level. The newer generations of India and Indian people worldwide have been trying to define the sexual and sensual vocabulary on their own rather than being influenced by external and foreign influences. In fact, it is a healthier approach and eventually when Indian people in India in one or two decades – when they become all formally educated and emancipated socially and have rather more space and time at their discretion will find that an open dialogue about sex matters is normal and acceptable. We should start talking about issues and focus light on dark areas, which create ignorance, ill-health and many social evils like failed marriages, rapes, divorces, disrespect for women, abuse of children and in general an unhappy people.

We could see the clarity in the Kāmaśāstra potential to address contemporary social issues like gender-based violence, sexual molestations, rape, gang-rape, sexual abuse and early/child marriage, deaths in love sports. Kāmaśāstra is a strong weapon in war against all these socio-psycho challenges and in creating awareness against it. In fact, the research clearly articulated the value of Kāmaśāstra and Āyurveda in handling chronic and difficult psychological disorders related to the sexuality in adolescence and young adulthood, homosexual and ambisexual behaviours, repressed sexuality, prostitution and pornography. Further, it has provided with the concept note on the sexuality influencing disease process and healing. Āyurveda's virility therapy, coupled with Kāmaśāstra's *rasa-bhāva* model, will be of immense potential and unique Indian therapeutic approach to all these diseases.

Moreover, Kāmaśāstra is readily linkable to the Indian philosophy and is well connected to the Hindu rituals and festivities like *garbhādhāna* and Vasanta celebration. The rightly designed social and educational programme based on Kāmaśāstra principles will easily prove its value in creating social awareness and adoption of the best sex and romance practices among the entire strata of society.

Very interestingly, we find eye-opening discussions and remarks from a recent thesis on the topic from the Kolkata region. It says (Dey 2015: 25):

> According to UNESCO, absence of proper sexuality education makes the young people potentially vulnerable to coercion, abuse and exploitation, unintended pregnancy and sexually transmitted infections (STIs), including HIV. Research shows that sexuality education programmes can help adolescents to abstain from or delay the debut of sexual relations; reduce the frequency of unprotected sexual activity; reduce the number of sexual partners and increase the use of protection against unintended pregnancy and STIs during sexual intercourse. UNESCO also affirms that school settings provide an important opportunity to reach large numbers of young people with sexuality education before they become sexually active. United Nations International Children's Emergency Fund's (UNICEF) reported in 2011 that adolescents constitute a very critical category in the global effort to eradicate poverty and inequality. As such promoting young people's sexual and reproductive health, including the provision of sexuality education in schools, is a key strategy towards achieving the Millennium Development Goals (MDGs), especially MDG 3 – achieving gender equality and empowerment of women, MDG 5 – reducing maternal mortality and achieving universal access to 1 Frontline, reproductive health and MDG 6 – combating HIV/AIDs. In 2003, United Nations Committee on the Rights of the Child also declared that international human rights standards recognize that adolescents have the right to access adequate information essential for their health and development and for their ability to participate meaningfully in society. Thus, sexuality education is not only a necessity, but it has also been

> recognized as a right of the adolescents and young people to be conferred by state. The global HIV epidemic has increased the necessity of sexuality education because it was realized that, in order to address HIV which is largely sexually transmitted, a better understanding of gender and sexuality is needed. In the context of the recent Delhi gang rape case, the Justice Verma Committee recommended (within Education and Perception Reforms) that sexuality education needs to be imparted because it will assist "young people in their physical, social, emotional and moral development as they prepare for adulthood, marriage, parenthood and ageing, as well as their social relationships in the context of family and society". It also stated, "appropriate education on sexuality is an important issue that parents and teachers must acknowledge and address if they want to make sure that their children are well adjusted and safe and will grow up to be mature and balanced individuals".

The above idea of sex education should be designed specifically for Indian society keeping Kāmaśāstra principles as the central theme. The significance of this recommendation can be judged by the below research conclusions drawn from different parts of the country and unique remedy Kāmaśāstra can bring in for the problems (Dey 2015: 378):

- Only 30 per cent of the schools practised high level of intervention so far as the adolescents' issues are concerned.
- Only a moderate section of parents and teachers reiterated that sexuality education has an integrated and holistic approach towards the development of the adolescents.
- It is found that higher percentages of parent-respondents avoided intimate topics involving human sexuality and sensitive issues.
- It is found that romantically involved female adolescents are found to suffer from mental stress; anxiety, guilt and depression than their sexually active male counterparts; male adolescents cherished their sexuality whereas the

female adolescents felt inhibited in expressing sexual desire or passion. As a result, girls directed their guilt though self-inflicted pain whereas boys sexually gratified them though watching pornography or practising self-pleasure.

- Further 67 per cent female adolescents are less likely to explore media and Internet for information. Whereas 55 per cent of the adolescents accessing media and Internet for information are male.
- Male adolescents also emerge as significant viewers of pornography and sexually explicit content given that the media market is mostly driven by the need to titillate male sexuality through various imagery of the female body and sexuality.

We have discussed above the prospect of Kāmaśāstra in addressing health, medical and social related issues. Moreover, I strongly recommend deploying Kāmaśāstra knowledge for the Sciemantic (Scientific and Romantic) Tourism.

I strongly propose that the educating bodies, especially sex education initiatives, should be designed using Kāmaśāstra theme to run the courses. These courses should be based on the scientific theory and visits to different monuments like Khajurāho to provide practical knowledge. The temples of Khajurāho were built in tenth century CE. These temples are famous for their erotic art. However, these temples also contain tremendous and marvellous sculptures of musical instruments. In walls of Khajurāho temples various musical instruments are depicted. Epigraphical sources (Varma and Dubey 2018) have great contribution in the reconstruction of history of Indian music. A course on Kāmaśāstra can be designed in multiple modules – starting with the classroom teaching on basic sex education, followed by visit to Khajurāho, wherein participants can enjoy and learn a music-oriented romantic module, followed by systematic tour on erotic sculptures, with audio–video aids and documentaries or films. This will certainly create necessary positivity about the romantic feeling and understanding of the truth – love between man and woman is a natural phenomenon; this is a specialty for the human beings unlike other species.

The appreciation of Indian architectural values along with Kāmaśāstra education should be the awareness and training theme for the common Indians. It will also help in preserving and increasing consciousness of ancient structures. We find today our great temples are becoming either as commercial places or picnic spots. No importance is being given to the architecture point of view. Unfortunately, no formal educating system today exists which has taken such initiatives for creating awareness and scientifically inculcating the sex education among visitors. Such things will help in preservations of the ancient monuments and go a long way in improving the taste, likings and maturity of the people on sexuality.

5

Summary and Conclusions

In this chapter, attempts are made to analyse the learning experience, which came through the research work. We will see here the presentation of the outcomes of the research arranged into a concise and summarized format.

5.1 Summary

Every culture and civilization of the world has its own history, especially related to various sciences prevailed in that civilization. The scope and applications of these sciences may range from pure sciences like physics, chemistry or mathematics and also spread in the integrated form of pure science applications like cosmology and philosophy, geology and geography, astrology and astronomy, psychology and sexology, algebra and geometry, ergonomics and ecology, mechanical and civil engineering, as well as biology and medical sciences. We could clearly mark the existence and prevalence of these sciences in Indian, Chinese and Greek cultures. India may be one of the few unique countries, where she has her own traditional science of sexology and social behaviour, which can be referred to as Kāmaśāstra. Also, it is the general acceptance among the scholars that Āyurveda is the oldest known medical science prevailed in the world. We could find many such unique features of Indian sciences.

Āyurveda can be regarded as the oldest treatise on medicine in the world. It is India's traditional, natural system of medicine that has been practised for more than 5,000 years. Āyurveda can be literally translated as the "science of life" or "practices of longevity". It clearly states that the mental and physical health depend on each other. The symptoms and diseases that could be categorized as mental thoughts or feelings are just as important as symptoms and diseases of the physical body. Both are due to imbalances within a person and both are treated by restoring the natural balance mentally and physically. Interestingly, Kāmaśāstra talks about the mind management and social behavioural aspects of human beings with special reference to sexology. It corresponds with the third human goal, viz. *kāma*. The key theme behind Kāmaśāstra is to guide and provide with prescriptions for the happy and sustained married life.

The present research is an attempt to discover the common understanding between Kāmaśāstra and Āyurveda. The main purpose is to analyse how Kāmaśāstra has adopted the key Āyurveda principles in its own theory. Efforts are made to explain the complete Kāmaśāstra theory based on Āyurveda.

Although many scholars have already put their efforts on the Āyurveda or Kāmaśāstra, we find untouched and ignored aspects in the literature especially related to interrelationships between these two sciences. We find that, so far, no scholar has defined precisely the theme and details adopted by Kāmaśāstra based on Āyurveda principles. There is no clue on demarcation, interdependence and independence of these sciences in existing literature. We will not see any relational study between Kāmaśāstra and Āyurveda. This lacuna has crept even in the works of modern scholars.

I have attempted exploring those interesting areas that link the confluence between these two sciences. A few examples are: human anatomy of Āyurveda and physical description of males and females appearing in Kāmaśāstra, Āyurveda outlook on *āsana* prescribed by Kāmaśāstra, importance of human character and philosophical approach assumed in both sciences, conceptual parity between the *dinacaryā* and *ṛtucaryā* prescribed by Vāgbhaṭa's *Aṣṭāṅga Hṛdayam* and the *dinacaryā* and *rātricaryā* described by Kāmaśāstra. Thus, the present research is aimed at filing these gaps in literature and presented the outcomes in three different categories:

- Analysing the Kāmaśāstra and Āyurveda theory.
- Exploring the areas of Āyurveda influence on Kāmaśāstra.
- Reinterpreting the Kāmaśāstra theory.

Attempts are made to review available and popular literature on the subject. The key idea here is to come up with the basic understanding of these sciences and their detailed application domains based on various treatises. Since Kāmaśāstra-based descriptions are available in many classical Sanskrit literature, attempts are made to review the same along with direct Kāmaśāstra literature. The following objectives are set:

- To review and analyse the conceptual origination and later evolution of Kāmaśāstra and Āyurveda basically using subject literature.
- To trace relevant references of Kāmaśāstra in classical Sanskrit literature.
- To come up with the key understanding of the subject matter, i.e. Kāmaśāstra and Āyurveda.
- To identify Āyurveda impact on each aspect of Kāmaśāstra.
- To explain the variations and deviations between the prescriptions provided by these two sciences.
- To classify the influence of Āyurveda on Kāmaśāstra in various areas to investigate if Kāmaśāstra is an applied science of Āyurveda.
- To develop a comprehensive framework for Kāmaśāstra based on analysis of various Kāmaśāstra treatises. This

yielded into theorizing all Kāmaśāstra aspects into a skeleton which contains all Kāmaśāstra *aṅgas* and provides a detailed reasoning of each Kāmaśāstra prescription based on Āyurveda.

- To develop a technical glossary of Kāmaśāstra with Āyurveda reference.

Thus, the primary objective of the research is to decipher the concepts, notions, scientific outlook and practising philosophy reflected from Kāmaśāstra treatises and to explain it in the Āyurveda context.

I have dealt with numerous research questions and aspects of influential validity of Āyurveda on Kāmaśāstra in my endeavour. We clearly see the originator of Āyurveda and Kāmaśāstra is the same, i.e. Brahmā. It has been further analysed how Āyurveda can be seen influencing Kāmaśāstra on four aspects, viz. structural influence on Kāmaśāstra texts, conceptual influence on the Kāmaśāstra theory, prescriptive influence on Kāmaśāstra practices and symbolic influence on Kāmaśāstra models. Below hypotheses are tested here to investigate the Āyurveda influence.

- Kāmaśāstra has used similar sequence of chapetrization theme as that of Āyurveda texts.
- Kāmaśāstra has adopted similar style of narration as observed typically and in general in Āyurveda texts.
- Kāmaśāstra has deployed Āyurveda terms and direct examples from Āyurveda texts thus leading to Āyurveda influence.
- *Concept of Homeostasis* (*Balance and Imbalance*): Āyurveda theory believes in a perfect balance between the natural elements and the *tridoṣa* to maintain a healthy state of living by following the principles of divine wisdom. Kāmaśāstra adopts the same concept of balance for the healthy state of mind and sustainable connubial relationships.

- *Concept of Anatomy*: Kāmaśāstra has adopted Āyurveda anatomy as the base for the classifications of male and female.
- Conceptual Elements in Therapy (*Sātmya Vicāra*): Āyurveda advocates to examine the constitution, morbidity, proportion of the elements, compactness and measurement as the key considerations before any therapy. Kāmaśāstra has adopted the same concept in its theory of pleasure maximization.
- Kāmaśāstra has adopted Āyurveda-compliant day and night routine.
- Kāmaśāstra has adopted methods of *āsana* based on the Āyurveda theory of prescribed behaviour and motions.
- Kāmaśāstra has prescribed the usage of the similar medicinal plants and materials as Āyurveda mentions for sexual power development.
- Kāmaśāstra has adopted Āyurveda coherent ideas of maintaining body hygiene, caring body organs and consumption of food and its quality.
- The regional significance on human behaviour and pleasure preference described in Kāmaśāstra is based on the regional considerations of the Āyurveda theory.
- There is a symbolic parity between Āyurveda model of patient, doctor, messenger and medicine and Kāmaśāstra model of male, female, messenger and pleasure techniques.
- Auspicious elements and description in Kāmaśāstra is in line with Āyurveda recommendations.

The author has adopted a structured methodology for this project. This included the following methods for data collection and analysis:

- Literature survey keeping research objectives in mind.
- Development of detailed research framework.
- Critical literature review keeping research questions in mind.

- Site visits.
- Interviews with field scholars.
- Theorizing the finding.

Initially, the project was started from surveying various popular and available literatures on the subject. This included various treatises, research papers, research articles and subject texts.

I had visited a few sites, which are significant from research standpoint. The list includes Khajurāho, the Sun Temple at Koṇārk and the Śrī Cennakeśava Svāmī Temple at Belūr (built by Vatsal dynasty in Karnataka). The key purpose of site visit was to discover the clues from erotic architecture of these temples that may support or contradict the theoretical views gathered from literature. This analysis was very important to understand the Kāmaśāstra concepts, especially those regarding the descriptions of various postures (*āsanas*) appearing in Kāmaśāstra and its depiction in architecture. These endeavours opened new dimensions of investigation within the research scope that led to enrich the overall research conclusions.

Further, interviews and discussions were conducted with renowned subject scholars. This helped in the validation of theory that was used to build the project outcome.

The thesis has been divided into four chapters, viz.:

1. Introduction,
2. Areas of Āyurveda Influence on Kāmaśāstra,
3. Reinterpreting the Kāmaśāstra Theory: Aṣṭāṅga Kāmaśāstra Concept, and
4. The Prospects of Kāmaśāstra.

The first chapter briefs about the Āyurveda as an ancient Indian medical science and Kāmaśāstra as a social behavioural science.

Āyurveda emphasizes prevention of disease, rejuvenation of

body systems and extension of lifespan. The profound premise and promise of Āyurveda is that through certain practices, not only can human prevent diseases but can also better understand self and the world, and live a long healthy life in balance and harmony, achieving fullest potential and express true inner nature on a daily basis. Lifestyle interventions are considered as the major preventive and natural therapeutic approach.

Vāgbhaṭa's *Aṣṭāṅga Hṛdayam* provides with a comprehensive overview of eight branches of Āyurveda touching all aspects of diagnosis, symptoms and therapy for a patient and a healthy person. It details the history of Āyurveda, its fundamental principles, human anatomy, hygiene, materia medica, therapeutics, diseases, diagnostic approach, surgery and surgical diseases, *pañca-karma*, paediatrics, etc. Vāgbhaṭa's *Aṣṭāṅga Hṛdayam* used as a basic literature source for this project.

The second chapter deals with the heart of the research, i.e. Āyurveda influence on Kāmaśāstra. It is indeed very interesting to study the interdisciplinary learning and relationships across these two sciences. The discussions highlight the positioning of Kāmaśāstra literature in overall Hindu value system and aiming at helping humans achieve *kāma* through satisfaction (management) of mind. On the similar line, we find Āyurveda advocates the balance of mind and body to manage diseases. In fact, Vāgbhaṭa's *Aṣṭāṅga Hṛdayam* categorically mentions the adoption of Kāmaśāstra principles along with Āyurveda prescriptions for better achieving *kāma*. Various hypotheses mentioned above are discussed in this chapter. It concludes with the premise that Kāmaśāstra describes the process and Āyurveda provides the reasoning behind prescription mentioned in Kāmaśāstra.

The third chapter deals with the unique outcome as the concept of Aṣṭāṅga Kāmasāstra, which can be regarded as the logical mechanism to comprehend the whole idea of Kāmaśāstra, which was evolved and culminated in our country. These elements (*aṅgas*) of Kāmaśāstra are the necessary and sufficient aspects of Kāmaśāstra to understand its scope and application. We can see that Āyurveda has direct relationships with these *aṅgas* on the conceptual levels, and the physiological and psychological levels. Their nomenclature and coverage are presented in the chapter.

The Concept of Aṣṭāṅga Kāmaśāstra: Kāmaśāstra has the following eight elements:

- *Nāyakas* (*Male*): Here various characteristics of the males are discussed including their classification based on physical attributes and skills. It further discusses aspects of horoscope, caste, education, skills, behaviour, character and their impact on males' overall performance of satisfaction creation.
- *Nāyikās* (*Female*): This aspect of Aṣṭāṅga Kāmaśāstra describes female types based on physical attributes, skills, relationship with males and even profession. The topic further discusses the role and responsibilities of females in their satisfaction creation.
- *Vāstu* (*Venue*): Right from the theory of hygiene for copulation up to the selection of a proper place, interior, designer furniture, various utility arrangements, etc. are discussed here.
- *Kāmadeva* (*Rituals*): This aspect of Aṣṭāṅga Kāmaśāstra supplies details on all types of required rituals like various sacrifices, *homa*, *yāga*, *śānti*, chanting, etc. which are performed by a *nāyaka* to yield progeny, prosperity, protection and happiness from the divinity of Kāmadeva.
- *Rasa and Bhāva* (*Morale and Feeling*): This aspect of Aṣṭāṅga Kāmaśāstra determines the rules of morale, taboos, best and preferred match of *nāyaka* and *nāyikā*, impacts of the external factors on the mind orientation of both – male and female. It discusses the significance of the right copulation mood and energy on progeny and pleasure.

- *Aāsana (Posture)*: Here we find the best possible body postures for the highest probability of conceiving and pleasure simultaneously. It describes the recommended positions and their benefits.
- *Bhojya (Consumption Rules)*: This deals with the different ingredients including food and medicinal materials that the *nāyaka* and *nāyikā* should consume for better performance. It also deals with the regular and typical process of consumption leading to desired effects. The term consumption is used in its wider meaning. It suggests the acceptance of tangibles or non-tangibles by body across senses including oral consumption (using different methods), application of medicines on body parts, inhalation of spray, consumption via viewing of different colour schemes and even listening to music. The ultimate impact of *bhojya* is seen in creation of the right mood and feelings.
- *Upakaraṇa (Instruments)*: This aspect of Aṣṭāṅga Kāmaśāstra suggests the usage of different instruments made from select materials that are used during copulation. It further discusses the fabrication of these instruments and most important is their regular maintenance.

Aṣṭāṅga Kāmaśāstra deals in detail with all the aspects of Kāmaśāstra, to name a few, male–female matching, emphasis on sanitation, sacrament and symbolization, morale and feelings, various types of body positions, consumption of food and medicinal ingredients, space, furniture and overall ambience, application and necessary hygiene of artificial instruments, etc.

I have proved here that anything related to Kāmaśāstra will be covered fewer than one of the issues of these elements. Further, this logic can be used to treat or rectify any imbalance or abnormality in the combinatory behavioural pattern of the *nāyaka*, *nāyikā* and other related aspects.

Chapter 4 deals with the prospect of Kāmaśāstra and its

contemporary relevance. Kāmaśāstra evolved over thousands of years and culminated as a full-fledged science of sexology and served as a unique solution for social and behavioural needs and problems. The uniqueness of Kāmaśāstra can be seen from its supreme creativity in recommendations on copulation, depth and width of a thought process, practical applications and highly human-centric relevance. Āyurveda has a significant influence on Kāmaśāstra and the key recommendations of Kāmaśāstra can be explained on **Āyurveda principles.** The interdisciplinary learning approach can be easily observed when both these sciences are compared. The chapter concludes that Kāmaśāstra should be seen as an extension of Āyurveda dealing specifically on sex psychology and behavioural therapy, and can be considered as **Āyurvedic branch of eugenics.** Apart from its social and therapeutic relevance, Kāmaśāstra should be used to design the innovative socially accepted sex education programme in schools and in general for public.

5.2 Limitations and Future Scope of the Research

A research study is always subjected to some limitations. It cannot be an error-free engagement especially when the topic is related to a social science and not a pure physical science. Since Kāmaśāstra deals with living entities and actual realities and situations which cannot always be manipulated as per the need of the study.

The limitations of the present study mostly arise from the peculiar nature of its subject matter and the resultant contradictions and ambiguities within the texts, reflections from the sculptures and opinions of field scholars. I have attempted to counter this by way of relying on the main Kāmaśāstra text, i.e. the *Kāmasūtra*. Thus, one of the main limitations of the study is that it failed validating the minute differences of prescriptions between all the other Kāmaśāstra texts like the *Rati Rahasya*, *Anaṅga Raṅga* and *Nāgarasarvasva* among others. Same thing goes with Āyurveda literature, where I have largely relied on Vāgbhaṭa's *Aṣṭāṅga Hṛdayam* assuming its virtue of concise nature.

I had faced terrible issues to take appointments, understand and later validate the findings from field scholars, especially Āyurveda practitioners and sex consultants due to their busy schedules and priorities. However, I have ensured the validations of findings from two Āyurveda practitioners. Many field scholars were reluctant to discuss because of the peculiar sensitivity attached with topic of sexuality and due to its chances of leading to controversies and misunderstandings. Similarly, many subjects, especially married couples, refused sharing their sexual experiences because either they are afraid or uncomfortable even after promising to maintain anonymity and assurance of academic usage of information. However, such conversations helped me to come up with strong Kāmaśāstra recommendations based on the firsthand experience.

Since most of the discussions are largely based on *Kāmasūtra* and Vāgbhaṭa's *Aṣṭāṅga Hṛdayam*, it may not be representative of Kāmaśāstra or Āyurveda respectively; hence the findings of the study cannot be generalized. However, it could remain relevant at broad therapeutic and sociocultural context with a significant conceptual theme.

One more limitation of the study that it has ignored is the conflicting prescriptions of Āyurveda and Kāmaśāstra. For example, a mix of ghee and milk is not recommended by Āyurveda, while Kāmaśāstra recommends the same. Although such observations are handful, a detailed analysis is not carried out.

Similarly, a few Kāmaśāstra prescriptions which have no mention in Āyurveda are ignored. For example, Kāmaśāstra recommends many techniques of mesmerism, on which Āyurveda is silent. I have mentioned those recommendations under Aṣṭāṅga Kāmaśāstra framework, however, I have not investigated its validity from the Āyurveda standpoint.

Finally, the major limitation might be, due to the lack of comprehensive knowledge of Āyurveda (the author being a graduate engineer with an Āyurveda certification), many mistakes might have happened in over or under interpretations and even ignorance of significant facts.

I believe that these limitations are the motivational elements for further researches. There is a lot of scope for further researches in this domain, based on the above-mentioned limitations.

Moreover, this study itself can be extended to include the married couples from the different parts of the country as key respondents and conduct exploration on their connubial relationships. This research can be planned to include Kāmaśāstra-based systematic diagnosis of various variables like anatomy, stress level, dissatisfaction and habits to validate on Āyurveda principles and evaluate the remedial fitness of the Aṣṭāṅga Kāmaśāstra framework. The outcome can be either in the form of root cause analytics of social mishaps including divorces, rapes, sexual crimes, human trafficking, gender violence, etc. An interesting element can be to experiment these issues with Āyurveda and Kāmaśāstra prescriptions with full rigour of clinical testing. Such successful experimentations will add immense value to the society and mankind in general.

The present research can be further used to design the generalized sex education course and academic programme for adolescents, women and young people within a specific regional and social set-up.

One more interesting area for further research is to analyse the medicinal plants and recipes described by Kāmaśāstra from the Āyurveda perspective. A focused research can be conducted to enlist all such prescriptions and identify the therapeutic significance on Āyurveda yardsticks. This will also help Āyurveda for cross learning from Kāmaśāstra.

5.3 Recommendations

In order to receive advantages from the Kāmaśāstra theory for the contemporary society, some recommendations are made below:

- The word *kāmaśāstra* must be used strictly in its pure and traditional sense – the social and behavioural science specific to sex psychology.
- The sexual diseases from Āyurveda therapy should be treated according to Kāmaśāstra or using its key principles.
- A new postgraduate level specialization course based on Kāmaśāstra dealing with sex psychology, which infuses Āyurveda principles, should be designed and taught in universities and colleges.
- Minimum two subjects completely based on Kāmaśāstra should be designed and included in the present syllabus of university level BAMS course and minimum one subject in the syllabus of MA psychology course. For availability of the necessary reference and reading materials on the subjects, government or autonomous institutions should release the funds for the printing of the appropriate Kāmaśāstra texts.
- In this regard, the responsibility of the field scholars is not only to teach Kāmaśāstra, but also to design the research programme that will unearth the strengths of classical Kāmaśāstra theory vis-à-vis the advantages of modern-day medicine and psychology education.
- A separate course on the Sciemantic (Scientific and Romantic) Tourism based on the theoretical sex education with practical appreciation of Kāmaśāstra sculptures and architecture for the common Indians should be run across the country. Such education will help the society know about the rich and scientific tradition of Indian eugenics and even the architectural skills to create a general awareness about the conservation of the monumental structures.
- Āyurveda companies, universities, sex consulting firms, Āyurveda practitioners should promote jointly, various research projects for students focusing on specific areas of

Kāmaśāstra. The objective should be to explore Kāmaśāstra applications in modern perspectives.

- Married couples should thoroughly analyse and use the knowledge, techniques and the rules of Kāmaśāstra for their sustainable and fulfilling married life.
- The thesis appeals to appreciate the Kāmaśāstra concept on the scientific Āyurveda grounds, especially to the modern societal elements – fresh Āyurveda practitioners and sex psychologists, youth and married couples.

5.4 Benefits of the Research

The benefits of this research are very much towards the personal knowledge gain and to the literature on Kāmaśāstra. The concept of Aṣṭāṅga Kāmaśāstra is developed first time to understand the Kāmaśāstra theory completely and easily. The attempts to explore the contemporary relevance and usage of Kāmaśāstra are also registered first time in the literatures published so far. The set of recommendations prescribed above promotes the practical and scientific applications of the Kāmaśāstra theory, validated on Āyurveda framework, that if followed, will enable the society improve the existing quality of life.

The thesis concludes with the hope that Kāmaśāstra is not to be seen as some sexual and mystic texts or even as an outdated concept. We can make its optimum use today as well as tomorrow if we could interpret and follow it properly. The thesis shows efforts, which are made to decode the scientific, aesthetic and symbolic propositions from Kāmaśāstra, based on Āyurveda and their presentation in the form of contemporary language of medical practitioners, sex psychologists and the overall learned society.

5.5 Conclusions

Kāmaśāstra evolved over thousands of years and culminated as a full-fledged science of sexology and served as a unique solution for social and behavioural needs and problems. The uniqueness

Table 5.1: Confluence between Āyurveda and Kāmaśāstra

	Āyurveda	*Kāmaśāstra*
Driving concept	*Tridoṣa* (three constituents)	*Puruṣārtha triṇī* (three life objectives)
Focuses on	*Svastha* and *Ātura* (healthy and patient)	*Nāyaka*, *nāyikā*, society (for patient and impatient)
Treatment	*Svasthya vṛtta* (best habitual routine) and medicine	*Nāgaraka-vṛtta* (best physio-Social-psycho routine) and restricted fleshly behaviour
Therapeutic approach	Aṣṭāṅga Āyurveda model with *Trisūtrī*	Aṣṭāṅga Kāmaśāstra model with therapeutic romance (developed in the research)
Ensures	Physical and mental health	Pleasure and positivity about life

of Kāmaśāstra can be seen from its supreme creativity in recommendations on copulation psychology, depth and width of thought process, practical applications and highly human-centric relevance. The same is based on the scientific grounds infused with sensuality, sexuality, morality, aesthetics and spirituality.

Āyurveda has a significant influence on Kāmaśāstra and the key recommendations of Kāmaśāstra can be explained on Āyurveda principles. The interdisciplinary learning approach can be easily observed when both these sciences are compared. I have proved many areas of confluence between these two sciences in the present research. A brief summarized view is presented in Table 5.1.

Like all other Indian sciences, both these disciplines must have synergistically evolved and Kāmaśāstra be an extension of Āyurveda dealing specifically on sex psychology and behavioural therapy, and can be considered as an Āyurvedic branch of eugenics.

Appendices

Appendix 1

Questionnaire

From: Rahul V. Altekar
20, Indraprasad Chs, Near Teachers' Colony
Bandra (East), Mumbai – 400 051
Phone: 9820053144

Dear Sir or Madam,

About Me

I am first class graduate engineer with postgraduate MBA qualification, working as Management Consultant in leading Indian industries and institutions.

I have completed MA (Sanskrit) and PhD in Vāstuśāstra. Currently, I am pursuing my second PhD in Āyurveda's influence on *Kāmaśāstra* from University of Mumbai. I have already worked on this subject for the last couple of years.

About Subject

Today we find various opinions on *Kāmaśāstra* prevailing in our society. Unfortunately, many are not aware of original Sanskrit literature, manuscripts, even translations in regional languages, and erotic sculptures & structures at various sites in India. The reasons may be lack of initiative by society, educating bodies and government. The subject is seen only in the sexual positioning or (less than) pornography point of view. We ignore the well-developed science dealing with physical anatomy, sociology, behavioural aspects, psychology, emotional models, hygiene and best practices, instruments, medications, and therapeutic approach.

The research objective is to determine the strength, relevance and prospects of *Kāmaśāstra*. In this connection one step is to measure the awareness of the subject in the society.

Your Help

Please fill up the the form attached herewith. You are requested to express frank and true opinions. This data is to be used for determining prospects of *Kāmaśāstra* in near future.

PROSPECTS OF KĀMAŚĀSTRA

FORM NO.: SAMPLE PROGRAM = 1A
PAGE NO.: 1
SITE:

---

1. CATEGORY CODE: [ ]

Academician – Private Educating Body – **A**; Academician – Government Institution – **B**; Āyurveda Practitioner – **C**; Sex & Psychologist Consultant – **D**; Sanskrit Scholar – **E**; Citizen - **F.**

2. STATUS: [ ]

REFERENCE ALLOWED – **Y**; NOT ALLOWED – **N**

("N" means your opinions will be used for analysis, but name will not be referred in thesis.)

NAME:
ADDRESS:
CONTACT:

A. SUBJECT KNOWLEDGE: [ ]

GOOD – **G**; AWARE – **W**; NIL – **L**

Please narrate briefly what you think important features of *Kāmaśāstra.*

QUERY? - RAHUL V. ALTEKAR, 20, INDRAPRASAD, BANDRA(E), M-51, PHONE: 9820053144

PROSPECTS OF KĀMAŚĀSTRA

FORM NO.: SAMPLE PROGRAM = 1A
PAGE NO.: 2
SITE:

B. SOURCE OF KNOWLEDGE: [ ]

FORMAL/INFORMALEDUCATION–**E**,EXPERIENCE–**X**,INTUITION–**I.**
Please narrate briefly about source of knowledge.

Please mention your opinions about prospects of *Kāmaśāstra.* You may use points like availability of authentic literature, case studies known, awareness in society and trend, role of sex consultants, Āyurveda Practitioners, Government & Private Academic Institutes, Internet & Pornography & *Kāmaśāstra/ Kāmasūtra* content available, *Kāmaśāstra* reflected from Art & Films, Consumer Protection Acts and Sex Consultants, recommendations.

QUERY? – RAHUL V. ALTEKAR, 20, INDRAPRASAD, BANDRA(E), M-51, PHONE: 9820053144

Appendix 2

Kokkoka's Literature Survey on Kāmaśāstra

KOKKOKA, the author of the *Rati Rahasya*, gratefully acknowledges the heavy debt he owes to his learned predecessors who contributed to the Kāmaśāstra literature. He provides an actual reference to their names and often to their works. He claims to place before his readers the quintessence or all the writings on the subject that had preceded him.

Kokkoka has used the generic term *muni* (sage) in referring to some of his predecessors. We must rely on the commentator Kāñcīnātha to identify these sages (Upadhyaya 1965: 1). There are nine such references, of which four are not identified even by Kāñcīnātha and the fifth is rather uncertainly mentioned.

The authors and their works referred to by Kokkoka, with their respective identities, are as follows:

Name of Sage	*Reference in Rati Rahasya*
Nandikeśvara	1.9, 2.5
Goṇikaputra	1.9, 2.5
Munīndra	6.8, 6.11, 8.4
Munibhiḥ	10.29
Karṇīsuta	4.21
Mūladeva	5.22
Guṇapātaka	4.3, 7, 25
Vātsyāyana	1.9, 3.17, 11.18-19, 22
Muni	10.13-14
Nāgārjuna	15.118

Cont.

Cont.

Name of Sage	*Reference in Rati Rahasya*
Śabdārṇava	14.1
Haramekhalā	14.1, 41
Uddiśa	14.1
Yogāvalī	14.1
Munayaḥ	10.26, 14.39

Appendix 3

Selected Plates of Kāmaśāstra-Related Sculptures from Site Surveys

Āsanādi Vidhi: Sculptures from Khajurāho

Pl. 1

Pl. 2

Pl. 3

Pl. 4

Pl. 5

Rasa-Bhāva: Sculptures from Khajurāho

Pl. 6

Pl. 7

Nāyaka and Nāyikā: Sculptures from Khajurāho

Pl. 8

Pl. 9

Appendix 4

Selected Celebration Moments of Kāmadeva Festival

1. Selected moments (*Pls* 1 to 4) are from "The Khajurāho Dance Festival", organized by the Department of Culture, Government of Madhya Pradesh. *Source*: https://chhatarpur.nic.in/en/gallery/khaiuraho-festival/

Pl. 1: Welcome Congression

Pl. 2: Dancers performing (Scene 1)

Pl. 3: Dancer performing (Scene 2)

Pl. 4: Dancers performing (Scene 3)

2. Poorotsavam, a unique nine-day festival of Kerala's North Malabar region, is being celebrated to invoke the blessings of Kāmadeva by young girls. During this festival several Devī temples dotted in the region would host cultural activities. The annual festival that is celebrated from Kārttika star till Pooram star of the Malayalam month Mīnam is being celebrated to rekindle the prayers of Deva-Kanyā to Lord Śiva for the rebirth of Kāmadeva. During the festival, young girls will decorate their houses with particular flowers to seek blessings of Kāmadeva to get a good husband while various Devī temples and other places of worship dotted across Kannur and Kasaragoḍ districts will become the stage for special cultural events like Poorakkali. The *Pls* 5-8 are from the celebrations (*source*: poorakali.com)

Pl. 5: Flowers used in Kāmadeva *pūjana*

Pl. 6: Kāmadeva depiction in the *raṅgolī* form

Pl. 7: Kāmadeva procession

Pl. 8: Children performing Kāmadeva *pūjana*

Appendix 5

Illustrative Āyurvedic Concepts

Concept of Homeostasis: Balance and Imbalance (Samāvasthā Vicāra)

- Imbalance in the state of bodily tissues is known as "disease" and equilibrium is called "health".
- *Dhātu-sāmya* is the term given for homeostasis in Āyurveda.
- The body is sustained by three opposing factors called *vāta*, *pitta* and *kapha*.
- The symptoms and diseases that could be categorized as mental thoughts or feelings are just as important as symptoms and diseases of the physical body.

Conceptual Elements in Therapy (Sātmya Vicāra)

- The definition of health in Āyurveda is not limited up to physical well-being only, but it includes the mental, spiritual and social well-being also.
- Efficacy of medicine depends upon it, as the diet or medicine which is not *sātmya* to the person does not act properly and homeostasis cannot be maintained.
- It advocates to examine the constitution of morbidity, constitution of the *dhātu*, compactness, measurement, suitability, psyche, power of intake and digestion of food, power of exercise and the age of the patient before application of medicine.

Concept of Anatomy and Physiology (Śārīra Vicāra)

- *Concept of a Cell*: The *Caraka Saṁhitā* has explained that the body parts can be divided and re-divided into innumerable individual components called *paramāṇu*.

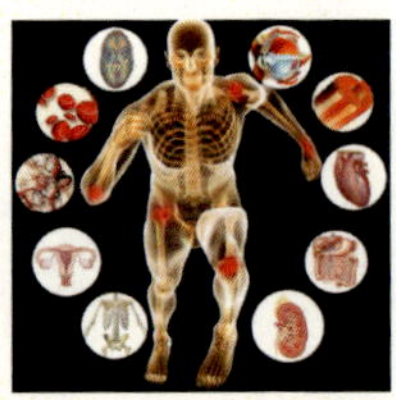

- *Basic Tissues*: Supplying the nourishment, delivery of life principle, providing covering or coating, providing lubrication, giving mechanical support, filling in the bony cavities and reproduction are the most important functions of these seven *dhātus* respectively.

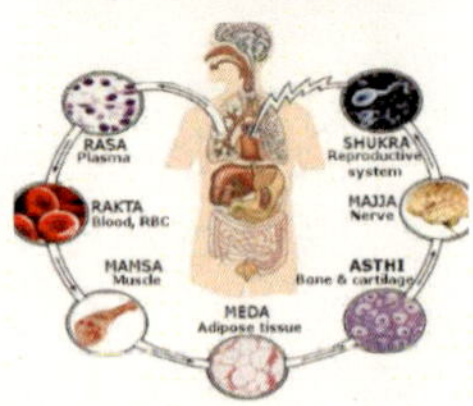

- *Reflexes*: The *Caraka Saṁhitā* suggests that one should not suppress the natural urges related to micturition, defecation, ejaculation, flatus, vomiting, sneezing, eructation, yawning, hunger, thirst, fears, sleep and dysponea developed after exertion.

Concept of Healthy Lifestyle (Svāsthya-vṛtta)

- *Characteristics of a Healthy Person*: The topic includes the avoidance of excessive utilization, non-utilization and wrong utilization of sense organs and mind.

- *Essential*: Personal hygiene, rejuvenation (*rasāyana*) and invigoration (*vājīkaraṇa*) yoga.
- The *key to health* does not lie in the application of drugs, but in the prime factors on which our life and vitality are based. The three most important ones are *food*, *sleep* and *sexual energy*.

Concepts in Therapeutical Approach (Cikitsā Vicāra)

- *Cikitsā* is defined as a process in which the vitiated *doṣas* are brought to normal state and their equilibrium state will be maintained.

- The method of treatment in Āyurvedic has ben classified into three categories:
  - Divine therapy
  - Rational therapy
  - Psychotherapy
- The rational therapy is primarily used for the treatment of somatic diseases. Psychotherapy deploys a special method of treatment, which is a non-pharmacological approach. It literally means overcoming of mind or victory over mind or control of mind.

Concepts in Eugenics, Virility and Aphrodisiac Therapy (Vājīkaraṇa Vicāra)

- By proper use of the *vājīkaraṇa* formulations, one becomes endowed with good physique, potency, strength, complexion and sexually strong as like an 8-year old horse.
- This therapy improves the function of the reproductive organs and vitalizes reproductive tissues increasing semen count and strengthening sperm motility in men and making eggs more viable for conception in women.
- *Vājikaraṇa* is a must for all those partners going to start the sexual life and who wishes to continue the sexual life in a better way.

Concepts in Eight Wings of Āyurveda (Aṣṭāṅga Āyurveda)

- Āyurveda is divided into eight branches, which are carefully chiseled out to meet specific needs in the process of maintaining health and preventing diseases.
  - *Kāya-cikitsā*: Internal and external treatments for the body.
  - *Bāla cikitsā*: Diseases related to infants.
  - *Graha cikitsā*: Healing of psychological problems.
  - *Ūrdhvāṅga cikitsā*: Treatments related to the ear, nose and throat region.
  - *Śalya cikitsā*: Sergeries and operations.
  - *Viṣa cikitsā*: Toxicology.
  - *Rasāyana cikitsā*: Methods to rejuvenate the *dhātu.*
  - *Vṛṣya cikitsā*: Science of aphrodisiacs, virility and improving health of progeny.

List of Concepts Reviewed

- Concept of digestion and metabolism (*agni vicāra*).
- Concept of vital points and traumatic effects (*marma vicāra*).
- Concept of materia medica and pharmacology (*dravya-guṇa vicāra*).
- Concept of diet (*āhāra vicāra*).
- Concepts in surgical approach (*śalya-tantra vicāra*).
- Concepts in medication (*bheṣaja vicāra*).
- Common medicinal plants in Āyurveda.

Appendix 6

Index of Kāmaśāstra Technical Terms

Below are the technical terms used in the context of Kāmaśāstra:

Āsanādi vidhi - This is the main celebration *nāyaka* and *nāyikā* do and achieve the supreme pleasure what Kāmaśāstra defines as achieving *rati rāga.* This process includes many substeps and not just the penetration.

Aṣṭāṅga Kāmaśāstra – It is the logical mechanism consisting of eight elements to comprehend the whole idea of *Kāmaśāstra.*

Aupariṣṭaka - The oral congress.

Bhāva dīpana vidhi – It is the process of *bhāva* creation.

Bhāvanirmiti cikitsā – The process *kāmavaidyā* (courtesan) follows to establish, build, and nurture the relationship with *nāyaka.*

Bhojya – These are the consumption rules suggested by *Kāmaśāstra* on food/eatables to enhance performance of *nāyaka* and *nāyikā.*

Ekacāriṇī - *Kāmaśāstra* has positioned the courtesan who is chaste as *ekacāriṇī.*

Garbhadhāraṇa vidhi - It is the ritual conducted to conceive post-wedding. This is performed during the post-nuptial conduct (strict observation of celibacy) from the three days of wedding.

Kāma therapy - It is the romantic treatment by a *nāyikā* (predominantly by a chaste courtesan) to *nāyaka,* wherein she assumes the role of his wife and ensures his complete pleasure without any attachment to him; however never makes him realize the same.

Kāmavaidyā - The courtesan especially chaste (*ekacāriṇī*) is *kāmavaidyā*. The broader definition is, a *nāyikā* who practices *kāma* therapy is *kāmavaidyā*.

Nakhavilekhanam - These are the romantic acts performed using nails during the copulation process for pleasure enhancement. Typically, it includes marking by nails on partner's body in a prescribed fashion.

Rasa and *bhāva* - This aspect of *aṣṭāṅga Kāmaśāstra* determines the rules of morale, taboos, best and preferred match of *nāyaka* and *nāyikā*, impacts of the external factors on the mind orientation of both - male and female. It discusses the significance of the right copulation mood and energy on progeny and pleasure.

Ratārambha vidhi - It is the process of creating essential sexual arousal and physical prerequisite.

Ratāvasānika vidhi - It is the process of achieving complete accomplishment and peaceful fulfilment leading to experience of *rati śānti*. After multiple rounds of unions and complete pleasure, *nāyaka* and *nāyikā* should progress for this process.

Rati-anurāga - It is the mental stage of the *nāyaka* and *nāyikā* developed through *ratārambha vidhi*.

Rati-rāga - It is the mental stage of the *nāyaka* and *nāyikā* developed through *āsanādi vidhi*.

Sciemantic (scientific and romantic) tourism - It is the prescription to the design of the contemporary sex education that should be based on the scientific theory and visits to different monuments like Khajurāho to provide practical knowledge through erotic art presented. Additionally, sciemantic tourism aims at running a course based on *Kāmaśāstra* and can be designed in multiple modules - starting with the classroom teaching on basic sex education, followed by visit to Khajurāho, wherein participants can enjoy and learn a music-oriented romantic module, followed by systematic tour on erotic sculptures, with audio-video aids and documentaries or films. This will certainly create necessary positivity about the romantic feeling and understanding of the truth – love between man and woman is a natural phenomenon; this is specialty for the human beings unlike other species.

Trisūtrī of *Kāmaśāstra* – These are the three considerations which *kāmavaidyā* should understand and follow for her patient who is nothing but her *nāyaka*. The *trisūtrī* of *Kāmaśāstra* is based on the Āyurveda theory, consisting of three elements namely, the objectives (*hetu*), symptoms (*lakṣaṇa*) and remedy (*samprāpti*) that the *kāmavaidyā* should analyse for her *nāyaka*.

Upakaraṇa – This aspect of *aṣṭāṅga Kāmaśāstra* suggests usage of different instruments made from select materials that are used during copulation. It further discusses the fabrication of these instruments and most important is their regular maintenance.

Bibliography

Agrawal, Akash Kumar et al., "Physiological Aspects of Agni", *Ayu: An International Quarterly Journal of Research in Ayurveda*, 31(3): 395-98. PMCID: PMC3221079, PMID: 22131747.

Agrawal, Kanhaiyalal, 1980, *Khajuraho* (in Hindi), Delhi: Macmillan.

Altekar, Rahul et al., 2020, "Reflection of Vāstu Element in Kāmaśāstra Theory", *Vidyavarta*, 1(69): 15-19.

Ananga-ranga (*Stage of the Bodiless One*), by Kalyāṇamalla, see Arbuthnot, 1907.

Arbuthnot, Forster Fitzgerald and Sir Richard Francis Burton, 1907, *The Hindu Art of Love* (*Ars Amoris Indica*) *or Ananga-ranga* (*Stage of the Bodiless One*), Charles Carrington.

Atreya, 1998, *Practical Ayurveda: Secrets for Physical, Sexual and Spiritual Health*, Newburyport, MA: Red Wheel/Weiser Publications.

Bagali Sachin S. et al., 2016, "Concept of Satwavajaya Chikitsa (Psychotherapy)", *Journal of Ayurveda and Integrated Medical Sciences*, 1(1): 56-63.

——, 2019, *Textbook of Swasthvritta*, New Delhi: Chaukhambha Publications.

Bagde, A.B. et al., 2013, "Vajikarana: A Unique Therapy of Ayurveda", *International Research Journal of Pharmacy*, 4(3): 4-7.

——, 2014, "Chikitsa Chatushpad: Four Pillars of Treatment in Ayurveda", *International Journal of Ayurveda & Alternative Medicine*, 2(2): 7-12.

Bargale, Sushant Sukumar et al., 2019, *Textbook of Swasthavritta evam Yoga*, repr., New Delhi: Chaukhambha Publications.

Behere, P.B. et al., 2013, "Ayurvedic Concepts Related to Psychotherapy", *Indian Journal of Psychiatry*, 55 (Suppl 2): pp. S310–S314, PMCID: PMC3705701, PMID: 23858273.

Bhishagratna, Kaviraj Kunja Lal, 2018, *Sushruta Samhita*, vol. 4: *Cikitsasthana*, London: Forgotton Books Classic Reprint Series.

Borakhade, V. et al., 2018, "Ahara Vichara: Ayurvedic Concept of Diet", *International Journal of Research – Granthalayah*, 6(2): 46-53.

Boulder, Andrew Schelling, 2019, *Erotic Love Poems from India: 101 Classics of Desire and Passion*, Shambhala.

Bṛhatsaṁhitā of Varāhamihira, ed. N. Chidambaram Iyer, New Delhi: Parimal Publication, 2013.

Caraka Saṁhitā, ed. Shree Gulab Kunverba Ayurvedic Society, Jamnagar, 1949.

——, 1948, part I, ed. Atridev ji Gupt, 2nd edn, Benares: Bhargava Pustakalaya.

Chakraborty Kaustav and Rajarshi Guha Thakurata, 2013, "Indian Concepts on Sexuality", *Indian Journal of Psychiatry* (January), 55(Suppl 2): S250–S255, PMCID: PMC3705691, PMID: 23858263.

Chandramouleeswaran, P. and K. Govadhan, 2012, "Ayurveda and Its Role in Sexual Health", *IJRAP*, 3(4): 619-21.

Chauhan, A., et al., 2015, "Ayurvedic Research and Methodology: Present Status and Future Strategies", *AYU: An International Quarterly Journal of Research in Āyurveda*, 36(4): 364–69.

Chouhan, D.S. et al., *Kāmakunjalatā*, ed. Dhundiraj Shastri, New Delhi: Chowkhambha Publications.

Danielou, Alain (tr.), 1993, *The Complete Kama Sutra: The First Unabridged Modern Translation of the Classic Indian Text.*

De, Sushil Kumar, 1959, *Ancient Indian Erotics and Erotic Literature*, Calcutta: Firma K.L. Mukhopadhyay.

Dewan, Shweta, 2014, "The Basics of Healthy Living (Swasthavritta): A Boon from Āyurveda", *International Ayurvedic Medical Journal*, 2(2): 211-18.

Dey, Amrita, 2015, "Formal and Informal Sexuality Education: A Study of Kolkata", dissertation, Department of Sociology, Jadavpur University, Kolkata.

Frawley, David, 1998, *Āyurveda and the Mind: The Healing of Consciousness*, Delhi: Motilal Banarsidass.

Ganguly, S., 2014, "Ayurveda for Cancer Therapy", *World Journal of Pharmaceutical Research*, 3(9): 1476-79.

Garde, Ganesh Krishna, 1983, *Sarth Vagbhatta*, Mumbai: Gajanana Book Depot.

Ghildiyal, Shivani and V.K. Joshi, 2012, "A Critical Review on Two Types of Laghupanchamula", *AYU*, 33(3): 343-47.

Gupta, Nisha, 2013, "Urjaskara – Rasayana factors in Ayurveda", *International Ayurvedic Medical Journal*, 1(3): 1-7.

Hampiholi, V.K., 1988, *Sex Education: Indian View*, Pune: Shubhada Publications.

——, 1988, *Kamashastra in Classical Sanskrit Literature*, Delhi: Ajanta Books.

Heinrich, M., J. Barnes, S. Gibbons and E. Williamson, 2004, *Fundamentals of Pharmacognosy and Phyto Pharmacy*, Edinburgh: Churchill Livingstone.

Introduction to Ayush Systems of Medicine, New Delhi: Ministry of Health & Family Welfare, Government of India. https://ayush.gov.in/alldomains.html#:~:text=Ayush%20is%20an%20acronym%20for,India%20for%20around%20100%20years.

Jaiswal, Y.S. and L.L. Williams, 2017, "A Glimpse of Ayurveda: The Forgotten History and Principles of Indian Traditional Medicine", *Journal of Traditional and Complementary Medicine*, 7: 50-53.

Jha, Rajdhar (ed.), 1929, *Nāgarasarvasva of Padmasri*, Calcutta: Venkateshvara Pustaka Agency.

Joshi, F. et al., 2016, "Concept of Shorthand Surgical Training w.s.r. to Yogasutriya Adhyaya: A Review", *International Ayurvedic Medical Journal*, 4(2): 225-28.

Kale, M.R., 2015, *The Meghaduta of Kalidasa: Text with Sanskrit Commentary of Mallinātha, English Translation, Notes, Appendices and a Map*, Delhi: Motilal Banarsidass.

Kapur, Malavika, 2016, *Psychological Perspectives on Childcare in Indian Indigenous Health Systems*, New Delhi: Springer India.

Kathuria, Richa, 2019, "'Self' in Indian Philosophy and Its Parallel in Western Philosophy", *The International Journal of Indian Psychology*, 7(1): 302-07.

Ketkar, Vaidya N.M., 1999, *Āyurveda Darshan*, Mumbai: N.M. Ketkar.

Kotecha, Rajesh, 2000, *Concept of Atattvabhinivesha in Ayurveda: New Way of Understanding the Minor Psychiatric Disorders on Ayurveda Parameters*, Jaipur: Publication Scheme.

Krishnamachariar, M., 1974, *History of Classical Sanskrit Literature*, Delhi: Motilal Banarsidass.

Kulshreshtha, Sushma, 2007, *Erotics in Kalidasa III: Experiencing Bliss: Samprayoga*, Kalidasa Academy of Sanskrit Music and Fine Arts Series No. 21, Delhi: Eastern Book Linkers.

——, 2007, *Kumarasambhava – Kamakelisati: Enjoyment of Bliss in Kumarasambhava: Erotica Indica – III*, New Delhi: Sanjay Prakashan.

Kumar, A. et al., 2011, "Principle of Dravyaguna (Ayurvedic Pharmacology)", *Biomedical and Pharmacology Journal*, 4(1): 147-52.

Lad, Vasant, 2002, *Āyurveda: The Science of Self-Healing*, Delhi: Motilal Banarsidass.

Loon, Gabriel van, 2013, *Charaka Samhita: Handbook on Ayurveda*, vol. I, North Carolina: Lulu.com, Reprinted with permission from P.V. Sharma and Chaukhambha Orientalia Publishers.

Madhavacharya, 2008, *Kamasutram of Shri Vatsyayana*, part I, Mumbai: Khemraj Srikrishna Das Publication.

——, 2008, *Kamasutram of Shri Vatsyayana*, Part II, Mumbai: Khemraj Srikrishna Das Publication.

McConnachie, James, 2005, *The Book of Love, the Story of the Kamasutra*, Dallas, TX: Metropolitan Press.

Mehar, Manjusha et al., 2017, "A Review on Therapeutic Use of Agadas in Ancient Ayurveda", *International Journal of Ayurveda and Pharmaceutical Chemistry*, 7(3): 214-22.

Mishra, Phani Kant, 2001, *Khajuraho: With Latest Discoveries*, New Delhi: Sundeep Prakashan.

Moscovici, Serge and Patricia Néve, 1973, "Studies in Social Influence: II. Instrumental and Symbolic Influence", *European Journal of Social Psychology*, 3(4): 461-71.

Mulchandani, Sandhya, 2006, *Erotic Literature of Ancient India*, Coimbatore: Mercury Books Publishers.

Nāgarasarvasva, ed. Rajdhar Jha, Kolkata: Lohiya Publication, originally published in 1929.

Neelam, S. et al., 2018, "Post-Operative Measures Described in Sushruta Samhita: An Overview", *International Journal of Advanced Research*, 6(3): 312-19.

Ninivaggi, Frank John, 2007, *Āyurveda: A Comprehensive Guide to Traditional Indian Medicine for the West*, Praeger Press.

Paliwal, Muralidhar, 2014, "The Concept of Satmya in Āyurveda", *Unique Journal of Ayurvedic and Herbal Medicines*, 2(4): 16-19.

Patil, Suma et al., 2017, "Concepts of Bhaishajya Kalpana in Charaka Samhita", *PIJAR, International Journal of Ayurvedic Research*, I(3): 26-31.

Patwardhan, Kishor, 2008, "Concepts of Human Physiology in Āyurveda", in *Sowarigpa and Āyurveda*, ed. Pabitra Kumar Roy, pp. 53-73, Samyak Vak Series 14, Sarnath, Varanasi: Central Institute of Higher Tibetan Studies.

Pokarna, K.L., 1994, *Social Beliefs, Cultural Practices in Health and Diseases*, Indian Sociological Series, Delhi: Rawat Publications.

Princy, Purwar and S.S. Yadav, 2018, "A Review on Yusha Kalpana", *International Journal of Green Pharmacy*, 11: S119.

Rathod, R.G. et al. 2016, "Comparative Study of Clinical Significance of Marma (Vital Points in Ayurveda) in Hands, Acupuncture and Acupressure: A Review", *Indian Journal of Medical Research and Pharmaceutical Sciences*, 3(8): 18-22.

Ravishankar, B. and V. Shukla, 2007, "Indian Systems of Medicine: A Brief Profile". *Air J Tradit Complement Altern Med.*, 3: 319-37.

Richard, Burton, 2006, *Kama Sutra of Vatsyayana*, (The Classic Burton Translation), NY (USA): Dover Publication.

Savrikar, S.S. et al., 2011, "Introduction to 'Rasashaastra': The Iatro-chemistry of Ayurveda", *African Journal of Traditional, Complementary and Alternative Medicines*, 8(5): 66-82.

Shastri, Ambikadatt (ed.), 1954, *Suśruta Saṁhitā*, Chaukhamba Sanskrit Series.

Shastri, Devadatta, 1992, *The Kamasutram of Shri Vatsyayana Muni*, Varanasi: Chaukhambha Sanskrit Sansthan.

Shilpa, S. et al., "Understanding Personality from Ayurvedic Perspective for Psychological Assessment: A Case", *Āyu.*, 32(1): 12–19.

Shridevi, P.G., 2020, "Bharata Muni's Concept of Rasa", *International Journal of Multidisciplinary Research*, VI(II).

Singh, Vineeta and Neeru Nathani, 2018, "Therapeutic Effects of Yusha Kalpana: A Critical Review", *International Journal of Physiology, Nutrition and Physical Education*, 3(1): 2132-35.

Steinbeck, John, 1952, *East of Eden*, Viking Press.

Sumantran, V.N. et al., 2012, "Insights on Personalized Medicine from Ayurveda", *The Journal of Alternative and Complementary Medicine*, 19(4): 1–6.

Svoboda, Robert E., 1999, *Āyurveda for Women: A Guide to Vitality and Health*, Santa Monica, CA: Healing Arts Publications.

Syal, Kumar et al., 2017, "The Significance of Ayurvedic Medicinal Plants", *Journal of Evidence-Based Complementary and Alternative Medicine*, 22(3): 494-501.

Thomas et al., 2019, "Controversial Identities of Medicinal Plants in Classical Literature of Ayurveda", *Journal of Ayurveda and Integrative Medicine*, September; available online https://www.sciencedirect.com/science/article/pii/S0975947618303747?via%3Dihub

Tillotson, Alan Keith, 2001, *The One Earth Herbal Sourcebook: Everything You Need to Know About Chinese, Western, and Ayurvedic Herbal Treatments*", New York: Kensington Publishing.

Trivedi, Pandit Ramgovind (tr.), 1954, *Ṛgveda*, Prayag: Indian Press Publications.

Upadhyaya, S.C., 1965, *Rati Rahasya of Pandit Kokkaka*, Bombay: Taraporevala & Sons.

Varma, Abhay and Anamica Dubey, 2018, "Vina (With Special Reference to Temples of Khajuraho)", *International Journal of Scientific Research in Science and Technology*, 4(7): 310-13.

Venil, N.S. and T. Girish, "Insights on Personalized Medicine from Ayurveda", *The Journal of Alternative and Complementary Medicine*, 0(0): 1-6.

Wilson, H.H. (tr.), 1888, *Rigveda Samhita*, London: Trübner.

Yerawar, P. et al., 2019, "Critical Review of Ashtanga Hridayam as per Chhanda Shastra (Sanskrit Prosody)", *World Journal of Pharmaceutical Research*, 8(12): 1705-10.

Online Internet Resources

Ayurvedic Herbs: A Clinical Guide to the Healing Plants of Traditional Indian Medicine, MS Premila https://books.google.co.in/s?id=r7JmIeAw9JAC&printsec=frontcover&dq=ayurvedic+drug+plants&hl=en&sa=X#v=onepage&q&f=false

Dr. Ram Mani Bhandari, https://ayurmantra.com/kamasutra-and-ayurveda.html

Jamadagni, Sameer, Dr. Samir Jamadagni's lecture for Ayurveda Vaidyas on Ayurvedic Treatment of Diseases of Back [Spine] and Gastrointestinal Tract Disorders on Sandu Foundation Day 8 May 2016 in Mumbai - https://www.youtube.com/watch?v=iMdQlydDPHM

Kama Sutra - It's Not about Sex । Bharat Gupt and Sanjay Dixit, https://www.youtube.com/watch?v=JIG7gCfnrKo

Madhav Chikitsa: https://europepmc.org/article/PMC/4995852

Vaidya Khadiwale Vaidyak Sanshodhan Sanstha: https://www.facebook.com/pg/Vaidya-Khadiwale-Vaidyak-Sanshodhan-Sanstha-405402022898630/about/?ref=page_internal

वैद्यराजआ.वा.दातारशास्त्री – Videos https://www.youtube.com/channel/UC5cM87Pio4ZSAysURDCB0Mw/featured

Shodh Ganga Handle

http://hdl.handle.net/10603/47473: A Critical Comparative Study of Kamapurusartha with Reference to Dharmasastra and Kamasastra.

http://hdl.handle.net/10603/94528 : Influence of Kamasastra on Classical Sanskrit Literature.

https://thoughtcatalog.com/eric-redding/2015/09/human-sexuality/

Institutional Resources

American Institute of Vedic Studies (NM)

California College of Ayurveda (CA)

Institute for Wholistic Education (WI)

New England Institute of Ayurvedic Medicines (MA)

Rocky Mountain Ayurvedic Health Retreat (CO)

The Ayurvedic Institute and Wellness Center (NM)

The Chopra Center for Well Being (CA)

Vinayak Ayurvedic Center (NM)

Index